How To Build A FLATHEAD FORD V-8

How To Build A
FLATHEAD FORD V-8

George McNicholl

MOTORBOOKS
INTERNATIONAL

About the author

George McNicholl was born in Vancouver, B.C. Canada more than fifty years ago. He purchased his first automobile engine (a Ford flathead V-8) when he was 12 years old. He sailed on deep-sea ships for 15 years with the last two years in the position of captain. Car and engine building have always been a hobbies for him and he has the greatest affection for the Ford flathead V-8. He is still involved in the shipping business, although he has been based ashore for 25 years.

First published in 2003 by MBI Publishing Company, 380 Jackson Street, Suite 200, St. Paul, MN 55101-3885 USA

MBI Publishing Company books are also available at discounts in bulk quantity for industrial or sales-promotional use. For details write to Special Sales Manager at Motorbooks International Wholesalers & Distributors, 380 Jackson Street, Suite 200, St. Paul, MN 55101-3885 USA

Library of Congress Cataloging-in-Publication Data

MiNicholl, George, 1947-
How to build a flathead Ford V-8 / by George McNicholl.
p. cm.
ISBN 0-7603-1493-4 (pbk. : alk. paper)
1. Ford Automobile—Motors—Design and Construction I. Title.

TL215.F35M36 2003
629.25'04—dc21

On the front cover: Tom Wilkerson's 1932 Ford roadster is heavily influenced by those hot rods he grew up admiring. That influence dictated that a Ford flathead V-8 would power his street rod. Tom chose a 1947 AB block, and then added finned Offenhauser (Offy) heads and a three deuce manifold that has been modified to accept three Holley 94 carburetors. *Dennis Parks.* **Left:** The crankshaft connecting rod journal is being measured with a micrometer to check the connecting rod bearing clearance. **Center:** A Serdi 60 valve grinding machine grinding the valve-seat inserts of a flathead engine block. **Right:** The main bearing bolts are in the final stage of being torqued to 105 ft-lb.

On the title page: Other vintage accessories on Tom Wilkerson's flathead include reproduction Fenton headers with glass packs and a dual-point ignition. Topping off the nostalgic engine are the obligatory acorn nuts securing the heads, which have all been hand-polished by the owner. *Dennis Parks*

On the back cover: This is the rare Ardun conversion flathead built in Section III.

Edited by Peter Bodensteiner
Designed by Chris Fayers

Printed in Hong Kong

CONTENTS

FOREWORD

Over 40 years ago, when I was at the grand age of 12, I bought my first engine in Vancouver, B.C., Canada. This was a complete 1949 Ford flathead V-8, for which I paid the huge sum (in those days) of $7.50 (Can.) cash. The engine was delivered totally dismantled to the back entrance of our house during the hours of darkness by two notorious local brothers. The fact that I was able to produce a bill of sale and the local police did not appear on our doorstep seemed to appease my father somewhat.

Over the next six months, I made numerous trips on my bicycle to the local library, where I wrote down information or traced drawings from various automotive manuals containing information on the Ford flathead V-8 engine. This was an enormous amount of work because no photocopiers were available in those days.

During this period I spent a lot of time on the weekends around the local garages where the older guys (17 and 18 years old) worked on their cars. In exchange for cleaning the dirtiest engine parts they had or sweeping out their garage, I was given parts that I needed for my engine. I was also privy to a lot of valuable information relating to engine building.

I managed to completely reassemble my engine within nine months, using a minimum of new parts. I spent many hours cleaning, painting, fitting, or breaking parts, and learning about the famous flathead. As soon as the engine was completed, I sold it for the amazing sum of $60 (Can.) cash. I had never seen so much money!

I built a few more engines in this manner, and then I bought my first car when I was 14 years old. That car was a 1950 Meteor (Canadian Ford) two-door sedan and I paid $25 (Can.) cash. I built a fantastic looking 276-ci Ford flathead V-8 engine for it. The block was ported, polished, and relieved. It featured Jahns 3 5/16″ cast aluminum pistons with Grant piston rings, Mercury 4″ cast alloy steel crankshaft, Iskenderian full-race camshaft with adjustable lifters, and Fenton polished aluminum cylinder heads. Rounding out my flathead were an Edelbrock 4-carb polished aluminum intake manifold with four Stromberg 97 polished carburetors, my own cylinder head-mounted generator bracket, and a Mallory dual point distributor and coil.

Approximately two years later I sold the complete car for $50 (Can.) and the engine for $300 to a really old (22 years of age) neighbor. With that amount of money in the bank at that stage of my life, I gave serious consideration to retiring and leading a life of leisure.

The day before my sixteenth birthday I started employment on a Swedish general cargo ship as a deckboy. I spent the next 15 years sailing on deep-sea cargo ships to many of the ports in the world, all the while working my way up through the ranks. I spent the last two years during my time at sea as captain.

During a port call at Long Beach, California, in 1963, I managed to obtain a ride to Reath Automotive, where I met the famous Joe Reath. I can remember standing at his counter and purchasing a set of Jahns flathead pistons while everyone else was buying goodies for their OHV Buick, Cadillac, Chevrolet, Chrysler, Ford, Oldsmobile, or Pontiac. A lot of people were looking at me as if I had just come out of a time warp. I then understood how the U.S. Immigration and Naturalization Service came up with the term "alien."

I came ashore almost 25 years ago and I have worked since then as the port captain, cargo superintendent, or project manager for shipping companies operating out of Northern Europe. I still do a lot of traveling in the shipping business, but now it is while comfortably seated on an airplane.

During the time that I have been permanently based ashore, I have built more than a dozen engines of various types and three award-winning custom cars from the ground up. Between shipping assignments I spend whatever time I can spare at Luke's Custom Machine & Design located in North Vancouver, B.C. I completely disassembled, cleaned, and inspected every part of the engines described in this book, and assisted Luke with the assembly and much of the detailing. I did that in order to correctly document each of the engines.

Luke tolerates my presence because I seem to know what I am doing around his shop. Once in a while I have a brain wave that helps him with his business, and he especially likes the fact he does not have to pay me!

I built this 1939-48 Edelbrock, polished, three-carb intake manifold with three Stromberg 97 polished carburetors in 1962. That is when this picture was taken, which explains why it is not the greatest. I sold this intake system the way it looks for $30.00 (Can.). Compare that to today's price. There is one Hellings-Stellings air cleaner missing due to a lack of funds in those days.

This photograph was taken in 1963 when I had just sold this engine for the enormous sum of $300.00 (Can.). I had not bolted the fourth Stromberg 97 carburetor on, and the fuel block is actually for a three-carb setup.

One of the sidelines I have undertaken over the past few years is the compiling of information relating to engines that Luke has built for his customers. I have done this for every engine and car that I have built for myself over the past 20 years. This complete build up documentation consists of all the part numbers, clearances, and prices along with a set of photographs taken during each stage of assembly. This information is very useful when determining the appraised value of a vehicle for insurance purposes. The vice president of a major insurance corporation recently complimented me on the detail and completeness of this work. I have used a lot of that information in this book.

Prior to sitting down and writing this book, I had decided I did not want to write about every modification that could be done to a flathead engine, or discuss all the different types of Ford flathead V-8 aftermarket parts available. I did decide to write about the complete build up of two distinct engines, a performance street engine and a blown street engine, and compile as much information as I could in one book about these specific engines. I believe I have succeeded in accomplishing that goal. The inclusion of the Ardun engine was an afterthought brought about by fortunate circumstances.

I would sincerely like to thank Luke Balogh for encouraging me to write this book and for providing me with a lot of valuable information, especially about the blown Ford flathead V-8 and Ardun engines. I would also like to thank my teenage son, Tyler, for his expertise with computers, in particular my computer, and his patience with me during the period I was putting all this together. I would like to thank my wife, Jillian, for having Tyler. Most important, I would like to thank my teenage daughter, Kristina, for teaching our cat Peppurr how to use my draft copies as scratching posts.

I would also like to offer Peter Bodensteiner, acquisitions editor at MBI Publishing Company, my gratitude for his keen interest in my manuscript. Without his support and assistance, this book would not have been published.

I have written this book for the benefit of the owners and those engaged in the field of automotive repair of the Ford flathead V-8. It is my hope that this publication will prove of considerable use to those parties. I welcome any comments or suggestions.

George McNicholl
North Vancouver, B.C.

INTRODUCTION

One of the reasons I decided to write this book was to share information with other Ford flathead V-8 engine owners and builders. I do not believe there should be a conspiracy of silence when it comes to building one of these old sweethearts! I shall be pleased if every reader is able to obtain even one piece of useful information from this book and apply it to his or her own flathead engine. The time I have spent writing this book will then have been worthwhile.

Section I covers the building of a street performance flathead engine, Section II covers the building of a blown street performance flathead engine, and Section III covers the building of an Ardun street performance engine. Although three completely different engines are described in this book, some of the information applicable to one engine is applicable to the other engines. Read the entire book.

I shall now explain the layout of the chapters in this book. The body of each chapter offers an explanation of the parts, clearances, and machining required in that chapter. In most instances, there is an explanation of where to locate these parts or services. At the end of each chapter is a summary providing the complete build up information and part numbers, clearances, and specifications along with the prices for those parts.

The Ford part numbers are those listed in the *Ford Motor Company of Canada, Master Repair Manual: Engine Including Cooling and Exhaust System*, manual number SE 384-B, 10/53, section number twelve. Shop manuals like this are available from Wilkinson's Automobilia (see the Resources section).

I appreciate that most automotive publications do not list the prices for the complete build up of an engine because those prices can change quickly over a very short period of time. I wanted to include the current prices in this book in order for the reader to fully understand what is involved financially when proceeding with the assembly of the engines described herein. There have been many recent rumors about the high cost of building these engines, and there is no doubt that some machine shops and companies are charging far too much. This is unfortunate because that situation will discourage many flathead fans from building their own motor. I believe the costs that I have indicated clearly show that a fine-quality flathead can be built for a reasonable amount of money. It is not cheap to build one of these engines, but it is not out of line, either. The cost of building an Ardun engine is another matter entirely.

Master

REPAIR MANUAL

ELKS GARAGE
PA 2022 129 CORDOVA ST.

ENGINE

INCLUDING COOLING AND EXHAUST SYSTEM

L-HEAD 239 AND 255 CUBIC INCH

This manual applies to the models listed below.

FORD CARS				1949	1950	1951	1952	1953
METEOR CARS				1949	1950	1951	1952	1953
MERCURY CARS				1949	1950	1951	1952	1953
MONARCH CARS				1949	1950	1951	1952	1953
TRUCKS								
MODEL SERIES								
47	1	100	1948	1949	1950	1951	1952	1953
—	—	250	—	—	—	—	—	1953
68	3	350	1948	1949	1950	1951	1952	1953
105	4	—	1948	1949	1950	1951	1952	—
135	5	500	1948	1949	1950	1951	1952	1953
155	6	600	1948	1949	1950	1951	1952	1953

MANUAL NUMBER SE 384-B 10/53

SECTION NUMBER TW

Ford Motor Company of Canada

PRIC

The Ford Motor Company Of Canada Master Repair Manual *for October 1953. The edge of the manual where the price was located is blocked out, but it cost 35 cents. This manual had some very interesting information and all the specifications for the stock flathead. Luke Balogh had this manual squirreled away at his shop along with a whole bunch of other NOS (new-old-stock) flathead engine parts.*

The difference in price between building a stock flathead engine and the performance street engine I have described in the first section of this book is only the cost of the aftermarket aluminum cylinder heads, the electronic ignition, and the high-performance fuel system. All the parts and labor for the short block assembly would be the same for both types of engines.

The prices I have listed are the retail prices in effect as of August 2002. These prices do not include any taxes or shipping and handling charges, but they do include the cost of the various machining procedures and any buffing, polishing, or chrome plating. These prices are in U.S. dollars. The prices indicated may vary in different parts of North America and are subject to change without notice.

The order in which I have listed the parts for the engine, such as the crankshaft, connecting rods and pistons, lubrication system, and camshaft, are not in the order in which the engine would normally be assembled. I have dedicated a chapter in each section of this book to the actual engine assembly.

If you are not experienced with the assembly of automobile engines, do not use your own engine as a learning tool. Use a friend's engine to practice on! Let an experienced engine builder assemble the engine. You will have spent a lot of hard-earned money prior to the assembly point of your little beauty, and it would be almost criminal to ruin the engine by making some dumb mistake when putting it together.

I have included some photographs of the engine boring, decking, valve grinding, and so forth. You will not be doing that type of machine work in your living room, so there is no need to concern yourself with how to do the work. If you are obsessed with this, approach your own engine builder and ask if you can watch the real thing. After all, you are going to be paying for it. If you have an engine builder with a gentle personality, he will probably allow you to watch, but if he is smart, he will charge you double for being such an irritating customer.

SECTION 1: PERFORMANCE STREET ENGINE

The first engine I am going to describe is somewhat unique by today's standards. The owner has requested the "crab-style" pre-1949 distributor be installed instead of the stock location 1949-53 Ford flathead V-8 distributor. This engine is designed as a street performance motor with a displacement of 276 cubic inches. The owner is going to install it in his daily-driven 1934 Ford five-window coupe.

From 1949 to 1953 the Ford Motor Company referred to the 239-ci Ford or the 255-ci Mercury as an "L-head" design. Over the years the name flathead has stayed with this engine and today it is almost a badge of honor.

The 1949-53 Ford specifications were:
- 239.4-ci displacement.
- Stock bore: 3 3/16" and stock stroke: 3 3/4"
- Stock compression ratio: 6.8:1
- 112 hp @ 3,600 rpm and 206 ft lb torque @ 2,000 rpm
- Casting numbers: 8BA (1949-50) and IBA (1951-53)

The 1949-53 Mercury specifications were:
- 255.4-ci displacement.
- Stock bore: 3 3/16" and stock stroke: 4.00"
- Stock compression ratio: 6.8:1
- 125 hp @ 3,700 rpm and 218 ft-lb torque @ 2,100 rpm
- Casting numbers: 8BA (1949-50) and IBA (1951-53)

The casting number for the 1949-50 Canadian Ford and Mercury blocks was C8BA, and the casting number for the 1951-1953 Canadian Ford and Mercury blocks was CIBA. The horsepower and torque ratings above are the maximum for the 1949-53 engines.

On a few occasions I have met people who have purchased an engine out of a Mercury car or truck believing the engine to be a Mercury flathead V-8. Only after the fact have they discovered the engine was not a Mercury but a Ford. There is no guarantee that what comes out of a car or truck is the real thing. The only way to ensure that a Mercury crankshaft is in an engine is to remove one of the cylinder heads and measure the stroke. The same engine block casting numbers have been used in both the Ford and Mercury cars and trucks. The casting numbers listed are the ones I am aware of. There may well be others, such as military or industrial models.

Over a 50-year period, it is impossible to tell how many times a Ford flathead V-8 engine has been taken apart and rebuilt. Parts from other engines may have been installed in a single engine just to keep it running. The serial number on the engine block may not match the vehicle serial number, or the serial number on the engine block may have been altered. None of this really matters because only three important things are necessary for the basis of building a fine street performance flathead: a decent block, a good Ford or Mercury crankshaft, and a set of late-model connecting rods. Find these items and forget about matching serial numbers!

Purchase and Magnaflux

The flathead V-8 engine block to locate as the basis for a street-performance engine is the 1949-53 Ford or Mercury. This block does not have the integral bellhousing. I believe this later generation of engine blocks is superior to the pre-1949 blocks for three distinct reasons: they have better cooling design due to the enlarged size of the coolant flow holes at the rear of the block; the rear crankshaft oil seal is a better design; and there is no integral bellhousing. This block is easier to adapt to a wider variety of late model transmissions.

There are two different depths of the right water pump opening (where the impeller fits) in some of the Canadian Ford engine blocks with the same C8BA casting number.

A 1950 Canadian Ford block, casting number C8BA. The distance from the front of the engine to the inside of the right and left water pump opening is approximately 3/4". The left and right openings are the same.

This photograph shows the depth of the right water pump opening to be approximately 2″. This is also a 1950 Canadian Ford block, casting number C8BA.

The right and left water pump openings were both $\frac{3}{4}''$ deep on some blocks, while the right water pump opening had a depth of approximately 2″ on other blocks.

It is entirely up to you as the potential builder of street performance flatheads to decide whether you want to purchase a complete engine or just certain parts of the engine. If you have a source for separate engine parts, then just buy the engine parts as they are needed.

If you do not know what to look for when purchasing an engine block, take a friend along who does. Better yet, see if the seller will agree to take the block to your local engine shop so the real professionals can examine it. If the seller will not agree to do this, insist upon a written agreement wherein your money is refunded if the block is found to be cracked or otherwise unacceptable. If the seller will not agree to this proposition, walk away and find another block and a more reasonable seller.

The first thing to do when you have located a block is to examine it for cracks. Do not be surprised if you find cracks around the cylinder head bolt holes between the cylinders. This is quite common and is probably the result of overtorquing the cylinder head bolts or a lack of antifreeze during the winter months in colder climates. The 1949-53 Ford flathead V-8s did not have any freeze plugs or even any engine block drain plugs. The cracks around the cylinder head bolt holes can be repaired by an experienced machine shop. Examine the cylinder head bolt holes to ensure they are not stripped or have not been drilled off-center by some Neanderthal who has attempted to repair damaged threads. It is best to try to find a block that is not cracked.

It is a far more serious situation if cracks are found around the valve seats and these cracks lead to the cylinder walls. If this is the case, I recommend you decline that block and press on with your search for a better one. These cracks could be repaired, but it involves eventually sleeving the cylinder, and this is going to be a costly proposition. Visually examine the sides of the block, the oil pan rails, and the main bearing webs and bolt holes for any obvious cracks or damage.

The maximum bore that a flathead block can safely sustain is usually $3\frac{5}{16}''$ + 0.030″ (3.3425″). Some blocks have been bored to $3\frac{3}{8}''$ (3.375″), providing there has been no core shift during the casting process. However, the cylinder walls are becoming pretty thin with a $3\frac{3}{8}''$ bore. Anyone wishing to bore a flathead block to $3\frac{3}{8}''$ (3.375″) should have the cylinders sonic tested to determine if the cylinder walls are thick enough. I would not recommend buying a block with a bore over $3\frac{5}{16}''$ (3.3125″). The engine I am using as an example in this section is going to be bored to $3\frac{5}{16}''$ (3.3125″), so if you want the same engine, you will have to locate a block that has been previously bored to a maximum of 0.060″ oversize (3.2475″).

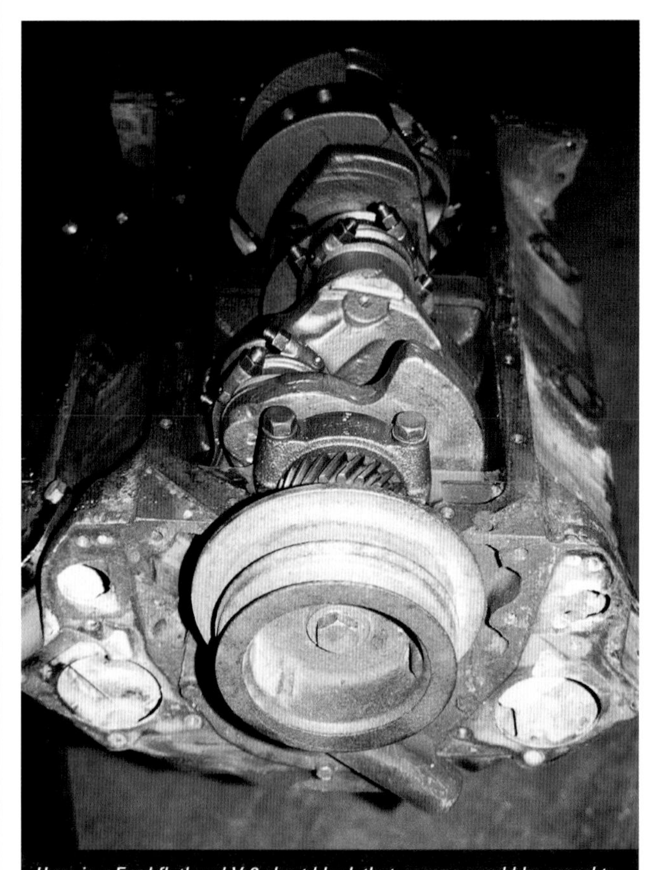

Here is a Ford flathead V-8 short block that anyone would be proud to exhibit in a car show due to the superior detailing. The poor old block had been sitting neglected in someone's garage for a lengthy period of time. This engine block is going to be the basis for the street performance engine described in this section.

This is a 1950 Canadian Ford engine block, casting number C8BA, with the fuel pump pushrod bushing removed. This block has just been redi-stripped.

When buying the block it should have the main bearing caps and bolts attached. It is not critical if the block is not fitted with the caps, but it will definitely necessitate spending additional money to have the block align honed, or even align bored, in order to properly fit other caps.

Have the engine block, the main bearing caps, and the main bearing cap bolts Magnafluxed, technically known as "Magnet Particle Testing." This will be the final test to determine if you are now the proud owner of an acceptable piece of history. The estimated cost for Magnafluxing the engine block and the main bearing caps is $45.

Cleaning

Remove every bolt, any fittings, the camshaft bearings, the fuel pump pushrod bushing, the rear upper oil seal retainer, and the oil line plug located at the front of the engine behind the camshaft timing gear. In order to remove the fuel pump pushrod bushing, the rear camshaft bearing must be removed first. Then drive the fuel pump pushrod bushing downward using a brass drift and a hammer. An impact driver may be required to remove the oil line plug, or it may even have to be drilled out. Just make certain it is removed.

It is a common practice with OHV (overhead valve) engines to grind the valve lifter gallery smooth in order to assist with the oil return to the oil pan. This procedure is not necessary with a flathead block due to the high quality of the block casting. The valve lifter gallery in a flathead motor is actually quite smooth. You have just saved yourself a lot of painstaking work!

Porting and Polishing

An opportune time to port and polish the engine block is after the block has been hot tanked. You do not want to go hog wild on the intake and exhaust ports. Apply some blue machinist's dye to the block and then use the intake manifold gasket and exhaust manifold gaskets that are going to be installed in the engine as templates to scribe around the respective ports. Use a high-speed grinder with a carbide bit to gasket-match the intake ports and exhaust ports. With the intake ports, clean them up all the way to the valve seats. Do not grind the valve seats. With the exhaust ports, grind as far up them as possible; clean up around the exhaust seats, being careful not to grind the seats themselves. The idea is not to remove a ton of metal but to smooth out the ports, removing a bare minimum of material.

The exhaust ports at each end and each side of the block should be finished up with a "D" shape that will be slightly bigger than the size of the exhaust port gasket. The "D" shape provides these exhaust ports with the optimum shape and is necessary in order to clean up the inside of the port close to the gasket area.

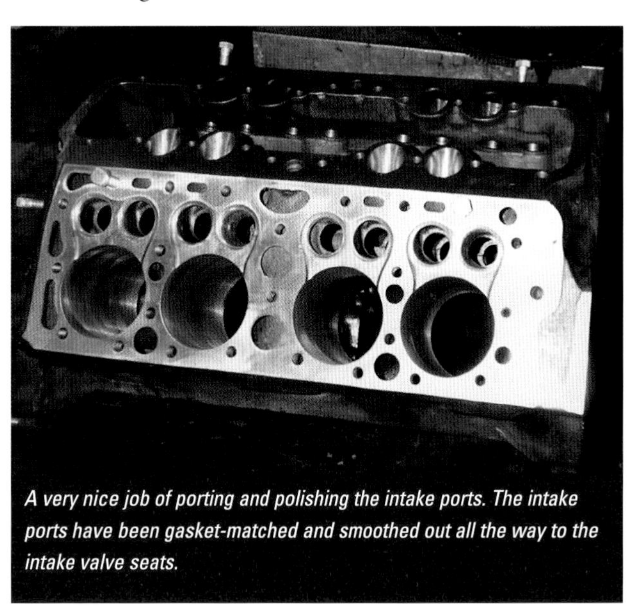

A very nice job of porting and polishing the intake ports. The intake ports have been gasket-matched and smoothed out all the way to the intake valve seats.

An excellent job porting and polishing the exhaust ports results in a "D" shape for the end ports on both sides of the block. The exterior surface of the block has been sanded and is now ready for paint.

Detailing the Block and Drilling Valve Lifter Bosses

Use a high-speed grinder with some small sanding discs to remove all the rough areas from the outside of the engine block. The entire outside surface should be as smooth as possible. This should not entail a lot of work, as the outside casting surface of the flathead block is usually fairly decent to start with.

Drill a 3/16" (0.1875") hole in the center of each of the valve lifter bosses. This hole should be approximately 1 to 1½" from the top of the lifter boss. The purpose of these holes is to simplify valve lifter adjustment. A 3/16" drill bit (use the chuck end) or a punch is inserted in the hole in order to prevent the valve lifter (tappet) from turning. The valve lifter is then easily adjusted using a thin tappet wrench. This method is far superior to smashing your knuckles using the Johnson adjustable lifter wrenches, and it takes half the time. Incidentally, this system will not work if you have adjustable lifters with a solid body that do not have the usual oval indents in the sides.

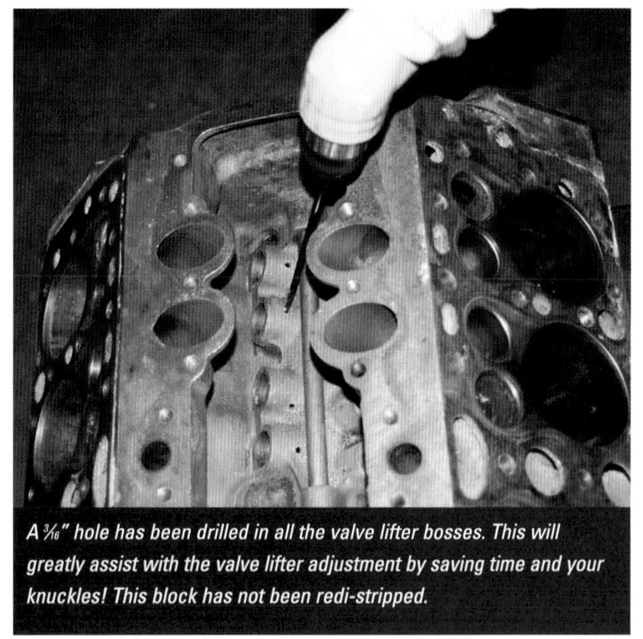

A 3/16" hole has been drilled in all the valve lifter bosses. This will greatly assist with the valve lifter adjustment by saving time and your knuckles! This block has not been redi-stripped.

Full-Flow Oiling

The one item that was missing on the flathead engine was a full-flow oil system through the oil filter. The horizontal hole for an oil line fitting on the lower left side near the back of the block should be drilled and tapped using a 3/8" N.P.T. tap. This hole leads to a horizontal crossover passage inside the block. Drill and tap the crossover passage using a 1/4" N.P.T. tap and then install a new stainless steel 1/4" N.P.T. plug in the passage using Permatex aviation form-a-gasket. The vertical inboard threaded oil line fitting hole at the top and back of the block, close to where the bellhousing is attached, should be drilled out and tapped using a 3/8" N.P.T. tap. The center vertical oil line fitting hole can be plugged using a 1/4" N.P.T. plug, or an oil pressure line can be connected.

It has been reported by some "knowledgeable" parties that the installation of a full-flow oil system does not directly filter the oil for the #3 main bearing and the #4 and #8 connecting rod bearings. Even if this is the case, at least 66% of the main bearing oil and 75% of the connecting rod bearing oil is being directly filtered. That is 100% better than what was happening with the stock Ford flathead V-8 oil filter system. Eventually the filtered oil will be returned to the #3 main bearing and the #4 and #8 connecting rod bearings. The installation of a full-flow oil system in a street performance flathead will greatly assist with ensuring long bearing life.

Relieving the Block

There has been a lot of discussion over the past few years regarding whether a Ford flathead V-8 engine block should be relieved or not. There is one critical point about this subject which is certain, and that is that the air/fuel mixture

Here we see how the "full-flow" oil system is created. The #1 flag position indicates where the horizontal oil fitting hole is for the pressure out line and the #2 flag position indicates where the vertical oil fitting hole is for the drain back line.

This flathead engine block has been relieved, and the 3/16" depth of the relief can be clearly seen. This mind-numbing work was performed using a hand grinder and involved hours of labor.

flows over the top and around the valves and not straight down from them in a flathead engine.

I do not intend to get into a great discussion about whether to relieve a flathead block or not. Relieving an engine block will lower the compression ratio approximately 0.5 to 0.75 of a point. I have not heard of a situation where the result of the lowering of a reasonable compression ratio in a normally aspirated engine leads to an increase in power. A street performance Ford flathead V-8 does not need to be relieved. Save a lot of money and forget about relieving the block.

Heat Risers

It used to be the practice to insert a penny in each heat riser passage in order to block them off. For street use, leave the passages unblocked, although this might be a non-issue because some aftermarket intake manifolds are not cast with heat riser passages. The purpose of the heat riser passages was to warm up the intake manifold as fast as possible when the weather was cold. If the heat riser passages are blocked off and you live in a colder climate, your vehicle will run horribly until the engine reaches normal operating temperature.

Re-Tap and Chamfer Bolt Holes

Run a tap through every bolt hole on the engine block. This is important and will ensure each and every thread is in perfect shape when it is time to reassemble the engine. Use a countersink bit in a drill and lightly chamfer all the cylinder head bolt holes. Take it easy when performing this procedure; the idea is not to see if you can push the countersink bit through to the other side of the block. This process will help to prevent these threads from being pulled when the bolts are torqued.

Redi-Strip Block

It is now time to send the engine block off to the strippers. Redi-stripping is a non-acidic chemical process that completely removes all foreign material from an engine block. This is a wonderful process and also an important one in order to have the water passages in a Ford flathead V-8 engine block completely cleaned out to prevent overheating. The estimated cost to hot tank and redi-strip an engine block is $155. For information on redi-stripping, see the Resources section.

Glyptal

Glyptal is the paint used on electrical motors. This paint will withstand very high temperatures and is as tough as nails. Glyptal is available from electrical repair outlets. I prefer to purchase this paint in the spray can form for ease of application. As soon as the engine block is returned from being redi-stripped, paint the valve lifter gallery.

This engine block has just returned from being redi-stripped. There are a few stains on the cylinder walls, but these will disappear when the block is bored. The block is absolutely clean, inside and out. The water passages must be thoroughly clean in a flathead in order to prevent overheating.

The valve lifter gallery has just been sprayed with Glyptal. This operation was carried out as soon as the block was returned from being redi-stripped.

Purchase 32 plastic 1″-diameter plugs from your local hardware store and insert them in the valve lifter bosses and the valve guide bosses. You can always wrap some masking tape around them if they don't quite fit. Use a rubber 1¼″-diameter bathtub plug in the hole for the valve lifter gallery breather tube, plug up the other five holes in the valve lifter gallery, and mask off the outside of the engine block with newspaper. Spray the valve lifter gallery and the front of the engine block behind the camshaft timing gear with Glyptal.

Glass bead the valve lifter gallery crankcase breather tube, the crankshaft oil slinger, and the two valve lifter gallery oil return hole baffles. Then spray them with Glyptal. Glass bead the timing gear cover, mask off the outside of it, and spray the inside with Glyptal.

Machining

It is extremely important to locate a machine shop that is capable of carrying out the machining procedures listed below, ensuring that close tolerances are adhered to. There is a huge difference between a machine shop that specializes in high-performance engine clearances and a machine shop that is routinely re-building average passenger car engines.

I once purchased an engine block that had been freshly bored 0.030″ oversize and align honed. That work was done so unprofessionally the cylinders had to be bored to 0.040″ oversize just to clean them up and the main bearing bosses had to be properly align honed. I am convinced the previous owner of the block must have done the boring and align honing in his backyard with a big drill. Fortunately, I was able to recover half the money I had paid for the block.

Cylinder Boring

The block will be bored and the cylinders honed and de-glazed resulting in a final bore of 3 5/16″ (3.3125″). The pistons should be purchased beforehand and delivered to the machine shop with the block. The machine shop will then measure each piston with a micrometer and bore the block accordingly to ensure there is 0.004″ piston-to-bore clearance (after cylinder honing), measured below the bottom of the wrist pin perpendicular to the wrist pin. This is the piston clearance Ross Racing Pistons recommends for these pistons. The engine block is usually bored to within 0.003″ to 0.004″ of the final bore and then honed and de-glazed, resulting in the final cylinder bore.

OHV engines should be bored and the cylinders honed using a torque plate. The purpose of the torque plate is to simulate the distortion caused to the engine block when the cylinder heads are torqued. On a flathead block, the cylinder head bolts are not spaced evenly around each cylinder, particularly where the valves are located. For this reason and the fact that the cylinder bore is relatively small, the use of a torque plate is not mandatory for the boring and final cylinder honing procedures of a flathead block.

The Ross pistons have been laid out for the boring operation. Each piston is measured with a micrometer, and the cylinders are bored accordingly, allowing for the recommended 0.004″ piston-to-bore clearance after cylinder honing.

An amazing 7.5 pounds of material have been removed from a flathead engine block as a result of increasing the cylinder bore from 3 3/16″ to 3 5/16″.

Photographed at High Performance Engines is a Rottler Boring Bar Company Model F2B boring bar. This is an older model boring bar but it does an excellent job of boring when used by an experienced operator.

A Sunnen Automatic Cylinder Re-Sizing Machine, Model CK-10, is honing and de-glazing the cylinder bores of the engine block featured in this section. This machine hones the cylinders to the final bore size with Sunnen 600-series 280-grit stones for cast iron rings. The finish is a cross-hatch pattern.

The main bearing caps must be installed and torqued to 105 ft-lb during the boring operation. This procedure places stress on the bottom end of the block and prevents the cylinders from distorting after they have been bored, when the crankshaft is installed and torqued in place. The cylinder banks in a flathead engine block are exactly 90 degrees to each other. The engine block described in this section had the stock bore of 3 3/16″ (3.1875″). In order to bore it to 3 5/16″ (3.3125″), three passes were made in each cylinder with the boring bar. The 0.125″ (1/8″) overbore on this block resulted in 7.5 lbs. of material being removed. The estimated cost for cylinder boring and honing and de-glazing is $125.

The cylinder boring is carried out using Rottler Boring Bar Company's Model F2B boring bar, or a similar type of machine. The engine block is set up in this machine, the centerline of the crankshaft is located using a dial indicator, and the block is then clamped into position, ready for the actual cylinder boring operation.

The final stage of the boring operation is the cylinder honing and de-glazing. This is a very important step and must be carried out correctly in order to ensure the proper seating of the piston rings. This procedure is undertaken using a Sunnen Automatic Cylinder Re-Sizing Machine, Model CK-10, or similar type of equipment. This machine is used to remove the last 0.003″ to 0.004″ of material from the cylinder walls using Sunnen 600-series 280-grit stones (for cast iron rings). The final result will be the finished bore. The finish on the cylinder walls will be a "cross-hatch" pattern.

This is a finished crankshaft that has been aligned and is guaranteed to be perfectly straight. It has been installed with the correct main bearings and torqued to 105 ft-lb in order to check the engine block main bearing bores and caps for proper alignment. This block did not require align honing.

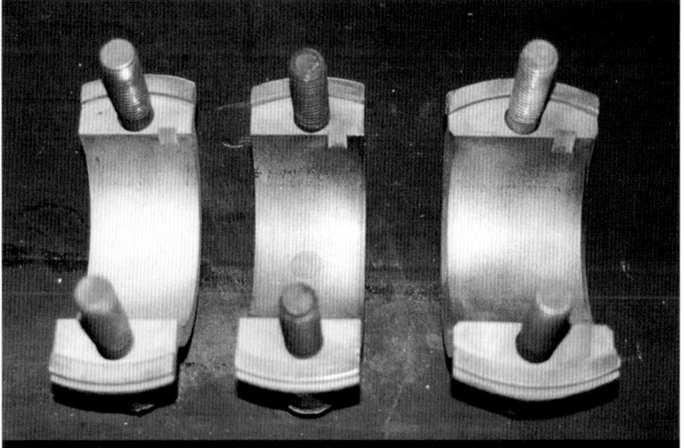

This picture of the underside of a set of flathead main bearing caps clearly shows the curved ridge near the outer edge of the caps. This ridge fits into a slot in the engine block. The result is a very strong interlocking system for the main bearing caps. The width of these caps is greater than the width of most OHV (overhead valve) engine main bearing caps.

Align Hone

The centerline of the crankshaft is the point from which all critical measurements are taken. The centerline of the crankshaft is used to ensure that the engine block main bearing housing bores, with the main bearing caps attached, are exactly parallel to it. The crankshaft centerline in a Ford flathead V-8 engine is offset 0.265″ to right.

The engine block main bearing housing bores must be measured to ensure they are all in perfect alignment with each other. If they are not, the block will have to be align honed. If the main bearing caps are not the original caps for the engine block, the block may have to be align honed or possibly even align bored. Each time the align honing operation is performed, 0.0005″ should be removed from the main bearing bores and main bearing caps. This process ensures they are exactly parallel with the centerline of the crankshaft. This procedure is so critical that it should only be done at a machine shop that builds high-performance engines. The estimated cost to align hone is $200.

A Sunnen Horizontal Hone, Model CH-100, align honing machine is being used to align hone a Keith Black aluminum hemi block that will be used for drag racing. You had better believe the operator of this machine knows what he is doing when something this expensive is being tackled! The flathead block described in this section did not require align honing.

An accepted method of checking the main bearing housing bore alignment of the engine block is to use a crankshaft that has been checked for alignment and is guaranteed to be straight. The correct main bearings for the crankshaft are installed in the block, the main bearings are well oiled, the crankshaft is installed, and the main bearing cap bolts are torqued to 105 ft-lb. The crankshaft should spin freely without any tight spots. If it does, the block is satisfactory. If it does not, the block should be align honed.

Use an inside micrometer or dial indicator to check the size of the main bearing housing bores with the main bearing caps installed and torqued to 105 ft-lb. Do this without installing the main bearings. The inside diameter measurement of all the main bearing housing bores should be 2.670″ to 2.671″ and they should all be perfectly round.

A Sunnen Horizontal Hone, Model CH-100, align honing machine, or similar type of machine, is used for align honing the engine block. The key to this whole procedure is the skill and experience of the operator. The best align honing machine operated by an unskilled align hone operator will destroy your engine block.

It is not often a flathead engine block appears on the scene that requires align honing. If the block is fitted with the original main bearing caps and there has not been a bearing problem in the past, such as a "spun" bearing or lack of lubrication, in all likelihood the block will not require align honing. The bottom end of a Ford flathead V-8 engine block is well-designed and built.

In most engines the mating surfaces, where the main bearing caps are attached to the block, are square and at 90 degrees. The main bearing caps on a flathead engine have a curved ridge on the underside that fits into a curved slot in the block. This interlocking system, along with the fact the flathead main bearing caps are almost twice the width of most OHV engine main bearing caps, results in a very rigid fixture.

Parallel Deck

An engine block is parallel decked to ensure the deck height is the same for all the cylinders. It also guarantees the deck is exactly 90 degrees to the cylinder bores. Most flathead engine blocks require the removal of 0.005″ to 0.012″ of deck material when they are parallel decked. The estimated cost for parallel decking is $110.

A Repco Automotive Equipment Company Type ASG parallel decking machine with the engine block described in this section.

A Repco Automotive Equipment Company Type ASG, or similar type of machine, is used to parallel deck the engine block. The crankshaft centerline is located using a dial indicator, the engine block is then clamped into position, and then one side of the block is parallel decked followed by the other side.

Shot Peen

While the engine block is at the machine shop, this is a good time to have the main bearing caps and main bearing cap bolts shot peened. This procedure assists removing any stress from these items.

These 1949-53 Ford flathead V-8 main bearing caps and main bearing cap bolts have been shot peened. The caps are in order, with the cap marked "F" for the front of the engine block, the cap marked "C" for the center of the engine block, and the big cap is always for the rear of the engine block.

Valve Seat Inserts

If the original intake valve seat inserts are badly pitted, they should be replaced. The engine described in this section will be fitted with 1.61″-diameter intake and exhaust valves. There is enough material left around the original intake valve seat inserts when this size of valve is installed. The intake valve seat inserts "run" cooler than the exhaust valve seat inserts so they do not need as much surface material around them.

The exhaust valve seat inserts "run" hotter and therefore require more surface material around them. There is enough material left around the original exhaust valve seat inserts when the 1.61″-diameter exhaust valves are installed.

The current consensus among the majority of engine builders is the exhaust valve seat inserts should be replaced

The Serdi 60 valve-seat grinding machine before it was "knocked down" for the valve job on the flathead block.

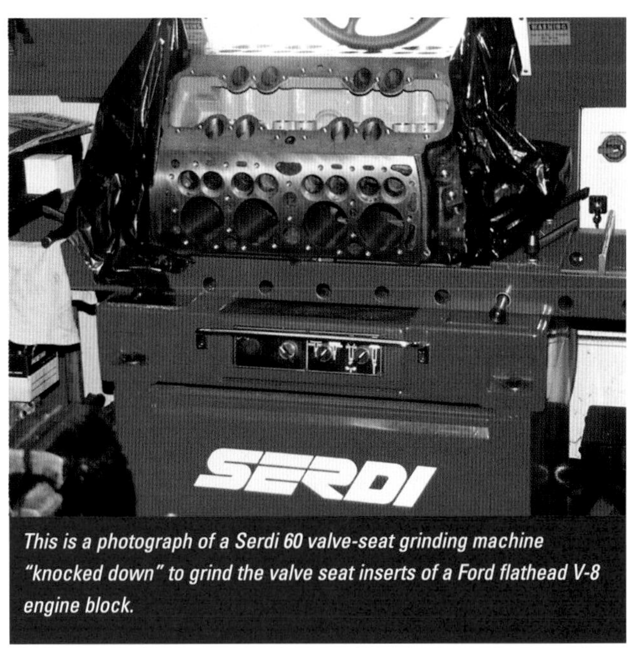

This is a photograph of a Serdi 60 valve-seat grinding machine "knocked down" to grind the valve seat inserts of a Ford flathead V-8 engine block.

with hardened ductile iron inserts for use with today's unleaded gasoline. If your vehicle is only going to be driven occasionally on the street, this is not a requirement. An associate of mine drove his car daily without hardened exhaust seat inserts for over 300,000 miles before the inserts finally packed it in!

Many flathead engine blocks came from the factory with hardened exhaust valve seat inserts. Your local machine shop will be able to tell you if your block has the hardened exhaust valve seat inserts installed when they start to grind the valve seat inserts. The engine block discussed in this section had hardened exhaust valve seat inserts, and all the valve seat inserts in the block were in good condition. As a result, no new valve seat inserts were required.

If new valve seat inserts are required for the installation of 1.60″-diameter valves, the parts necessary are the Ertel Manufacturing Company #80780 intake valve seat inserts and #80810 hardened ductile iron exhaust valve seat inserts. The valve seat inserts can be purchased from most automotive supply outlets, or your local machine shop can probably provide them. The installation of the valve seat inserts should be left to an experienced machine shop. The estimated cost for the installation of 16 new valve seat inserts is $200, not including the cost of the inserts.

Valve Grind

Locate a machine shop that has a reputation for performing top-quality Serdi-machined, multi-angle "blueprint" valve grinds. The Serdi valve grinding machine is fitted with a boring bar that machines the valve seat inserts, rather than the old-style method of grinding the valve seat inserts using stones. This boring bar enables the valve seat inserts to be blended in with the intake and exhaust ports and ensures all the valves are at the same equal depth in the valve seat inserts. Obviously, you will have to purchase the valves prior to the Serdi machine operation. The estimated cost for a Serdi-machined multi-angle "blueprint" valve grind is $200.

Here is a flathead engine block with all the machining procedures completed. The block has been thoroughly cleaned, and it is now time to mask the block prior to the external paint being applied.

A Serdi 60 Automatic Centering By Spherical and Flat Air Cushion valve seat grinding machine should be used. The Serdi machine is a top-of-the-line machine that performs outstanding valve seat grinding. This is simply the best way to grind Ford flathead V-8 valve seat inserts.

High Performance Engines "knocks down" the Serdi valve grinding machine in order to grind the valve seat inserts in a Ford flathead V-8 engine block. They have designed two different types of jigs, for centering purposes, to use with the Serdi machine that allow them to grind the valve seat inserts with or without the valve guide bushings installed.

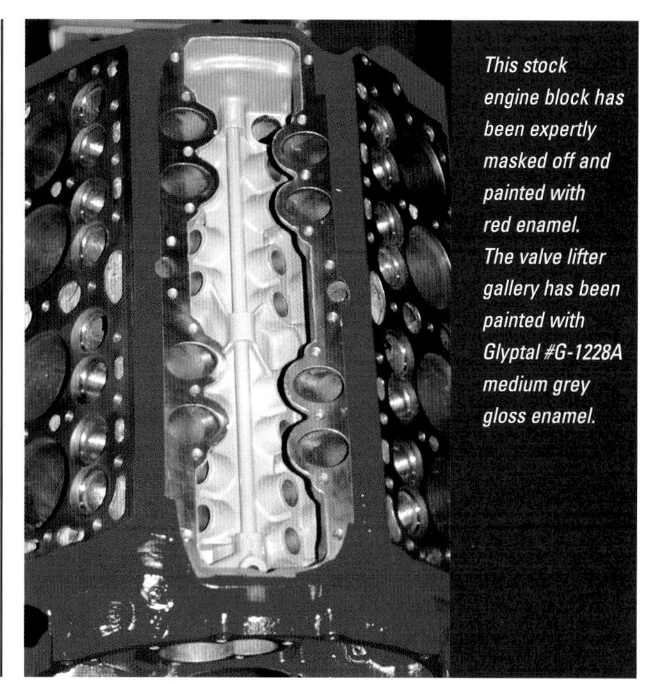

This stock engine block has been expertly masked off and painted with red enamel. The valve lifter gallery has been painted with Glyptal #G-1228A medium grey gloss enamel.

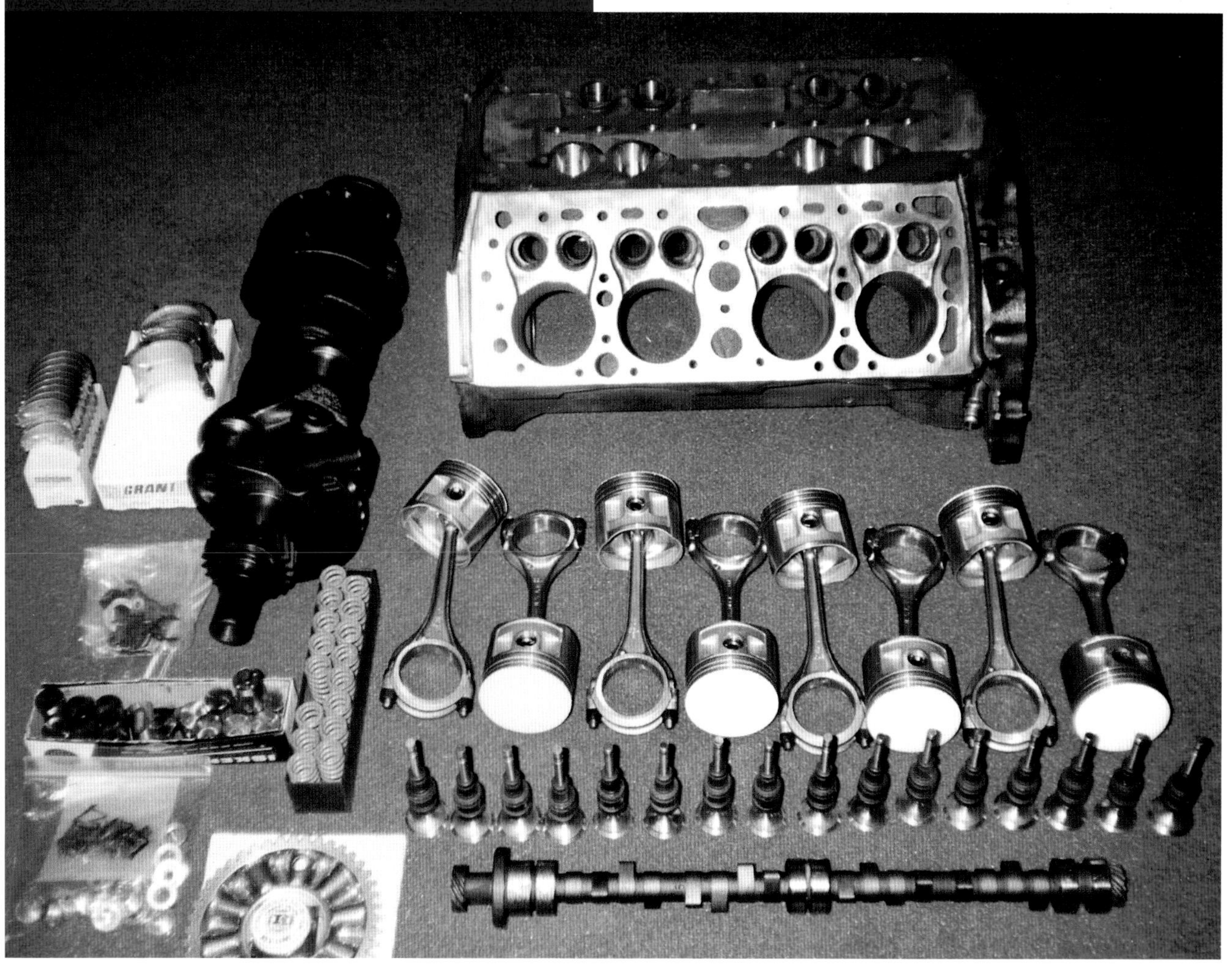

Here are the parts for a street performance flathead short block before going to the machine shop. The engine block is a 1950 Canadian Ford C8BA casting. Also seen are a Mercury 4" cast alloy steel crankshaft, Jahns C90 three-ring cast aluminum pistons with Grant piston rings, Clevite 77 bearings, and Iskenderian #818800 "88 grind" camshaft and adjustable lifters. Rounding out the display are Iskenderian #185-G single valve springs, retainers, locks, and keepers; new 1.60" intake valves and 1.50" exhaust valves with new guides; and an aluminum camshaft timing gear.

De-Glaze

De-glaze the valve lifter bosses and the valve guide bosses using a wheel cylinder hone. Do just enough honing to clean up these bosses. An absolute minimum of material should be removed in order to avoid excess valve lifter and guide clearance, which will result in oiling problems. Do not pretend you are boring out a cylinder when you do this!

Cracks

If there were any cracks in the block around the cylinder head bolt holes, have them "stitched" by an expert machine shop. This is absolutely not a job for the home engine builder or even a regular welder. There is a procedure to repairing the cracks in the block, and it must be followed closely, or the block could be ruined. Having gone through a lot of trouble to locate a fairly decent engine block, you do not want it to end up in the cargo hold of a ship bound for a scrap yard in India!

Cleaning and Painting

After all the machining procedures in this chapter have been performed, thoroughly clean the engine block with hot water and soap. Use long, thin engine brushes to reach as far into the oil passages as possible. Spend the time to do this job properly. The term "surgically clean" applies here.

Mask off the engine with newspaper and use the intake manifold gasket, cylinder head gaskets, oil pan gaskets, timing cover gasket, oil pump idler gear cover gasket, and water pump gaskets as templates for masking. This way all the exposed areas of the engine block will be painted. This procedure is referred to as detailing. You might want to trim the intake manifold gasket to the shape of the intake manifold in order to avoid having a lot of bare gasket material exposed.

One of the best paint products I have found for use on engine blocks is Endura #EX-2C black 160 hi-gloss polyurethane. This is really tough paint that seems to be impervious to gasoline, oil, antifreeze, or brake fluid, and will give a beautiful finish to the engine block. I have always used black as my choice of color for blocks. However, this product is available in different colors, and there are a number of other manufacturers of polyurethane paint, such as RM and PPG. You can purchase polyurethane paint from any industrial paint supply store or even your local body shop.

Engine Block Summary

1950 Canadian Ford 239.4-ci L-head V-8 engine block; Casting Number: C8BA; 2-bolt main bearing caps; 24 stud block; Stock Bore: 3³⁄₁₆" (3.1875"); Stock Stroke: 3½"; Stock Compression Ratio: 6.8:1; 100 hp @ 3,600 rpm and 181 ft-lb torque @ 2,000 rpm. Engine block weight (bare): 200 lbs.	$200.00
Engine block hot tanked and redi-stripped. Engine block, main bearing caps, and main bearing cap bolts Magnafluxed.	$205.00
All threads re-tapped; main bearing caps and main bearing cap bolts shot peened; cylinder head bolt holes chamfered; valve lifter bosses de-glazed allowing for 0.0015" valve lifter clearance; valve lifter bosses drilled with ³⁄₁₆" (0.1875") hole for valve lifter adjustment. Exterior surface of engine block sanded and detailed. Valve lifter gallery and front of engine block painted with Glyptal #G-1228A medium grey gloss enamel. Exterior surface of engine block painted with Endura #EX-2C black 160 hi-gloss polyurethane.	$373.06
Engine block converted to "full-flow" oil system.	$65.00
Engine block bored 0.125" (⅛") oversize and cylinders honed and de-glazed using Sunnen 600-series 280-grit stones, final bore: 3⁵⁄₁₆" (3.3125"). Piston-to-bore clearance: 0.004" measured below bottom of wrist pin perpendicular to wrist pin.	$125.00
Engine block parallel decked to 0.010" average, below deck.	$110.00
Serdi-machined multi-angle "blueprint" valve grind performed.	$200.00
Intake and exhaust ports fully ported and polished and gasket matched.	$216.67
ENGINE BLOCK TOTAL:	**$1,494.73**

CHAPTER 2
CRANKSHAFT

Purchase

The best crankshaft to use for a street performance Ford flathead V-8 engine is the 1949-53 Mercury with the 4.00″ stroke. The Mercury crankshaft is manufactured from cast alloy steel and is a fine-quality item. A Mercury crankshaft in good condition is getting harder to find and, as a result, the price is going up. Currently, the price for one of these crankshafts is in the $300 to $400 range, depending on how many times it has been previously ground.

If your engine is still assembled and a cylinder head has been removed, measure the stroke to see if it is 4.00″. If the crankshaft is out of the engine block, have a machine shop or a professional engine builder measure the stroke. This is important because the difference between the stroke of a Ford and Mercury flathead V-8 crankshaft is only ¼″ (0.250″), and trying to measure it with a pair of calipers on a garage floor could give an incorrect reading.

Some of the Mercury crankshafts had a small oval ("jellybean") indent, approximately ¾″ length x ⅜″ width, in the front of the forward counterweight. The crankshaft may even have the Mercury casting or model number left on it. Look for the model number CM or the casting number 61402 on the counterweights.

The crankshaft will probably have to be re-ground. *The Ford Motor Company of Canada Master Repair Manual* specifies the out-of-round service limit at 0.0015″, the taper service limit at 0.001″, and the maximum runout at 0.002″. This manual also indicated connecting rod bearings up to 0.040″ undersize could be installed and were available at one time from the Ford Motor Company.

A 1949-53 Mercury 4″-stroke crankshaft with a "jellybean" on the front counterweight is shown with a 1946-48 Ford #6306 cast iron helical crankshaft gear with 22 teeth. The engine block this crankshaft will be installed in is a 1950 Ford. However, it will have the pre-1949 Ford "crab-like" distributor.

Magnaflux

The first thing to do after you have purchased a crankshaft is to have it Magnafluxed. Just make certain that you have an agreement in place with the seller whereby you can return the crankshaft for a full refund if it is found to be cracked or otherwise unusable. The estimated cost to Magnaflux a flathead crankshaft is $20.

Shot Peen and Plug Removal

If the crankshaft passes the Magnaflux test, have it shot peened to assist removing any stress. Remove the four pressed-in oil passage plugs from the ends of the connecting rod journals. These plugs may have to be drilled out. The holes are to be re-tapped for ⅛″ N.P.T. plugs (some crankshafts require ¼″ N.P.T. or ⅜″ N.P.T. plugs). New stainless steel connecting rod journal oil passage plugs should be installed using Loctite. Do this after the crankshaft has been ground, chamfered, and polished. Remove the crankshaft gear with a gear puller.

Straightness, Chamfer, and Polish

Check the crankshaft for alignment and runout with the use of a dial indicator and have it straightened, if necessary. All the oil holes should be chamfered by just lightly grinding the sharp surface off around the oil hole. This means you do not make deep oval craters around the holes. The estimated cost to chamfer the oil holes is $20.

After the crankshaft has been ground and the oil holes have been chamfered, the journals should be polished. This ensures an absolutely smooth bearing surface. The estimated cost of polishing the crankshaft journals is $30.

A 1949-53 Mercury 4"-stroke crankshaft with the oil holes lightly chamfered. The freshly drilled holes in the bottom of the counterweight indicate this crankshaft has just been balanced.

Re-Grinding and Cleaning

If the crankshaft journals are standard size and it is necessary to re-grind the crankshaft, then re-grind the journals to 0.010″ undersize; if the journals have been ground to 0.010″ undersize, then re-grind them to 0.020″ undersize, and so on. A quality machine shop will ensure the crankshaft is ground and polished allowing for the correct bearing clearances. The estimated cost for re-grinding a crankshaft is $105.

After all the procedures mentioned in this chapter have been carried out, thoroughly clean the crankshaft with hot water and soap. Use long, thin engine brushes to clean out the oil holes in the main bearing and connecting rod journals. Once again, the term "surgically clean" applies.

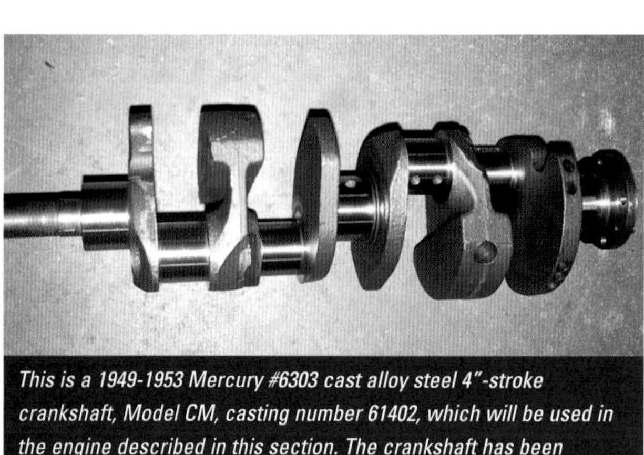

This is a 1949-1953 Mercury #6303 cast alloy steel 4"-stroke crankshaft, Model CM, casting number 61402, which will be used in the engine described in this section. The crankshaft has been Magnafluxed, shot peened, aligned, main journals and connecting rod journals ground 0.020" undersize, balanced, oil holes chamfered, and the journals polished.

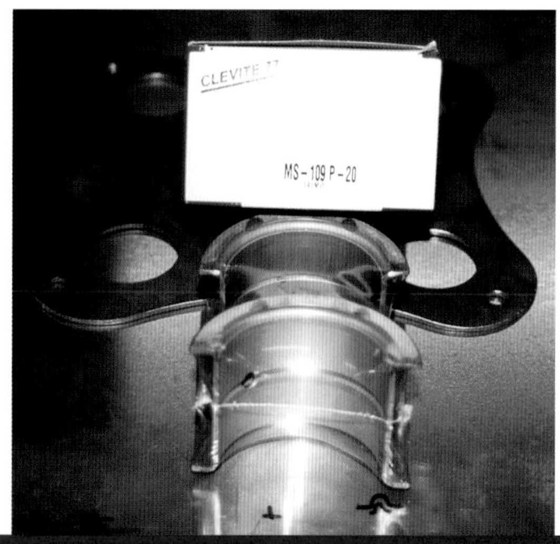

These Clevite "77" #MS-109P-20 main bearings are for the crankshaft being used in the engine described in this section and they are 0.020" oversize.

Main Bearings

I have been using Clevite "77" main bearings by Michigan Bearings for the past number of years in all my engines. They are an excellent bearing and they are competitive in price. These bearings are available for the Ford flathead V-8. Clevite "77" bearings are a tri-metal construction: soft lead alloy outer layer, copper-lead center, and a steel backing.

The main bearings should be inserted in the engine block main bearing bores and the main bearing caps; install the main bearing caps and torque the main bearing cap bolts to 105 ft-lb. Use an inside micrometer, or dial indicator, to measure the inside diameter of the main bearings and a micrometer to measure the main bearing journals on the crankshaft. The difference between these two measurements is the main bearing clearance. *The Ford Motor Company of Canada Master Repair Manual* specifies this clearance to be 0.000″ to 0.0026″.

The crankshaft end play is checked by inserting the main bearings in the main bearing bores and the main bearing caps. Oil the bearings, install the crankshaft, and torque the main bearing cap bolts to 105 ft-lb. Then, insert a socket extension bar into one of the crankshaft counterweight balancing holes, attach a dial indicator to the end of the snout (at the front) or the end of the flywheel flange (at the rear) of the crankshaft, and move the crankshaft forward and backward. The reading on the dial indicator is the crankshaft end play. *The Ford Motor Company of Canada Master Repair Manual* specifies the crankshaft end play to be 0.002″ to 0.006″. The rear main bearing is the "thrust bearing" that controls end play.

It is seldom that a Ford flathead V-8 engine block fitted with a Mercury 4″ stroke crankshaft has a problem with

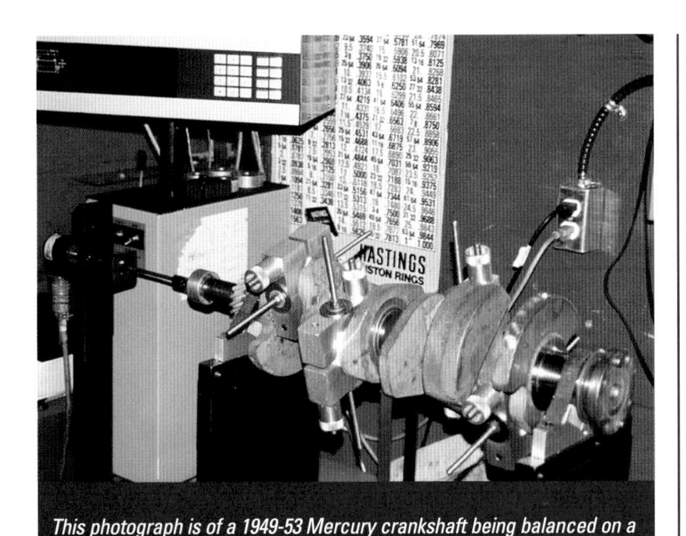

This photograph is of a 1949-53 Mercury crankshaft being balanced on a Hines Industries balancer with digital readout. The bob weights bolted to each of the connecting rod journals simulates the exact weight of the connecting rod/piston assemblies attached to that journal.

crankshaft end play. These blocks and cranks were made of sturdy material. As long as quality main bearings are installed with the correct clearance, the crankshaft is perfectly straight, and the original main bearing caps are in place, there should not be a problem with crankshaft end play.

It is usually a good idea to have the machine shop that grinds your crankshaft supply the crankshaft bearings. This way you are certain to be in possession of the correct bearings and not something that fits a 1985 Yugo. If you do know what bearings the re-ground crankshaft requires and you want to purchase them yourself, they are available through most automotive supply outlets.

Crankshaft Gear and Pulley

The stock Ford crankshaft gear will be reused, provided none of the gear teeth are chipped or missing. These are tough gears and they do not usually wear out, because the camshaft gear is made of aluminum or a fiber material. The Ford crankshaft gear and crankshaft pulley woodruff keys will be reused provided they are in good condition. If a new crankshaft gear is required, use a Melling #2701 crankshaft gear (1949-53), available at most automotive parts outlets.

A 1949-53 Ford Truck #GAUB241815 double-groove crankshaft pulley will be installed. This pulley utilizes the "wide" ⅝″ V-belt in order to be compatible with the 1949-53 Ford Truck water pumps. The crankshaft pulley diameter was reduced to 4¾″ in order to clear the 1942-48 distributor housing.

Luke's produces a crankshaft sleeve that is required when using the Speedway Motors one-piece front crankshaft oil seal; more about that seal later.

Crankshaft Summary

Item	Cost
1949-53 Mercury #6303 cast alloy steel crankshaft; Model CM; Casting Number: 61402; main journal diameter: 2.498″-2.499″; connecting rod journal diameter: 2.138″-2.139″; non-floating connecting rod bearings; Stock Stroke: 4.00″. Crankshaft weight: 67 lbs.	$400.00
Crankshaft Magnafluxed, aligned, and shot peened; main journals ground 0.020″ undersize; connecting rod journals ground 0.020″ undersize; oil holes chamfered; journals polished; and crankshaft balanced. Factory crankshaft connecting rod journal oil plugs removed and new stainless steel ⅛″ N.P.T. plugs installed using Loctite.	$270.00
New Clevite "77" #MS-109P-20 main bearings, 0.020″ oversize, installed allowing for 0.002″ crankshaft clearance and 0.004″ end play. Main bearing cap bolts torqued to 105 ft-lb using Molykote.	$117.11
1946-1948 Ford #6306 cast iron helical crankshaft gear, 22 teeth, and Ford #6310 oil slinger installed with Ford #357654-S crankshaft gear woodruff key. Luke's new crankshaft oil seal sleeve installed. 1949-53 Ford Truck #GAUB241815 crankshaft pulley, 4½″ diameter, double groove, installed with Ford #74153-S crankshaft pulley woodruff key and Ford #351590-S crankshaft pulley bolt washer with Ford #20639-S crankshaft pulley bolt. Crankshaft pulley bolt installed using Loctite and torqued to 50 ft-lb. Oil slinger painted with Glyptal #G-1228A medium grey gloss enamel.	$135.87
CRANKSHAFT TOTAL:	**$922.98**

CHAPTER 3
CONNECTING RODS AND PISTONS

Purchase

The connecting rods to use in a street performance or blown street engine are those found in the 1949-53 Ford flathead V-8 engine. The casting number for these connecting rods is 8BA6205A or 8BA and they use non-floating connecting rod bearings. Fortunately, lot of these rods are still available at very reasonable prices.

These connecting rods are forged steel of an "I" beam construction with integral studs. The flathead connecting rods may look frail when placed next to a connecting rod from a large cubic-inch OHV engine, but these Ford connecting rods are tough little critters! The connecting rod studs cannot be updated because they cannot be removed from the rod.

The 1949-53 Ford flathead V-8 connecting rods are 7.00″ length, center to center—that is, from the center of the big end to the center of the small end. There is a rod ratio of 1.75 when a 4″ stroke crankshaft is used. The connecting rod studs are 3/8″ N.F. thread.

Magnaflux and Shot Peen

The connecting rods must be Magnafluxed to ensure there are no hidden flaws. Shot peen the connecting rods to assist removing any stress points. Do not shot peen the studs. Mask the studs with duct tape. Purchase new connecting rod nuts, Pioneer #CRN-731, worth about $3.30 for 16 nuts. The estimated cost to Magnaflux eight connecting rods is $30.

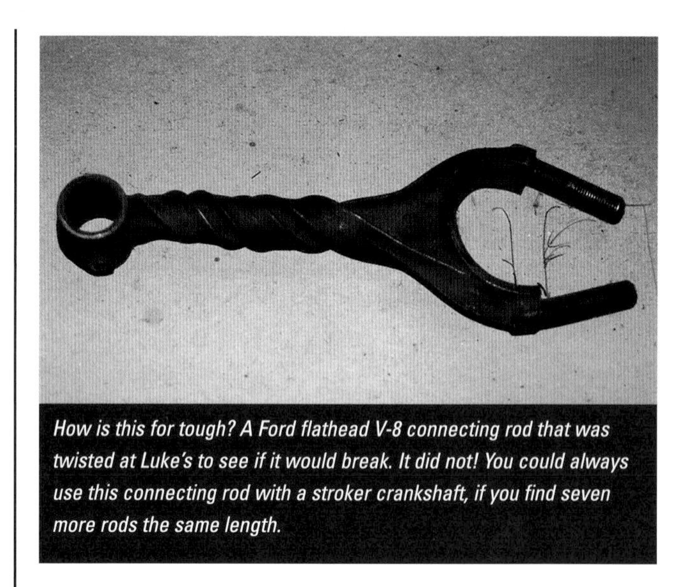

How is this for tough? A Ford flathead V-8 connecting rod that was twisted at Luke's to see if it would break. It did not! You could always use this connecting rod with a stroker crankshaft, if you find seven more rods the same length.

Align, Re-Size, and Re-Bush

The connecting rods should be aligned using a Sunnen connecting rod alignment tool, or a similar type instrument, and a connecting rod vise. Aligning ensures the connecting rods are vertically straight in both the front and side position: in other words, not twisted or bent.

The crankshaft end of the connecting rod ("the big end") should be re-sized on a Sunnen Heavy Duty Precision Honing Machine, Powerstroker Model LBB-1810, or a similar type of machine. This process will ensure the big

Anyone for flathead connecting rods? Just one box of the stash of connecting rods that I discovered at Luke's Custom Machine & Design. Full floating and non-floating connecting rods are pictured here.

This is a Sunnen connecting rod alignment tool. After the connecting rods are checked for alignment and, if necessary, aligned, they will be absolutely straight.

Here is the crankshaft end ("the big end") of a connecting rod being honed on a Sunnen Heavy Duty Precision Honing Machine, Powerstroker Model LBB-1810.

The wrist pin end ("the small end") of a connecting rod is being honed on a Sunnen Heavy Duty Precision Honing Machine, Model LBB-1499.

ends are perfectly round and all the connecting rods are the same length, center to center. The estimated cost for re-sizing a set of connecting rods is $80.

Install new wrist pin bushings in the connecting rods. After more than 50 years, it is very likely the original rod bushings are worn out. Sealed Power (Federal Mogul) manufactures the wrist pin bushings in two types: #9024VA for the 0.8125″ wrist pin bore and #9024XBS for the 0.819″ wrist pin bore.

Here are seven of a set of connecting rods with new wrist pin bushings installed and honed, and the big ends re-sized. New Pioneer #CRN-731 connecting rod nuts have been installed.

Now here is a rare instrument: a gauge used to check the size of the crankshaft end ("the big end") of a Ford or Mercury connecting rod. Printed on it is: "Ford V-8-Mercury con rod gauge #105 mfg. by All-Power Mfg. Co. Los Angeles Cal."

There is a rumor that only the Sealed Power (Federal Mogul) #9024XBS connecting rod wrist pin bushing is still available. If that wrist pin bushing is used, the small end of the connecting rod must be honed in order for it to fit. If the Sealed Power (Federal Mogul) #9024VA wrist pin bushing can be located, no honing of the small end of the connecting rod is required. Do not confuse the foregoing explanation of the honing of the small end of the connecting rod with the actual honing of the wrist pin bushing after it is installed.

The pistons should be brought to the machine shop when the wrist pin bushings are being replaced. The machine shop can then hone the bushings to fit the wrist pins allowing for the correct clearance. *The Ford Motor Company of Canada Master Repair Manual* specifies 0.001″ to 0.003″ wrist pin clearance in the connecting rod.

The honing of the wrist pin end ("the small end") of the connecting rod is carried out on a Sunnen Heavy Duty Precision Honing Machine, Model LBB-1499, or similar type of machine. The estimated cost for re-bushing and wrist pin fitting a set of connecting rods is $120, which does not include the price of the wrist pin bushing.

De-Beam

It is not recommended to de-beam the Ford flathead V-8 connecting rods for street performance use. There is not a lot of material to play with on these rods, and sometimes things are best left alone. If the rods were going to be "boxed," then the subject of de-beaming could be reviewed (see Section II, Chapter 23).

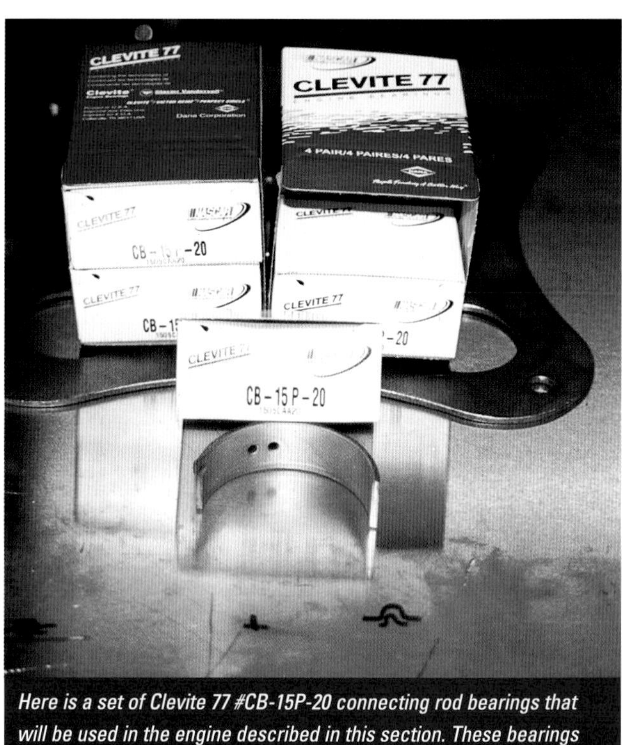

Here is a set of Clevite 77 #CB-15P-20 connecting rod bearings that will be used in the engine described in this section. These bearings are 0.020″ oversize.

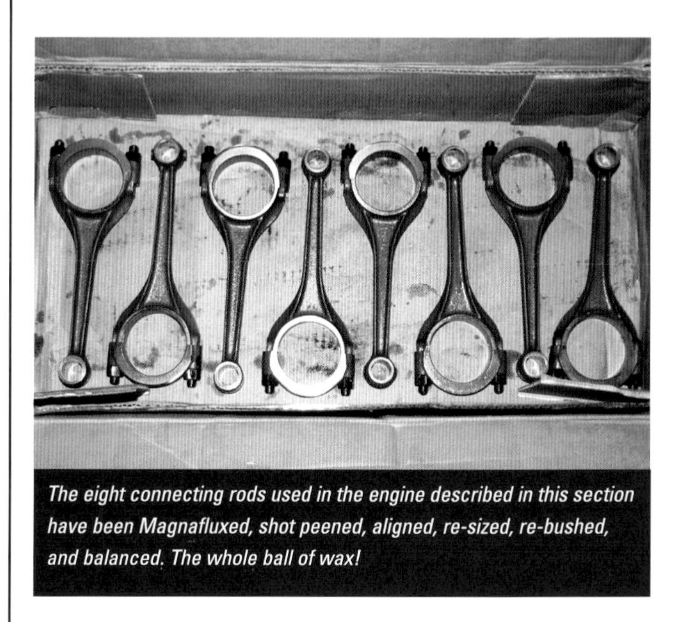

The eight connecting rods used in the engine described in this section have been Magnafluxed, shot peened, aligned, re-sized, re-bushed, and balanced. The whole ball of wax!

Connecting Rod Bearings

I believe the best connecting rod bearings to use in the Ford flathead V-8 engine are the Clevite "77" by Michigan Bearings. They are of excellent quality, reasonably priced, and can be purchased at your local automotive supply outlet.

Here is another treasure trove of NOS (new-old-stock) parts. They are: Ford #B-9243-A fuel line fittings ¼" line for the fuel pump; Ford #48-12148 distributor to front cover screws; Ford #C21A-6761-B oil level indicator gasket (felt dipstick gasket); and a Ford #C49A-6200 connecting rod still wrapped in the factory greased cloth!

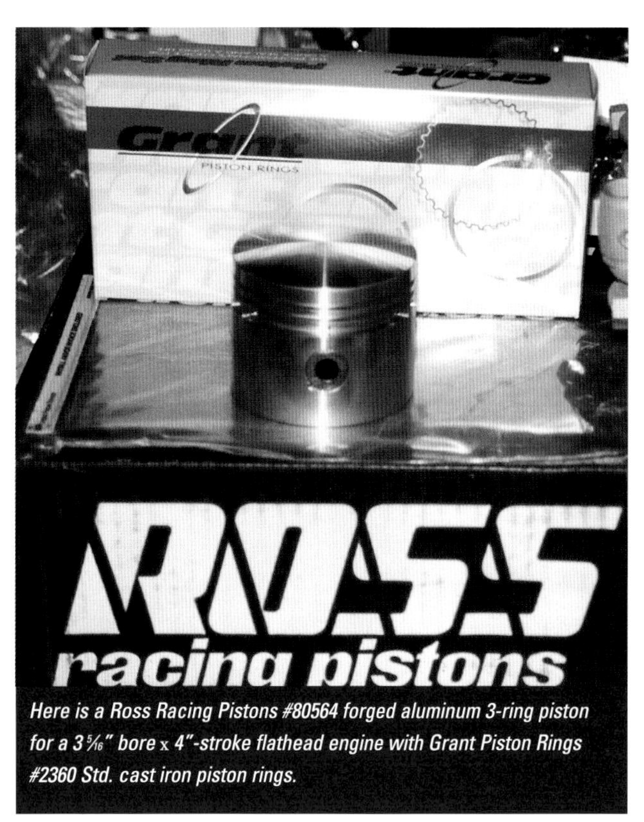

Here is a Ross Racing Pistons #80564 forged aluminum 3-ring piston for a 3 5/16" bore x 4"-stroke flathead engine with Grant Piston Rings #2360 Std. cast iron piston rings.

The correct method of checking the connecting rod bearing clearance is to insert the connecting rod bearings in the connecting rods and the connecting rod caps, torque the connecting rod nuts to 45 ft-lb in a connecting rod vise, and then measure the bores with an inside micrometer or dial indicator. Measure the connecting rod journals of the crankshaft with a micrometer. The difference between these two measurements is the clearance. *The Ford Motor Company of Canada Master Repair Manual* specifies the connecting rod bearing clearance to be 0.0005″ to 0.003″.

The correct procedure for checking the side clearance of a pair of connecting rods is to measure the distance across the connecting rod journal with an inside micrometer, clamp the two connecting rods for that journal together in a connecting rod vise, and use a micrometer to measure the thickness of the two connecting rods. The difference between these two measurements is the connecting rod side clearance, per pair of connecting rods. This clearance should be re-checked with a feeler gauge when the connecting rods are installed on the crankshaft. *The Ford Motor Company of Canada Master Repair Manual* specifies the connecting rod side clearance, per pair of connecting rods, to be 0.006″ to 0.020″.

Pistons

The pistons that will be used in the engine described in this section are manufactured by Ross Racing Pistons using forged 2618 T-61 aluminum and have a slight domed top. The pistons are the three-ring design and weigh 310 grams. The wrist pins are chrome moly straight-wall steel weighing 120 grams. Spiro Lox retainers are supplied with the pistons.

The Ross Racing Pistons #80564 pistons are for a 3 5/16″ (3.3125″) bore and a 4.00″ stroke. The rings supplied are Grant Piston Rings #2360 Std. cast iron top and second-compression ring. This is an excellent package at a great price. These Ross forged pistons, wrist pins, and piston

This is a Ross Racing Piston #80564 forged piston with the "straight wall" wrist pin.

This is a set of Jahns C90 cast aluminum 3-ring pistons for a 3⅜" bore x 4" stroke flathead engine. The piston tops are painted with V.H.T. #SP-101 flat white high temperature coating. This is an old drag racing trick. The theory behind this is the paint will help to promote "flame travel" across the piston top during initial start-up. The paint will eventually burn off. I recently examined a set of pistons that had been painted like this, from an engine driven on the street for over 3,000 miles. The paint was just starting to burn off and the piston tops appeared brand new. Whether this theory actually works, it is hard to say, but it certainly does no harm. Besides, when the piston tops are painted, they look great in photographs!

rings cost around $100 more than the old-style cast pistons and rings. Forget about nostalgia and go with quality!

Grant Piston Rings recommends the end gaps to be 0.003" to 0.004" per inch of cylinder bore. This would be 0.010" to 0.013" for an engine with a 3⁵⁄₁₆" (3.3125") bore. The oil ring is set at 0.014". Some experts would argue that only moly rings should be used in today's engines. There is no question that moly rings are good, but do not underestimate the quality and lifespan of good cast iron rings. They work just fine in the old Ford flathead V-8.

The Grant piston rings, supplied for the engine described in this section, did not require gapping. The top and second compression rings, as they came out of the box, had 0.012" gap, and the oil rings had a gap of 0.014". This is apparently quite normal for the Grant piston rings, as they are not really considered "file fit" rings. This is a sweet benefit and makes the price of the Ross pistons with Grant rings look even better.

An accepted method of checking the end gap of the piston rings is to place a piston ring approximately 1" from the top of the cylinder in which it is going to be used. The ring must be perfectly "square" in the cylinder to obtain an accurate measurement. Use a feeler gauge to determine the end gap of the ring. If this end gap is in accordance with the end gap called for by the piston ring manufacturer, then move on to the next piston ring and continue until all the rings for all the cylinders are checked.

If the piston ring end gap is not wide enough, you must file the end of the piston ring until you obtain the correct end gap. File the piston ring using a rotary piston ring filing tool in order to ensure the ends of the piston ring remain parallel to each other.

After all the piston rings are correctly gapped, install them on the pistons using a piston ring installation tool. This tool expands the rings enough to install them without scratching and gouging the aluminum pistons or breaking the rings. Prior to installation of the piston assemblies in the engine, the piston rings are individually turned on the pistons within the piston ring manufacturer's recommended arc. This means that each of the three rings on a piston are turned and positioned so the end gap is not in the same location for all three rings. Install the piston assemblies in

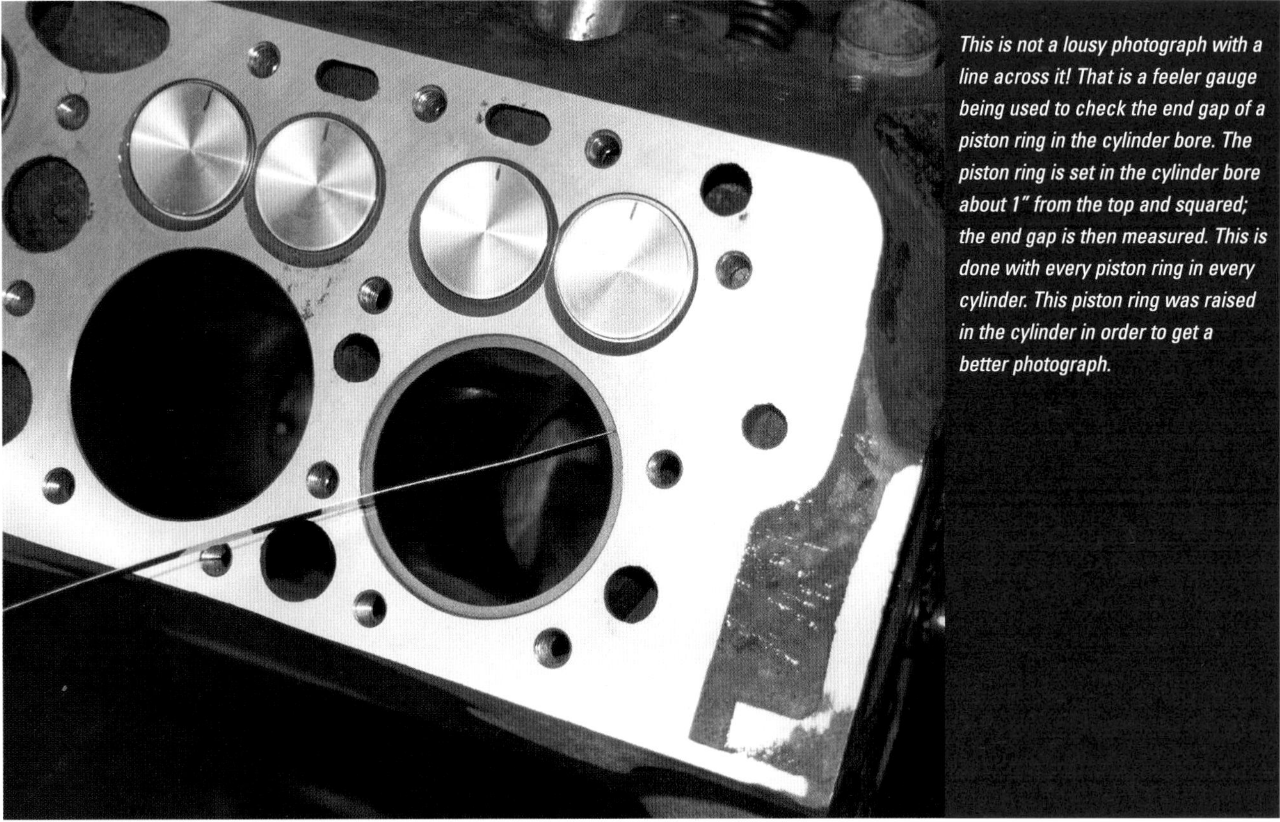

This is not a lousy photograph with a line across it! That is a feeler gauge being used to check the end gap of a piston ring in the cylinder bore. The piston ring is set in the cylinder bore about 1" from the top and squared; the end gap is then measured. This is done with every piston ring in every cylinder. This piston ring was raised in the cylinder in order to get a better photograph.

The Ross Racing Pistons forged aluminum pistons with wrist pins are of exceptional quality.

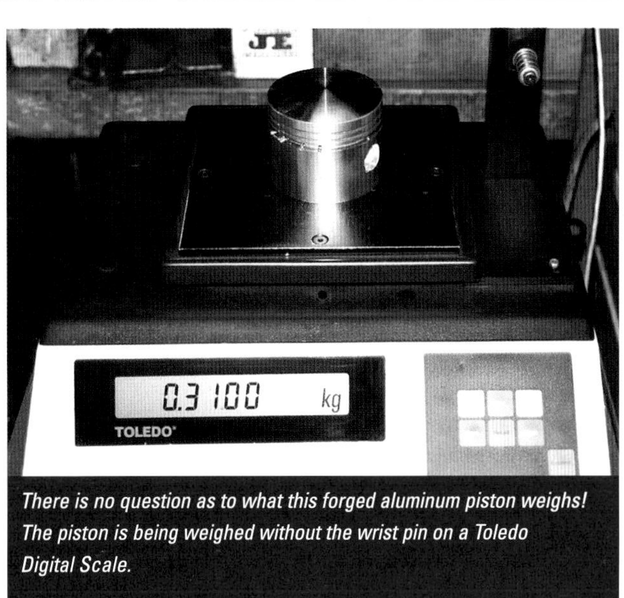

There is no question as to what this forged aluminum piston weighs! The piston is being weighed without the wrist pin on a Toledo Digital Scale.

the engine block using a piston ring compressor, which compresses the rings evenly around the piston. Then insert the piston in the cylinder bore by gently tapping the piston top with a piece of wood or the handle end of a rubber hammer. Use plastic connecting rod bolt protectors when installing the connecting rod/piston assemblies so as not to nick the crankshaft connecting rod journals.

Balancing

One of the most important steps in building a reliable engine is to have it properly balanced. This is a job for an experienced machine shop. Do not start drilling metal out of the pistons, rods, etc., and think you are helping the situation. Proper engine balancing is a real art that should be left to the professionals.

This connecting rod is being balanced on a Stewart-Warner Connecting Rod Balancer, Model 329738. This is a rotating balance with the big end mounted on the balancing machine.

A connecting rod is being balanced on a Stewart-Warner Connecting rod balancer, Model 329738. This is a reciprocating balance with the small end placed on the balancing machine.

You should weigh the pistons on a Toledo Digital Scale, or similar type of instrument, in order to find the lightest weight piston. The other seven pistons are then lightened to that weight. The proper method of reducing the weight of a piston is to remove material by milling from the outside (the bottom) of the wrist pin bosses.

The connecting rods are weighed on a Stewart-Warner Connecting Rod Balancer, Model 329738, or a similar type instrument, in order to find the lightest connecting rod. The lightest connecting rod is then balanced by placing the crankshaft end (the big end) on the balancing machine and suspending the wrist pin end (the small end). This is called a rotating balance. Then the wrist pin end is placed on the balancing machine and the crankshaft end is suspended. This is called a reciprocating balance. All the other connecting rods are balanced in the same manner and have material removed in order to be the same weight as the lightest rod. Material is removed from the top of the connecting rod, above the wrist pin hole, or from the sides of the connecting rod and cap using a belt sander. Do not remove material from the bottom of the flathead connecting rod cap, because there is a limited amount of material in this area. If the numbers on the side of a connecting rod are ground off as a result of the balancing, re-stamp them.

The crankshaft is balanced using a Hines Industries Digital Balancer, or a similar type of machine. The pistons, wrist pins, wrist pin locks, piston rings, connecting rod bearings, connecting rods, connecting rod nuts, and even an estimated amount of lubricating oil is calculated and a final weight is tallied up. This exact amount of weight, in the form of an attachable bob weight, is bolted to each crankshaft connecting rod journal. The crankshaft is then spun on the balancing machine, and additional weight is either removed by drilling material from the bottom edges of the crankshaft counterweights, or added by drilling and inserting heavy metal (Mallory metal) in the sides of the crankshaft counterweights in order to compensate for any imbalance.

The bob weight is calculated by adding the following weights:

Piston weight (each):	____ x 1 =	____ grams
Wrist pin (each):	____ x 1 =	____ grams
Wrist pin locks (pair/piston):	____ x 1 =	____ grams
Piston rings (set/piston):	____ x 1 =	____ grams
Reciprocating connecting rod (each):	____ x 1 =	____ grams
Rotating connecting rod (each):	____ x 2 =	____ grams
Connecting rod bearings (set/rod):	____ x 2 =	____ grams
Connecting rod nuts (pair):	____ x 2 =	____ grams
Oil (estimated):	____ x 1 =	____ grams
Total "Bob" weight:		____ grams

My sincere thanks to Bud Child, of High Performance Engines, for this valuable information.

If a standard transmission is to be used, the crankshaft pulley, flywheel, clutch disc, and pressure plate should be delivered to the machine shop for balancing with the

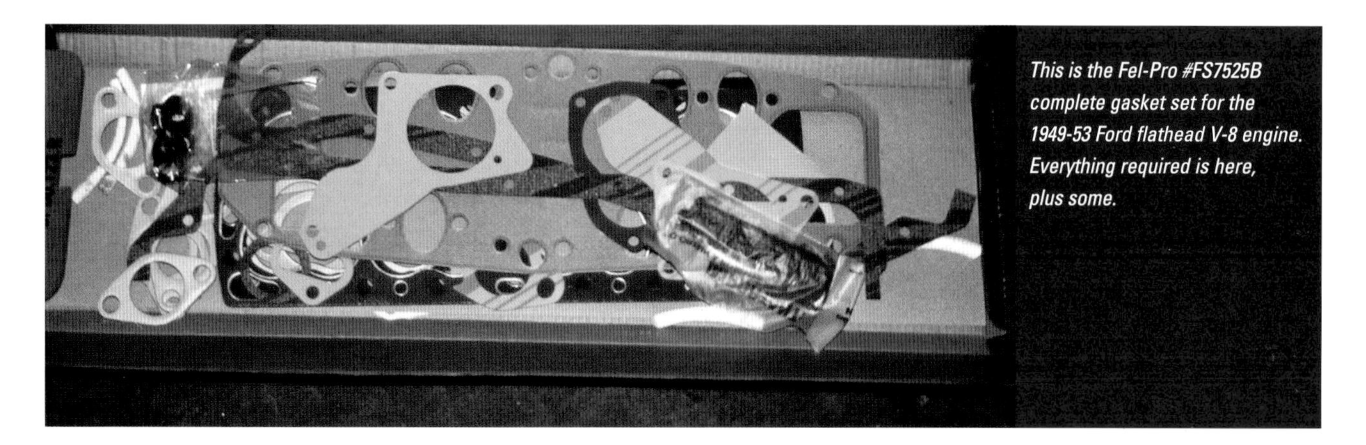

This is the Fel-Pro #FS7525B complete gasket set for the 1949-53 Ford flathead V-8 engine. Everything required is here, plus some.

rotating assembly. The crankshaft pulley and the flexplate should be delivered to the machine shop if an automatic transmission is to be used.

A complete V-8 engine balance will eliminate any engine vibration, which in turn will ensure the engine bearings enjoy a long and happy life. The estimated cost for a complete V-8 engine balance is $190.

Gaskets

Fel-Pro produces a good, complete gasket set for the 1949-53 Ford or Mercury flathead V-8 engine. This kit is available from Speedway Motors or your local automotive parts dealer.

Connecting Rods and Pistons Summary

1949–53 Ford #6200 forged steel connecting rods; Model Number: 8BA; Casting Number: 8BA6205A; non-floating connecting rod bearings. Connecting rod length: 7.00″. Connecting rod ratio: 1.75 (with 4″ stroke crankshaft).	$80.00
Connecting rods Magnafluxed, shot peened, aligned, re-sized, and balanced. New Sealed Power (Federal Mogul) #9024VA wrist pin bushings, 0.8125″ o.d., installed allowing for 0.002″ clearance. New Pioneer #CRN-731 connecting rod nuts installed using Loctite and torqued to 45 ft-lb.	$286.85
New Clevite "77" #CB-15P-20 connecting rod bearings, 0.020″ oversize, installed allowing for 0.002″ connecting rod clearance and 0.014″-0.018″ side clearance per pair of connecting rods.	$160.00
New Ross Racing Pistons #80564 forged 2618T-61 aluminum pistons; 9.1:1 compression ratio; 0.125″ (1/8″) oversize; piston weight: 310 grams, each. 3/32″ width top and 2nd compression ring and 5/32″ width oil ring. "Full floating" heat treated and case hardened 4340 chrome moly steel straight-wall wrist pins with new Ross Racing Pistons #4004-J Spiro Lox retainers. Wrist pin diameter: 0.750″; wrist pin length: 2.770″; wrist pin weight: 120 grams. New Grant Piston Rings #2360 Std. cast iron piston ring set installed within manufacturer's recommended arc. Top and 2nd compression ring gap: 0.012″; oil ring gap: 0.014″.	$409.60
Complete V-8 engine balance.	$190.00
New Fel-Pro #FS7525B gasket set installed (valve guide O-rings included).	$54.95
CONNECTING RODS AND PISTONS TOTAL:	**$1,181.40**

CHAPTER 4
LUBRICATION SYSTEM

Purchase

The 1949-53 Ford #6603 oil pump is considered the best of all the flathead oil pumps. A new oil pump is a requirement for any street performance Ford flathead V-8 engine.

Aftermarket oil pumps that are direct replacements for the original Ford oil pumps are available. These are the Melling #M-19, the Pioneer #OP-19, and the Sealed Power (Federal Mogul) #224-41108. They are all standard-volume oil pumps and can be purchased at your local automotive parts outlet.

The Melling #M-15 and the Pioneer #OP-15 are high-volume oil pumps for the Ford flathead V-8. There is no reason to use a high-volume oil pump in a street performance motor when the standard volume oil pump provides all the lubrication required. A high-volume oil pump for a Ford flathead is twice the cost of the standard-volume oil pump and a totally unnecessary expenditure.

A new Melling #M-19 standard volume oil pump for a 1949-953 Ford is shown with a 1949-53 Ford passenger car oil pump cover and inlet tube. The oil pump pick-up is for the center sump oil pans.

Here is the Melling #M-19 oil pump and the Ford passenger car oil pump cover and inlet tube installed. The oil pump pick-up is almost at the center of the engine.

This is a beautifully chromed 1949-53 Ford passenger car oil pan with the center sump and three-quart capacity (four quarts with the large oil filter). This engine was shipped to the owner in Colorado, and when it reached the truck depot in Denver, a forklift operator managed to drive one of the forks through the side of the oil pan.

The clearance between the gears and the top cover of the oil pump should be checked. This clearance should be 0.00025″ (without the gasket) and is accomplished by either sanding the top of the housing on a piece of thick glass if there is excessive clearance, or sanding the gears on a piece of thick glass if the clearance is not adequate. After correctly clearancing the oil pump, thoroughly clean the oil pump, apply some motor oil to the gears, reinstall the top cover gasket with silicone sealant, and torque the bolts to 80 in-lb using Loctite.

Oil Pan and Pick-up

The best oil pans to use for a street performance flathead are those for the 1949-53 Mercury passenger car or the 1949-53 Ford Truck models with a four-quart capacity (five quarts with a large oil filter). These oil pans have the sump at the rear, and the Mercury model has a built-in oil baffle. Try to locate one of these oil pans with the matching oil pump pick-up tube and screen. The Mercury pick-up tube and screen has an attached baffle. After cleaning the pick-up tube assembly with screen filter, bolt the assembly to the oil pump body using silicone sealant on the gasket, and torque the two bolts to 80 in-lb using Loctite.

Install the oil pump with a stainless steel 5/16" N.C. x 1"-length bolt and lock washer using Loctite, and torque to 15 ft-lb.

As soon as you receive the gasket set, remove the cord material rear oil seals and place them in a can of motor oil. Let them soak in the oil for at least a week to become thoroughly saturated. When these seals are new and dry they are extremely tough and very difficult to install. After they have been soaked in oil they become much more pliable. Install the rear oil seal in the oil pan by rolling it in using a large socket.

Prior to cleaning the oil pan, remove the Ford #6751 dipstick tube boss from the oil pan. The dipstick boss gasket should be replaced due to age. This is accomplished by grinding the ends off the three Ford #63359-S rivets on the inside of the oil pan and then driving them out with a punch. After the oil pan has been cleaned and before it is painted, reinstall the dipstick boss with three each of 10-32 x 1/2"- length pan head screws and nuts using Loctite. You will have to fabricate a new gasket from good quality gasket material and install it using silicone sealant. Grind any excess material off the ends of the screws and stake them with a center punch.

The oil pan may have some surface rust on it; if so, glass bead the oil pan inside and out. If the oil pan has a lot of rust on it, it should be sandblasted or redi-stripped. After the oil pan has been cleaned up, paint it with the same paint as the engine block. You will need 16 stainless steel bolts, 5/16" N.C. x 1/2"-length with lock washers and AN flat washers for installing the oil pan.

The dipstick used in the 1949-53 Ford Truck had "8T" stamped on the handle, and the dipstick used in the 1949-53 Ford passenger cars had "8A" on the handle.

A Melling #M-19 standard volume oil pump for a 1949-53 Ford is shown with a 1949-53 Ford Truck #6615 oil pump cover and inlet tube. This oil pump pick-up is for the rear sump oil pans.

This 1949-53 Ford Truck #6675 rear sump oil pan was covered in rust prior to being redi-stripped. Now it looks almost like new.

Oil Pump Idler Gear

Many used blocks still have the oil pump idler gear installed, and it will be necessary to remove this gear prior to redi-stripping the engine block. There is a 3/8" N.C. threaded hole in the face of the oil pump idler gear shaft. Insert a bolt of approximately 1 1/2" length in this hole with a thick, flat washer. Attach the jaws of a slide hammer to the bolt and washer and pull the idler gear out of the block.

If the engine block did not come equipped with the oil pump idler gear, you will have to find one. The idler gear and shaft as well as the cover are not difficult to locate, and they should be cheap. It is seldom you will see a damaged oil pump idler gear. The oil pump idler gear cover was originally installed with five cap screw bolts that had a hole in the head of each bolt. The ends of a piece of wire were passed through the bolt heads and twisted together in order to prevent the bolts from coming loose. If you do not have those bolts, use five new stainless steel bolts: 5/16" N.C. x 1/2" length with lock washers. If you have the bolts, find a nice piece of stainless steel wire and use it like the factory did. No one will ever see it, but you will know it is there.

Fuel Pump Pushrod Bushing

The fuel pump pushrod bushing was removed prior to the engine block being hot tanked. This particular engine will have three carburetors and therefore will require an electric fuel pump. The stock flathead fuel pump is not suitable for multi-carb applications.

The fuel pump pushrod bushing has a hole in it that lines up with a hole in the block that feeds oil to the bushing in order to lubricate it. If the pushrod is removed and the hole is not plugged, there will be a loss of oil pressure. Braze the hole closed and then reinstall the fuel pump pushrod bushing in the block.

This picture contains a lot of trinkets! They are: the 1949-53 Ford #6310 crankshaft oil slinger, #6658 oil pump idler gear cover, #6524 valve lifter gallery oil return hole baffles (2), and #6756 valve lifter gallery crankcase breather tube. All of those items have been painted with Glyptal. There is also a 1949-53 Ford #6754 dipstick tube, #6655 oil pump idler gear with #6657 bushing, #6656 oil pump idler gear shaft, #6258 camshaft gear lock washer plate with #350400 camshaft bolts (4), #8BA-6335 rear upper oil seal retainer, and a 1946-48 Ford #6306 crankshaft gear. The item of real interest is the rare NOS (new-old-stock) 1946-48 Canadian Ford Military #59A-6256 cast iron camshaft gear. The center section of the gear has been painted with Glyptal.

The hoses for the full-flow oil system. The pressure-out hose (the lower hose) is connected to the inlet side of the remote oil filter and the drain-back (upper hose) is connected to the outlet side of the remote oil filter.

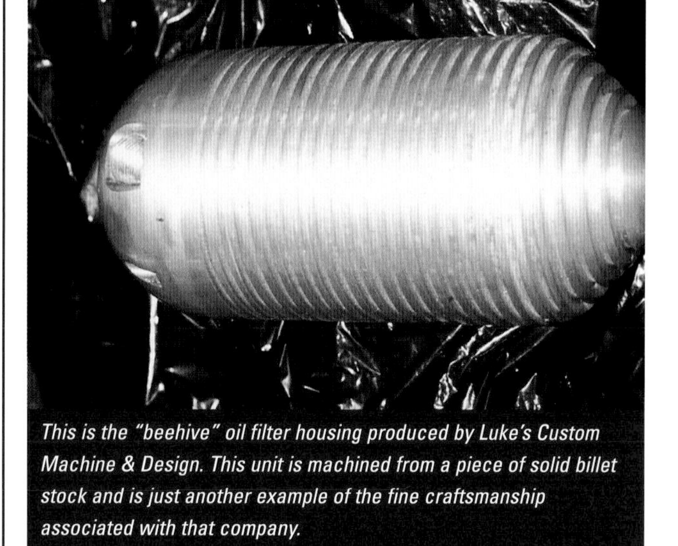

This is the "beehive" oil filter housing produced by Luke's Custom Machine & Design. This unit is machined from a piece of solid billet stock and is just another example of the fine craftsmanship associated with that company.

Baffles and Breather Tube

Earlier in this book, the two valve lifter gallery oil return hole baffles and the valve lifter gallery crankcase breather tube were mentioned. If these items were not in the engine block when you purchased it, you will have to find a source for them. They are not expensive items and should be f airly easy to locate.

Oil Filter

In order to attach the remote oil filter bracket to the left cylinder head for the full-flow oil system, you will need a mounting bracket. For the remote oil filter bracket Luke's fabricates a very nice polished stainless steel model that bolts to the left-hand cylinder head in the same position as the stock unit. Luke's also produces a beautiful "beehive" oil filter for a lot more money than the oil filter bracket.

The Trans-Dapt #1045 remote oil filter bracket, with horizontal inlet and outlets, will be required. This is a fairly presentable unit with a chrome-like finish, or it can be polished. It uses the Fram #PH8A (Ford) oil filter, although you might want to use a Moroso #22400 chrome filter. These parts are available from your local speed shop dealer.

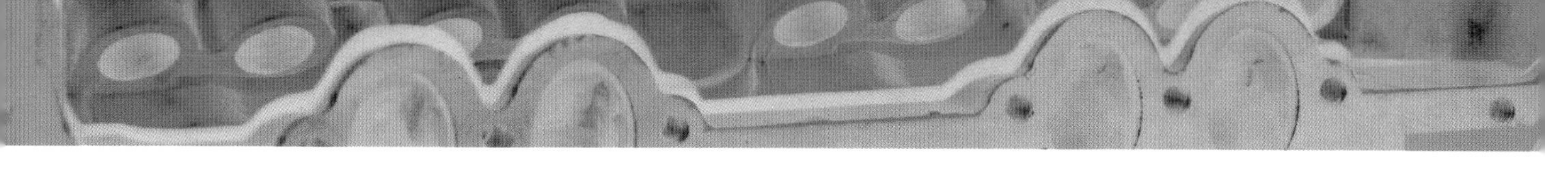

The Trans-Dapt #1032 neoprene rubber hoses, 24″ length x ½″ N.PT., are the last items required to hook up the oil filter. Some engine owners like the look of the braided stainless steel lines and the blue/red anodized AN fittings. I usually cover the neoprene hoses with Spectre #3001A black nylabraid and Spectre #3308B chrome champclamps, which are available from your preferred speed equipment dealer.

The outboard horizontal oil line hole in the block is for the pressure out. The line from here is attached to the inlet side of the oil filter adapter. The inboard vertical oil line hole in the block is for the drain back. The line from here is attached to the outlet side of the oil filter adapter.

The owner of the engine being described in this section did not want the oil filter mounted on the left cylinder head. Instead, he chose to mount the unit on the firewall.

Lubrication System Summary

New stainless steel ⅜″ N.P.T. plug (Ford #6026), front of oil gallery line plug, installed using Permatex aviation-form-a-gasket. Ford #6025 fuel pump pushrod bushing oil hole brazed closed. Ford #6657 oil pump idler gear bushing installed with Ford #6655 oil pump idler gear and Ford #6656 oil pump idler gear shaft allowing for 0.002″ clearance. Ford #6658 oil pump idler gear cover installed with Ford #22507 oil pump idler gear cover bolts and lock washers using Loctite and torqued to 80 in-lb with stainless steel safety wire. Oil pump idler gear cover gasket installed using silicone sealant. Inside of oil pump idler gear cover, Ford #6756 valve lifter gallery crankcase breather tube, and Ford #6524 valve lifter gallery oil return hole baffles (2), painted with Glyptal #G-1228A medium grey gloss enamel.	$153.43
New Melling #M-19 standard volume oil pump (for 1949-53 Ford) installed with 1949-53 Ford Truck #6615 oil pump cover and inlet tube, Ford #6623 oil pump cover screen, and Ford #6628 oil pump cover screen spring retainer. Oil pump end clearance: 0.00025″. Oil pump cover and inlet tube gasket installed using silicone sealant and bolts torqued to 80 in-lb using Loctite. 1949-53 Ford #8BA-6335 rear upper oil seal retainer installed. Rear oil seal packings (Ford #6700) soaked in SAE 30 Wt. motor oil and installed. New Speedway Motors #912-S12853 front one-piece oil seal installed using silicone sealant.	$159.10
1949-53 Ford Truck #6675 oil pan, 4 quart capacity, installed with new stainless steel bolts, lock washers, and AN flat washers using Loctite and torqued to 15 ft-lb. Gaskets installed using silicone sealant. Ford #6754 dipstick tube, Ford #6750 dipstick, and NOS. (new-old-stock) Ford #C21A-6761-B felt dipstick gasket installed. Oil pan, dipstick tube, and dipstick redi-stripped and painted with Endura #EX-2C black 160 hi-gloss polyurethane. Engine lubricated with 5 quarts Penzoil HD-30 Wt. motor oil.	$209.70
New Trans-Dapt #1045 polished remote oil filter bracket with horizontal inlet/outlet; new Moroso #22400 chrome oil filter; and new Trans-Dapt #1032 neoprene rubber hoses, 2′ length x ½″ N.P.T. New Weatherhead #3200-8-6 polished brass reducers, ½″ N.P.T. to ⅜″ N.P.T., new Weatherhead #3328-6 polished brass extension, ⅜″ N.P.T.; new Weatherhead #3300-6 polished brass coupling, ⅜″ N.P.T.; and new Weatherhead #3400-6 polished brass 90 degree elbow, ⅜″ N.P.T., installed using teflon tape. Hoses covered with new Spectre #3001A black nylabraid and new Spectre #3308B chrome champclamps.	$75.00
LUBRICATION SYSTEM TOTAL:	**$597.23**

CHAPTER 5
CAMSHAFT AND CYLINDER HEADS

Camshaft Bearings

Install a set of Clevite "77" (Michigan Bearings) camshaft bearings. The #1 and #3 bearing are #SH-21, with a housing bore of 1.9275″ to 1.9285; #2 bearing, #SH-22, has a housing bore of 1.9275″ to 1.9285″. *The Ford Motor Company of Canada Master Repair Manual* specifies 0.007″ to 0.016″ camshaft end play, 0.001″-0.002″ camshaft bearing clearance, and the camshaft journal diameter to be 1.7965″ to 1.7970″.

The camshaft bearings should be removed with a camshaft bearing installation tool, and they must be installed using it. By using this tool you will avoid damage to the camshaft housing bores and especially to the camshaft bearings.

Camshaft

The camshaft is quite possibly the single most important part of an automobile engine, and it will also be the center of most discussions relating to the engine. I am certain if you ask seven different people what the best camshaft is to use in your vehicle, you will get twelve different opinions. Do not believe that the highest valve lift and the most duration will result in the most horsepower or torque. See the Dyno Printouts chapter for camshaft comparisons.

The people who know exactly what camshaft to use are the camshaft manufacturers, and there are some very good camshaft manufacturing companies in the United States. I have been using Crower camshafts and valvetrain components for my own engines. The reader may well have his own preference of camshaft manufacturer, which is fine, providing the end result is that the correct camshaft is installed in the engine.

This is a set of Clevite 77 camshaft bearings, part #SH-21S, for the engine being described in this section.

A Crane Cams #BF5528 "400 grind" camshaft has been installed in order to check the camshaft-to-bearing clearance. This is a 0.396″ net valve lift racing camshaft and really should not be considered for street use.

Some flathead camshafts are supplied without the Ford #6254 rear camshaft gear that drives the oil pump idler gear. This gear is available from Speedway Motors at low cost as part #910-16254. Some 1949-53 camshafts are supplied without the Ford front gear that drives the distributor. This drive gear is also inexpensive and available from Speedway Motors: #910-16255.

I shall give a brief explanation of a few of the most common terms used when discussing camshafts. The catalogs most camshaft manufacturers distribute have a section on camshaft terminology and the mathematics associated with camshafts, if the reader would like a more in-depth explanation.

Advertised Duration: Duration is the number of crankshaft degrees the intake and exhaust valves are held open. The advertised duration of a camshaft could mean anything. Camshaft manufacturers specified a camshaft had a duration of so many degrees; however, they did not explain at which point of tappet (camshaft lifter) lift that duration was calculated. This could have been 0.004″ lift, 0.006″ lift, 0.007″ lift, 0.010″ lift, 0.020″ lift, or any lift. It seems as though none of the camshaft manufacturers used a similar method to calculate the duration, and this made it nearly impossible to compare camshafts from different companies.

Duration @ 0.050″ Lift: A number of years ago, camshaft manufacturers started to measure the duration at 0.050″ of tappet (camshaft lifter) lift. This is now the standard to use when comparing camshafts.

This is the 1946-48 camshaft Crower Cams & Equipment has recommended for the 1949-53 engine described in this section. The camshaft has duration @ 0.050" lift of 224 degrees, intake and exhaust, and a lobe separation angle of 110 degrees. The net valve lift is 0.322"/0.320" intake and exhaust.

Valve Lift: This is the maximum net lift of the valve, expressed in decimals of an inch. It will be less than the camshaft lobe lift in a Ford flathead V-8 engine due to the valve lash, which is deducted. There are no rocker arms in a flathead engine, so the valve lift will be less than the camshaft lobe lift.

Overlap: Overlap is the number of crankshaft degrees the intake and exhaust valves are open together. A camshaft with a lot of overlap creates a rough idle and is not recommended for a street performance flathead engine.

The Lobe Separation Angle: The lobe separation angle (or lobe centerline angle) is the angle between the intake and exhaust lobes, at the maximum lift point, expressed in degrees. A large lobe separation angle (110 to 116 degrees) will result in a smoother idle and a greater power range. A smaller lobe separation angle (104 to 110 degrees) will result in a rougher idle and a narrower power range. The engine described in this section will be driven daily on the street, which dictates that a camshaft with a larger lobe separation angle be used. The larger lobe separation angle will ensure the car idles properly and the engine has vacuum at idle. The camshaft that Crower Cams & Equipment Company recommends for a 1949-53 Ford flathead V-8 street performance engine described in this section is the #SPL59A "street grind." The advertised duration is: 264 degrees intake and exhaust; duration @ 0.050" lift: 224 degrees intake and exhaust; net valve lift: 0.322"/0.320" intake and exhaust; lobe separation angle: 110 degrees.

Note: This camshaft, ground by Crower for the engine discussed in this section, is a 1946-48 camshaft that is being used in a 1949-53 engine. It is an excellent camshaft for street use. Crower's price is competitive and outright, with no core exchange.

I strongly recommend purchasing only a new camshaft. A used camshaft must have the lifters that were used with that camshaft matched exactly to the lobes on the camshaft, the same way they were installed in the engine. If the lifters are mixed up, the camshaft will be destroyed when the engine is started. Buying a used camshaft is a real gamble. The camshaft may have some company's name stamped on it, but it may well have been re-ground or one or more of the lobes may have gone flat. A used camshaft could be taken to a reputable camshaft company for inspection, but why bother? New camshafts are not expensive, and you know exactly what you are buying.

The cost of having a camshaft ground for a specific engine is about the same as buying an off-the-shelf camshaft. Some of the camshafts being sold today are based on the same technology that was offered over 40 years ago. I prefer to have a camshaft ground for a specific engine by Crower using their latest state-of-the-art technology. This way the optimum engine output is realized.

Camshaft Interchange

Some flathead engine owners like to install a pre-1949 camshaft in a 1949-53 motor, or a 1949-53 camshaft in a pre-1949 motor. The camshafts are interchangeable. However, there is one major point to remember, and that is that the angle between the valves is different. Prior to 1946 the angle was 101½ degrees and the angle from 1946-53 was 100 degrees. A pre-1949 camshaft will not work well in a 1949-53 engine block unless it has a 1946-48 camshaft. If you want to install a 1949-53 camshaft in a pre-1949 motor, it will have to be in a 1946-48 engine block (model 59A). The only other solution to this problem is to have a camshaft manufacturer grind a camshaft for a particular year of engine block.

This is a 1942 Canadian Ford #21A-6019FMCC cast iron timing gear cover for use with the two-bolt crab-style distributor. The inside of the timing gear cover has been painted with Glyptal. The connecting rods are ready for shot peening, and those are brand-new stainless steel valves and valve guide bushings.

The teeth on the 1949-53 Ford flathead V-8 camshaft and crankshaft gears are slanted in the opposite direction of the teeth on the 1946-48 Ford flathead V-8 camshaft and crankshaft gears. The 1949-53 camshaft and crankshaft gears provide the thrust against the timing gear cover, and the 1946-48 camshaft and crankshaft gears provide the thrust against the engine block. If a 1949-53 camshaft is going to be installed in a 1946-48 block, the 1949-53 camshaft and crankshaft gears should be installed. If a 1946-48 camshaft is going to be installed in a 1949-53 block, the 1946-1948 camshaft and crankshaft gears should be installed. It should be noted that some of the early 1949 Ford engines were factory equipped with the 1946-48 camshaft and crankshaft gears. This was possibly due to the Ford Motor Company cleaning out old stock.

Degree Camshaft

The tools required to degree a camshaft are a 9″-diameter degree wheel, 1″ travel dial indicator with a long stem, magnetic adjustable dial indicator stand, and a heavy gauge wire pointer (such as coat hanger material). The crankshaft, connecting rod and piston assemblies, camshaft, and intake and exhaust lifters for the #1 cylinder must be installed in order to degree the camshaft.

Locate the TDC (top dead center) of the #1 piston with the dial indicator. Install the degree wheel on the nose of the crankshaft and attach the wire pointer to the engine block so it is as close as possible to the edge of the degree wheel. With the #1 piston at TDC, turn the degree wheel until the pointer is at the zero degree mark on the wheel and then securely clamp the degree wheel in this position so that it cannot move. Turn the crankshaft in one direction until the #1 piston reaches TDC; the wire pointer should be at the zero position on the degree wheel. Rotate the engine in the opposite direction until the #1 piston reaches TDC; the wire pointer should be at the zero position on the degree wheel. The degree wheel is now perfectly positioned. Remove the dial indicator from the #1 piston.

Place the magnetic dial indicator stand on the block near the #1 intake valve seat and align the dial indicator so it passes through the valve guide bushing boss and touches the top of the #1 intake valve lifter. The dial indicator must be at the same angle as the intake valve lifter in order to obtain an accurate reading.

Rotate the crankshaft until the maximum lift point for the #1 intake lifter is located. Rotate the crankshaft one revolution past the maximum lift point. The lifter is now in the center of the base circle. Set the dial indicator to the zero position. Turn the crankshaft in the normal direction of rotation until a reading of 0.050″ is reached on the dial indicator. The degree wheel will now show the number of degrees BTC (before top center) for the #1 intake valve. Rotate the crankshaft past the maximum lift point of #1 intake valve until the dial indicator again reaches 0.050″. The degree wheel will now show the number of degrees ABC (after bottom center) for #1 intake valve.

Remove the dial indicator and stand from near the #1 intake valve seat and set them up near the #1 exhaust valve seat. Align the dial indicator so it passes through the valve guide bushing boss and touches the top of the #1 exhaust valve lifter. The dial indicator must be at the same angle as the exhaust valve lifter in order to obtain an accurate reading.

Rotate the crankshaft until the maximum lift point for the #1 exhaust valve is located. Rotate the crankshaft 1 revolution past the maximum lift point. The lifter is now in the center of the base circle. Set the dial indicator to the zero position. Turn the crankshaft in the normal direction of rotation until a reading of 0.050″ is reached on the dial indicator. The degree wheel will now show the number of degrees BBC (before bottom center) for #1 exhaust valve. Rotate the crankshaft past the maximum lift point of #1 exhaust valve until the dial indicator again reaches 0.050″. The degree wheel will now show the number of degrees ATC (after top center) for #1 exhaust valve.

All the readings from the degree wheel for BTC (before top center), ABC (after bottom center), BBC, and ATC should be in accordance with the manufacturer's camshaft specification card (timing tag). Maximum engine performance will be reached if the camshaft is degreed according to those specifications.

Valve Lifters

The Ford #6500 flathead V-8 stock camshaft lifters (or tappets, or cam followers) will not be utilized for the simple fact they are not adjustable. The lifters that will be used are the Johnson adjustable solid lifters. They are available from Iskenderian Racing Cams: #F85-02; Speedway Motors: #450-F8502; or Sealed Power (Federal Mogul) #AT-770. Crower Cams & Equipment also manufacturers a solid flat tappet camshaft adjustable lifter for the Ford flathead V-8: #66913. The Crower lifter is in the same price range as the Johnson adjustable lifter, but it is a special order item.

There have been many types of adjustable lifters available throughout the years. The Johnson types are hollow or solid, and not all have the oval slots on the side. The Federal Mogul #RMT787 adjustable lifters had a solid body with a deep groove around the middle. If a used set of adjustable lifters is in otherwise good condition, the face and the top of the adjusting screw can be re-surfaced by a reputable camshaft company for a minimal amount of money. I would recommend buying only new lifters.

The Iskenderian Racing Cams #F85-02 and the Sealed Power (Federal Mogul) #AT-770 Johnson adjustable lifters for the Ford flathead V-8 engine are the solid body design. The Johnson adjustable lifter used to be available in the hollow body design, but that model has been discontinued for a number of years. It is highly doubtful there would be any noticeable difference in the performance or longevity of a flathead street engine due to the difference in weight of a set of solid body or a set of hollow body lifters. Flatattack Racing Products, an Australian company, has introduced a 79 gram hollow body adjustable lifter for the flathead engine at a cost of $200 for a set.

Although the camshaft lifters are referred to as flat tappet, the face of the camshaft lifters is actually convex in order to permit the lifters to rotate and thereby encourage even wear on the lifter face and camshaft lobe. Always install new camshaft lifters with a new camshaft. If new lifters are installed on a used camshaft or used lifters are installed on a new camshaft, camshaft failure is almost certainly guaranteed.

Here are three different Johnson adjustable lifters, all with the same height body and adjusting screw. The one on the far left has a solid body, and the other two have hollow bodies but with different side slots.

Johnson solid adjustable lifters available from Speedway Motors or Iskenderian Racing Cams are pictured with the famous "knuckle buster" adjusting wrenches that are usually supplied with the lifters.

The subject of roller camshafts and roller lifters for the flathead occasionally arises. The problem with roller lifters for this application is the diameter of the lifter body is 1.00″ and the lifter body height is 1.50″, which would result in a heavy body if a roller were included within those dimensions. This situation would necessitate the use of a higher tension valve spring with no room to install it. The use of Groove-Lock or Radius Lifters will overcome this problem.

This is one solution to roller lifters in a flathead engine. The lifters are very lightweight Schubeck Racing Engine Products "diamond hard" radius lifters, for use with a roller camshaft. The custom roller camshaft has stock diameter small-block Chevrolet journals.

Four different types of lifters, from the left, are the Ford #6500 stock lifter, Johnson hollow-body adjustable lifter, Crower Groove-Lock roller lifter for a Chrysler 392-ci hemi engine (a flathead adjustable lifter was not available), and a Schubeck Racing Engine Products "diamond hard" radius lifter for an Ardun race engine.

Schubeck Racing Engine Products manufactures very lightweight (43 grams) "diamond hard" radius lifters, 0.687″ diameter, for use with a roller camshaft. A sleeve is machined for the lifter bosses in order to fit the lifters. A roller camshaft with small block Chevrolet journals is used with these lifters. This set up is for an Ardun race engine and is extremely expensive, but could be produced for a regular Ford flathead V-8 engine.

Crower Cams & Equipment custom manufactures roller camshafts and a Groove-Lock anodized aluminum adjustable roller lifter for the Ford flathead V-8 engine: #66273 (order drill jig #66575). These lifters are the stock 1.00″ diameter and are approximately 1.75″ in height. A slot is machined in each valve lifter boss to accommodate the 2 "buttons" on the lifter, which prevent the lifter from rotating. These lifters are of the highest quality and they are expensive.

Here are the weights of four different lifters:

- Ford flathead V-8 #6500 stock lifter: 44.0 grams.
- Johnson adjustable lifter with hollow body: 80.5 grams.
- Johnson adjustable lifter with solid body: 114 grams.
- Crower Hemi Groove-Lock anodized aluminum roller lifter: 48.0 grams.

A roller camshaft and roller lifters are not a requirement for a street performance Ford flathead V-8 engine. If the engine is to be used for drag racing, salt flat racing, or you have just located the Lost Dutchman's Mine, then you could consider using the roller camshaft and roller lifters.

Valves

Stainless steel valves should be used for the intake and exhaust in a street performance Ford flathead V-8 engine. Stainless steel valves are very durable and will last a lot longer than the stock valves. Exhaust valves can be used as intake valves, but intake valves cannot be used as exhaust valves.

The use of 1.61″ head diameter intake and exhaust valves is quite adequate for a flathead engine that is going to be used on the street daily. This size of valve does not necessitate any major modifications to the valve seats or the Edelbrock #1115 cylinder head combustion chambers (1949-53) when camshafts with 0.350″ net valve lift, or less, are used. These valves are installed in some small-block Chevrolet engines and are readily available at reasonable prices. The valves should be of the one-piece design, swirl polished, 11/32″ stem diameter, stock length, and have hardened tips.

This nice looking set of stainless steel valves supplied by Dale Wilch's RPM Catalog is the #40961 "small block" Chevrolet with 1.61″ head diameter, 11/32″ stem diameter, stock length, and swirl polished.

The Sioux Tools Model 2075HP "accu-chuck" valve grinder does an excellent job of multi-angle blueprint valve grinds. The valve pictured in the chuck is not a flathead valve that shrunk!

The best price I have found for stainless steel valves is through Dale Wilch's RPM Catalog. Speedway Motors sells a slightly higher priced version, and Manley Performance Parts has a number of different types of valves in a variety of prices. It is only a small matter of money!

You may have wondered how to distinguish a stock Ford flathead V-8 intake valve from a stock Ford flathead V-8 exhaust valve. Use a magnet. The intake valves are magnetic and the exhaust valves are not. (I would like to thank Tom Hood, a local Ford guru, for that tidbit of useful information).

The actual valves should be ground on a Sioux Tools Model 2075HP "accu-chuck" valve grinder, or a similar type of machine, in order to obtain a quality multi-angle "blueprint" valve grind. A multi-angle blueprint valve grind can comprise up to seven different angles. The most common is three angles consisting of 45 degrees on the valve as it sits on the valve seat insert, 30 degrees above where the valve sits, and 70 degrees below where the valve sits.

Valve Guide Bushings

After years of faithful service, the valve guide bushings (or valve guides) should be replaced. The valve guide bushing to valve stem clearance will be approximately 0.0015″ with new valves and valve guide bushings. The Ford intake valve guide bushings had a groove around them for the installation of an oil-control O-ring. The Ford exhaust valve guide bushings were a solid body design. The intake and exhaust valve guide bushings are the same diameter. It is not uncommon to find intake valve guide bushings installed with exhaust valves. The replacement valve guide bushings available today are all the intake design. The valve guide bushing O-rings are included in the Fel-Pro gasket set.

The best source I have found for new heat-treated, one-piece valve guide bushings is Speedway Motors, part #910-15315. They are for the 1949-53 Ford—although they can be used for the earlier year engines with 1949-53 valve components—and they cost $3.49 each.

If the valve guide bushings in an engine appear to be in very good shape and therefore could possibly be reused, *The Ford Motor Company of Canada Master Repair Manual* specifies the maximum valve stem-to-valve guide bushing clearance for the intake valves to be 0.004″ and for the exhaust valves to be 0.005″.

It used to be a common practice to machine the valve guide bushings to a cone shape in order to keep the valve guide bushings from protruding into the ports and thereby interfering with the intake and exhaust flow. If this is necessary, measure 5/16″ (0.3125″) from the center of the valve stem hole (at the top of the valve guide) outward, and measure 1/8″ (0.125″) from the side of the valve guide bushing downward. Then remove the material between these two points in a lathe, which results in the cone shape. If you use the new valve guide bushings available from Speedway Motors, they do not protrude into the ports, so this machining exercise is not required.

A brand-new set of heat-treated, one-piece valve guide bushings purchased from Speedway Motors is a very inexpensive item and should be used when building up a street performance Ford flathead V-8.

Valve Springs

The stock Ford valve springs were adequate when used with the stock Ford camshaft and valvetrain. They are not suitable for a flathead engine that is equipped with a higher lift camshaft. In days past, these camshafts were referred to as "3/4" or "full race" cams.

The best valve springs to use are the Iskenderian Racing Cams single- or dual-valve springs. Even other camshaft manufacturers recommend them. These valve springs are top quality oil tempered, shot peened, and silicon chrome.

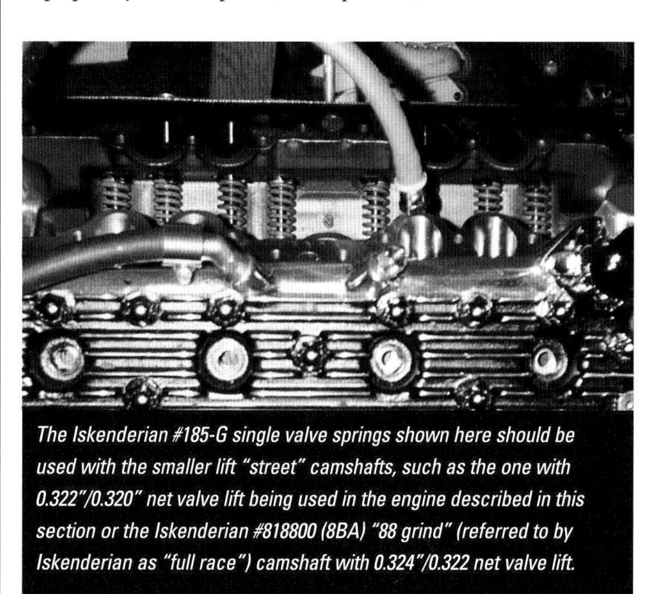

The Iskenderian #185-G single valve springs shown here should be used with the smaller lift "street" camshafts, such as the one with 0.322″/0.320″ net valve lift being used in the engine described in this section or the Iskenderian #818800 (8BA) "88 grind" (referred to by Iskenderian as "full race") camshaft with 0.324″/0.322 net valve lift.

These brand-new Iskenderian #185-G single-valve springs are of good quality and can probably be used with just about all the Ford flathead V-8 "street" camshafts produced by all the camshaft manufacturers.

They are available from Speedway Motors or directly from Iskenderian and they are very reasonably priced.

The Iskenderian #185-G single valve springs are very good for street camshafts with valve lifts up to 0.370″. Their specifications are:

- Installed height, valves closed: 85 lbs. @ 2.00″ or 120 lbs. @ 1.875″.
- Installed height, valves open: 208 lbs. @ 1.543″ (0.332″ lift) or 218 lbs. @ 1.505″ (0.370″ lift).
- 1.010″ o.d. and 0.690″ i.d.
- Coil bind: 1.345″
- Color: grey

The Iskenderian #4005 dual-valve springs (#205-G and #206-G) are very good for blower camshafts and race camshafts with valve lifts of 0.370″ or higher. Their specifications are:

- Installed height: 60 lbs. @ 1.90625″ ($1\frac{29}{32}$″) or 82 lbs. @ 1.8125″ or 115 lbs. @ 1.6875″
- Installed height, valves open: 152 lbs. @ 1.53625″ or 163 lbs. @ 1.50625″ or 170 lbs. @ 1.4625″ (0.350″ lift).
- 1.240″ o.d. and 0.925″/0.690″ i.d.
- Coil bind: 0.960″
- Maximum lift: 0.500″
- Color: grey

The Iskenderian #4005 dual-valve springs require a lot of extra work to install. Unlike the Iskenderian #185-G single valve springs, the dual springs cannot be pre-assembled with the valves and valve guide bushings and then slid into the valve guide bushing bosses. The dual-valve springs are larger than the valve guide bushing bosses, so the dual-valve springs must be placed in position in the valve lifter gallery and assembled from there with the valves, valve guide bushings, two valve spring retainers, and locks.

Iskenderian #4005 dual-valve springs are of good quality and should be used with the higher-lift racing camshafts.

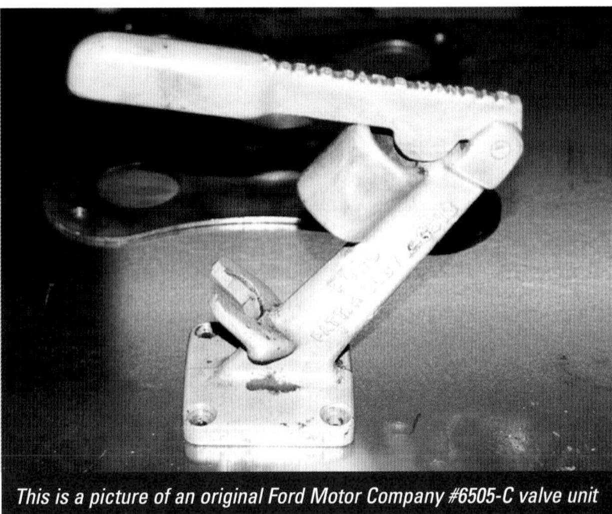

This is a picture of an original Ford Motor Company #6505-C valve unit assembly tool. You place the valve spring retainer in the bottom; insert the valve spring, valve guide bushing, and valve; and then compress the whole assembly with the handle so you can install the valve stem locks. The valve unit assemblies can be put together in seconds.

A flathead engine can use valve springs with less spring tension than the valve springs used in an OHV engine since the valves "sit" in a flathead block while the valves "hang" in an OHV cylinder head. Use the Iskenderian Racing Cams #404 valve spring shims to obtain the correct installed height for the valve springs.

Valve Spring Retainers and Locks

The Iskenderian #185-G single valve spring is used with the 1949-53 Ford #6514 stock valve spring retainer. It should be fairly easy to locate a 16-piece set of these valve spring retainers at minimal cost.

The valve, valve guide bushing, Iskenderian #185-G single valve spring, valve spring retainer, and valve stem locks are being assembled using the Ford #6505-C valve unit assembly tool. Unfortunately, this tool does not work with double valve springs because the springs are wider than the neck of the tool.

The Iskenderian dual-valve springs require the use of the Iskenderian #87-F dual-valve spring retainer and the 1949-53 Ford #6514 stock valve spring retainer. Do not confuse the Ford #6517 valve spring retainer sleeve for the rotatable valve with the Ford #6514 valve spring retainer. The Iskenderian dual-valve spring retainers are available directly from Iskenderian or through Speedway Motors.

Good quality small block Chevrolet valve stem locks are readily available and are appropriate for use in a flathead. The locks that are required should be 4140 chrome moly stamped steel, heat treated, 7 degree, and 11/32″ stem diameter. These are available from Crower, part #86100; Iskenderian #VL-11/32; Manley #13127-16; Crane #99041-1; or Speedway Motors #910-15316.

You will also need a 16-piece set of the Ford flathead V-8 valve guide bushing retainers. The pre-1949 Ford engine utilized the same "crow's foot" retainer, so they should be easy to locate at a dirt-cheap price or even free.

Camshaft Gear and Timing Cover

The stock 1949-53 Ford fiber camshaft timing gear should not be installed in a street-performance flathead because it will not withstand the increased stress caused by the after-market performance valvetrain. Instead, you should purchase a new aluminum camshaft timing gear. This part is not expensive, so do not bother with a used aluminum camshaft timing gear. This gear is available from Speedway Motors, part #910-14625L, or your local automotive parts outlet will have a Melling #2702 camshaft gear (for 1949-53).

One other item of importance that you must obtain is the Ford flathead V-8 camshaft locking plate and the four bolts specially constructed to secure the camshaft gear to the camshaft. The pre-1949 Ford locking plate and bolts are the same, so it should not be a major problem to find these pieces.

The camshaft gear will only bolt onto the camshaft in one position because the bolt holes in the camshaft are asymmetrical and not evenly spaced. This prevents someone from installing the camshaft gear improperly and obtaining incorrect results when the camshaft is degreed. The crankshaft gear will only fit on the crankshaft in one

Here are some valvetrain components: Iskenderian #87-F dual-valve springs retainers; Iskenderian #VL-11/32 valve stem locks, 7 degree and 11/32″ stem; 1949-53 Ford #6514 stock valve spring retainers; and the Ford #6512 crow's foot valve guide bushing retainers.

The Gray #FT57 valve spring compressor bar is used for the installation of the valve guide bushing retainer. If you do not have one of these bars, you are out of luck as far as assembling the valvetrain on a Ford flathead V-8 engine.

position. If the camshaft and crankshaft are aligned correctly, it is highly unlikely the results of degreeing a camshaft will differ from the camshaft manufacturer's specifications. If the results do differ greatly, then the problem most likely lies with the camshaft itself.

A point of interest that is hardly ever mentioned is that Ford Motor Company offered the fiber and aluminum camshaft timing gears in standard size and 0.006″ oversize. The purpose of the oversize camshaft timing gears was to assist in eliminating excessive timing gear noise and erratic ignition timing, better known as "spark chatter."

If you are going to use the pre-1949 crab-style distributor with the two-bolt mounting on a 1949-53 flathead V-8 engine, you will have to purchase a 1942-48 Ford #59A-6256 cast iron timing gear cover. This part, which was the type used on the performance street engine described in this section, is fairly easy to locate and should not be expensive.

If you decide to use the 1949-53 Ford flathead V-8 stock distributor location, you will need a 1949-53 flathead timing gear cover, and there are two models available. One is of aluminum construction with a bushing cast into the cover. This bushing is used to support the end of the distributor shaft. The other timing gear cover is manufactured of cast iron without the bushing. The type of distributor and distributor gear you use (more about that subject later in the book) will determine which timing gear cover is required. Timing gear covers are not an expensive item and should be readily available. There is a pointer installed in the front of both of these timing gear covers. This is not a nail that somehow got stuck in the timing gear cover, so do not attempt to pull it out with a hammer! This pointer is for the timing adjustment. Purchase some stainless steel bolts for installing the timing gear cover: five pieces of 5/16″ N.C. x 3/4″ length with lock washers.

The Speedway Motors #912-S12853 flathead one-piece front oil seal is a terrific item and is on the mandatory purchase list! The main bearing cap behind it was fabricated by Luke's Custom Machine & Design for the blown flathead engine featured in Section II.

One Piece Oil Seal and Sleeve

Speedway Motors markets a one-piece front oil seal for the flathead engine, part #912-S12853. This is an excellent product that actually works and should have been introduced years ago. Buy one!

One thing that is missing with the one-piece oil seal is the crankshaft sleeve. The stock 1949-53 Ford flathead V-8 crankshaft sleeve is not designed to work with a one-piece oil seal as a result of the spiral grooves in the sleeve. The only place I know of that manufactures the correct crankshaft sleeve is Luke's Custom Machine & Design.

Cylinder Heads

I do not recommend the purchase of used aluminum cylinder heads for the flathead engine unless they are in excellent condition. Many used cylinder heads have been seriously abused over the years; some have been "planed," and some are badly corroded. New aluminum cylinder heads are not cheap, but they are trouble free.

There are a limited number of manufacturers of aluminum cylinder heads for the 1949-53 Ford flathead V-8 engine. I prefer the Edelbrock #1115 cylinder heads. These are a quality product manufactured from 356 aluminum and T-6 tempered. The compression ratio is 8.1:1 with the stock 3 3/16″ bore and 3 3/4″ stroke and a block relieved to a depth of 3/16″. Edelbrock used to market the #1115 cylinder head with a 7.5:1, 8.0:1, 8.5:1, 9.0:1, or 9.5:1 compression ratio being available with a block relieved to a depth of 3/16″. The Edelbrocks are good-looking cylinder heads with a greater spacing between the "fins" compared to other cylinder heads that have the "fins" spaced closer together.

It is very difficult and costly to buff between the fins when they are closer together, and for that reason many engine owners paint between the fins. The Edelbrock heads, with the greater fin spacing, can be buffed between the fins, or left natural, so it is totally unnecessary to paint these heads. I believe anyone who paints between the fins of an Edelbrock head should have their head(s) repossessed!

One process that should not be done to the cylinder heads of a street performance Ford flathead V-8 engine is to plane the heads. Years ago, this was a common practice in order to raise the compression ratio of the engine. If the cylinder heads are planed, there is a good possibility the upper combustion chamber portion of the heads will have to be milled to permit adequate valve-to-cylinder-head clearance. The engine described in this section will have a 9.1:1 compression ratio with the Edelbrock #1115 cylinder heads (as they came out of the box) and the Ross pistons. This is very close to the maximum compression ratio at which a

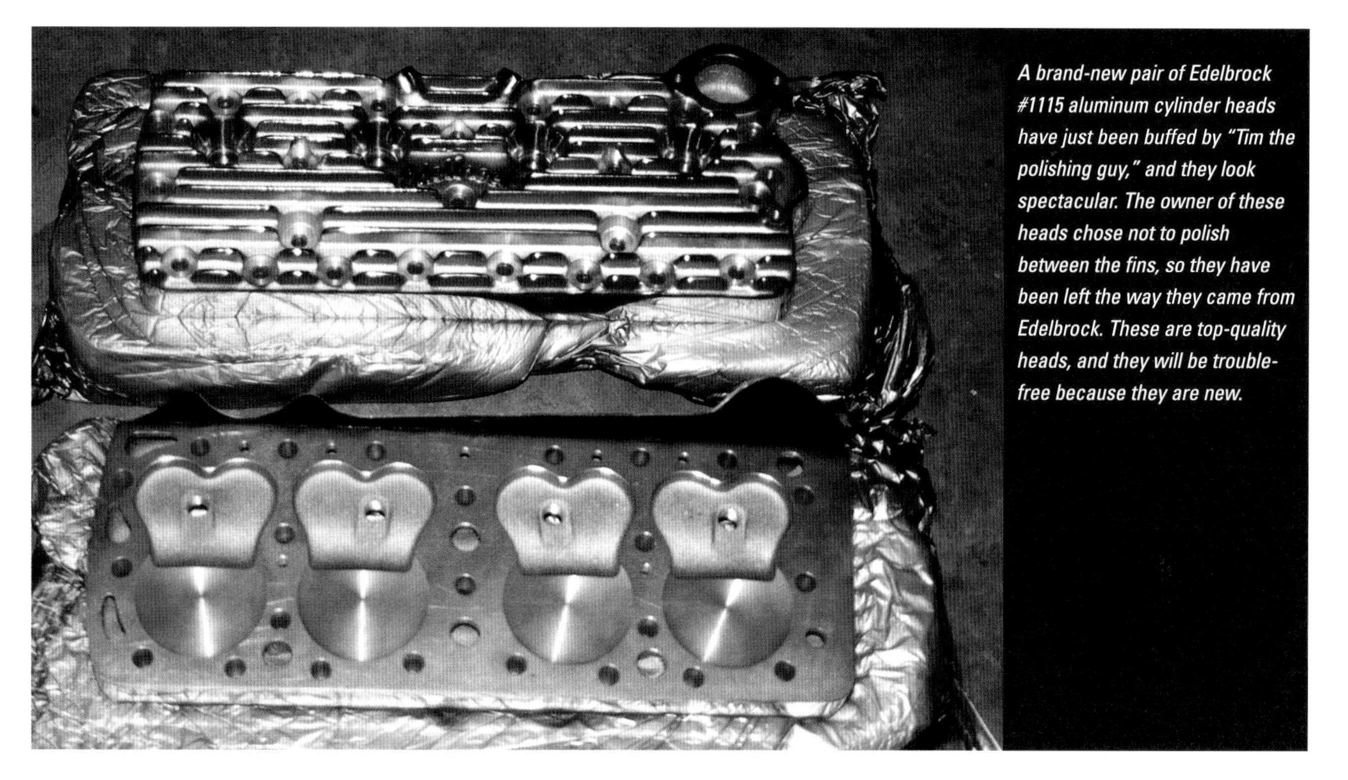
A brand-new pair of Edelbrock #1115 aluminum cylinder heads have just been buffed by "Tim the polishing guy," and they look spectacular. The owner of these heads chose not to polish between the fins, so they have been left the way they came from Edelbrock. These are top-quality heads, and they will be trouble-free because they are new.

street performance flathead engine can properly function when using today's highest octane unleaded gasoline.

Offenhauser has previously published a chart indicating the compression ratio of the flathead engines based on the bore, stroke, and the part number of the Offenhauser cylinder head used. This chart might be available through an Offenhauser dealer. Offenhauser #1069 aluminum cylinder heads (1949-53) are still available in different compression ratios based on their part numbers 425, 400, 375, 350, and 325. The lower the number, the higher the compression ratio (non-relieved block). The number represents the valve-to-cylinder head clearance. The number of the cylinder head is supposed to be stamped near the water outlet opening on the cylinder head, providing it hasn't been polished off. Offenhauser parts are available directly from Offenhauser or your local speed equipment outlet.

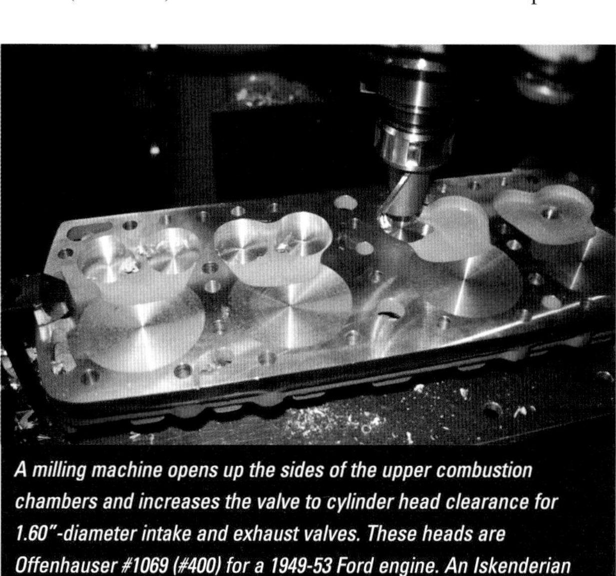
A milling machine opens up the sides of the upper combustion chambers and increases the valve to cylinder head clearance for 1.60"-diameter intake and exhaust valves. These heads are Offenhauser #1069 (#400) for a 1949-53 Ford engine. An Iskenderian #814000 (8BA) "400 JR. grind" camshaft with 0.396" net valve lift will be used with these cylinder heads.

The 1949-53 Ford flathead cylinder head bolts can be reused, although they have probably been beaten, overtorqued, and otherwise neglected over the years. The stock bolts are a good-quality item. If you cannot locate a set of the stock bolts, purchase a new set of Grade "8" (150,000 psi) hex-head bolts: 28 pieces of 7⁄16" N.C. x 2¾" length and 20 pieces of 7⁄16" N.C. x 2" length. You must use a set of hardened steel cylinder-head bolt flat washers when installing aluminum cylinder heads. Manley Performance Parts #42102 flat washers are heat treated and of very high quality. The bolts are available from industrial supply outlets, and the washers are available from your local speed shop.

I have heard many discussions regarding the installation of aluminum cylinder heads on engines and whether bolts or studs should be used. I have installed aluminum cylinder heads on my own engines using bolts and have never encountered any problems. Remember, the cylinder-head bolts are only torqued to 40 ft-lb when using aluminum cylinder heads. There should not be a problem if the cylinder heads are new and absolutely straight, the engine block decks are absolutely straight, and the bolts are in good

Here is a pair of 1949-50 Ford #8BA-8592-A2 water outlet elbows. These happy campers are ready for the chrome plating shop!

condition. It is important to re-torque the aluminum cylinder heads immediately after the initial fire-up. If your heart is set on using studs, Speedway Motors sells the complete set, part #910-15310, for $99.95.

Most flathead owners install the chrome acorn nut covers on the cylinder-head bolts of their engines. If you are using the stock cylinder-head bolts, you will require the covers that fit the bolts with a head size of 11/16" from Speedway Motors, part #910-10115. If you have changed to new cylinder-head bolts, then you will require the chrome acorn nut covers that fit the bolts with a head size of 5/8" from J.C. Whitney & Company, part #38BB2776R. These are very inexpensive items.

Cylinder Head Gaskets

The engine block described in this section is being bored to 3 5/16" (3.3125"). The cylinder head gaskets supplied with the Fel-Pro gasket kit are not suited for large-bore flathead engines. The alternative is to use the Fel-Pro #1055 (right side) and #1056 (left side) copper "sandwiched" cylinder head gaskets for 1949-53 Ford flathead V-8 engines. These gaskets will fit an engine with up to a 3.420" bore; their thickness is 0.062", and they have a compressed volume of 14 cc. Edelbrock recommends the use of these gaskets with their #1115 aluminum cylinder heads (1949-53). These gaskets can be purchased from your local automotive supply outlet or from Speedway Motors, part #910-15895.

There is a slick trick to use for copper sandwiched cylinder head gaskets if the center section is composed of asbestos. Soak the cylinder head gaskets in water in the bath tub for one hour (this should really get the wife's attention!) and then install them. The gaskets will compress to the maximum when they are wet and torqued. This will ensure a great seal. I thank Bud Child for this "pearl of wisdom."

The Speedway Motors #916-15201 exhaust baffle kit is shown along with some brand new stainless steel valves and valve guide bushings.

Water Outlets

The 1949-53 flathead cylinder heads were designed with a water outlet elbow bolted onto each head. The water outlet elbows are cast iron and the neck is vertical. These items should be readily available at a very low cost. The water outlet elbows should be chrome plated to look presentable with the polished aluminum heads. You will require the following stainless steel fasteners for the two water outlet elbows: four pieces of 5/16" N.C. x 1" length bolts and four pieces of 5/16" lock washers. Polish the bolt heads.

If you cannot locate a pair of water outlet elbows, or the ones you find are badly corroded, do not despair. Speedway Motors sells brand-new stock-style aluminum water outlet elbows, part #910-15852, for $12.95 each. Have them buffed.

Your vehicle is to be driven on the street, and therefore it should have thermostats installed. Removing the thermostats will cause the coolant in the engine to start to move too fast for the heat to be dissipated. Chevrolet small block 180 degree F thermostats will properly fit the Ford flathead water outlet elbows. You can also purchase thermostats from Speedway Motors, part #910-15802.

Exhaust Baffles

It is very important to install exhaust baffles in the Ford flathead engine in order to keep the exhaust gases from the two center cylinders on each side of the block from mixing with each other. Without the baffles, the exhaust gases from the two center cylinders collide with each other before they exit the block. These baffles are held in place by an extended cylinder head stud. I strongly recommend that you additionally secure these baffles in the block with an irontite plug, drilled through the block (exhaust port) into the baffle and secured with Loctite. This prevents the baffle from ever coming loose and dropping into the exhaust port, thereby restricting the exhaust exit from the center cylinders.

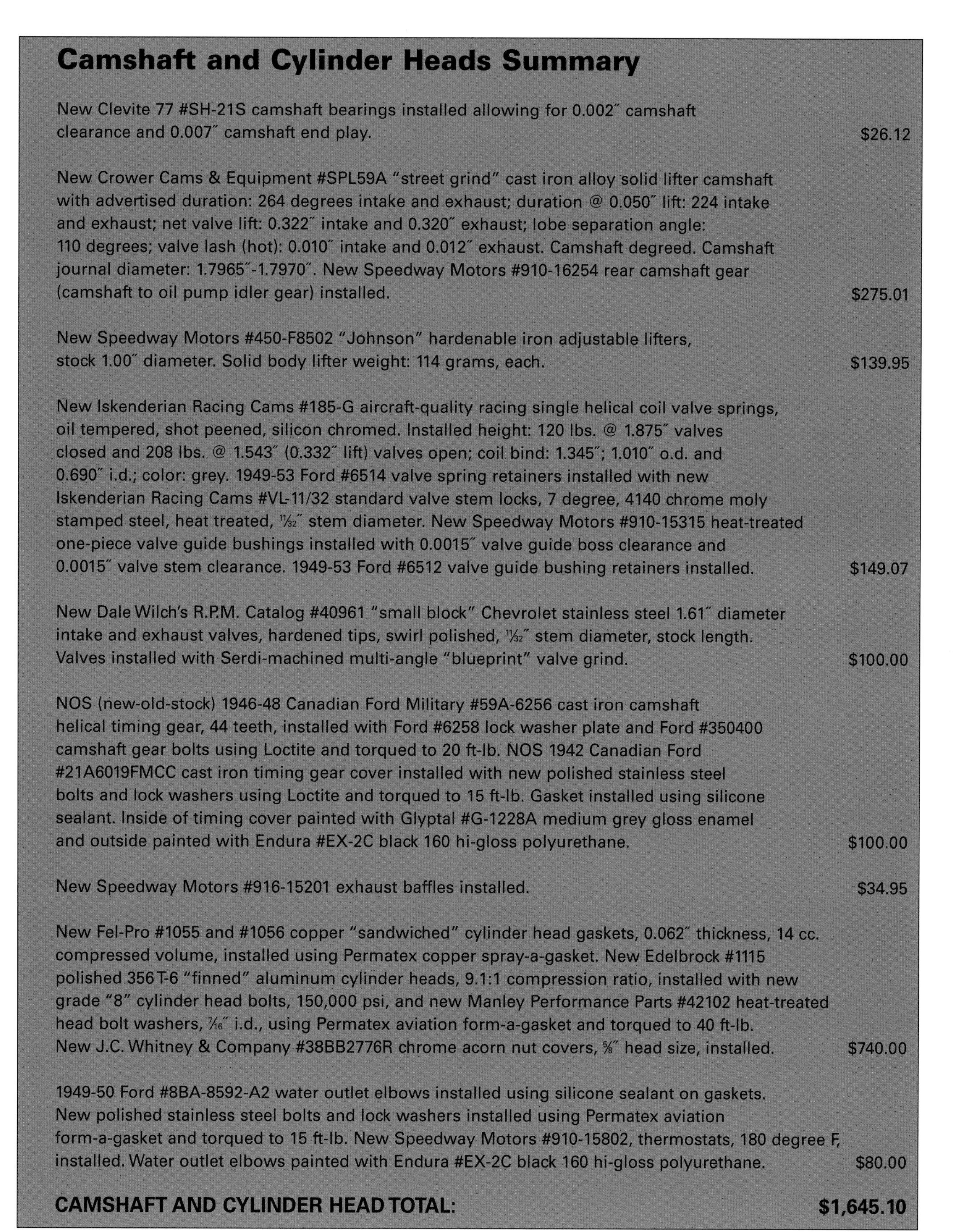

Camshaft and Cylinder Heads Summary

New Clevite 77 #SH-21S camshaft bearings installed allowing for 0.002″ camshaft clearance and 0.007″ camshaft end play.	$26.12
New Crower Cams & Equipment #SPL59A "street grind" cast iron alloy solid lifter camshaft with advertised duration: 264 degrees intake and exhaust; duration @ 0.050″ lift: 224 intake and exhaust; net valve lift: 0.322″ intake and 0.320″ exhaust; lobe separation angle: 110 degrees; valve lash (hot): 0.010″ intake and 0.012″ exhaust. Camshaft degreed. Camshaft journal diameter: 1.7965″-1.7970″. New Speedway Motors #910-16254 rear camshaft gear (camshaft to oil pump idler gear) installed.	$275.01
New Speedway Motors #450-F8502 "Johnson" hardenable iron adjustable lifters, stock 1.00″ diameter. Solid body lifter weight: 114 grams, each.	$139.95
New Iskenderian Racing Cams #185-G aircraft-quality racing single helical coil valve springs, oil tempered, shot peened, silicon chromed. Installed height: 120 lbs. @ 1.875″ valves closed and 208 lbs. @ 1.543″ (0.332″ lift) valves open; coil bind: 1.345″; 1.010″ o.d. and 0.690″ i.d.; color: grey. 1949-53 Ford #6514 valve spring retainers installed with new Iskenderian Racing Cams #VL-11/32 standard valve stem locks, 7 degree, 4140 chrome moly stamped steel, heat treated, 11/32″ stem diameter. New Speedway Motors #910-15315 heat-treated one-piece valve guide bushings installed with 0.0015″ valve guide boss clearance and 0.0015″ valve stem clearance. 1949-53 Ford #6512 valve guide bushing retainers installed.	$149.07
New Dale Wilch's R.P.M. Catalog #40961 "small block" Chevrolet stainless steel 1.61″ diameter intake and exhaust valves, hardened tips, swirl polished, 11/32″ stem diameter, stock length. Valves installed with Serdi-machined multi-angle "blueprint" valve grind.	$100.00
NOS (new-old-stock) 1946-48 Canadian Ford Military #59A-6256 cast iron camshaft helical timing gear, 44 teeth, installed with Ford #6258 lock washer plate and Ford #350400 camshaft gear bolts using Loctite and torqued to 20 ft-lb. NOS 1942 Canadian Ford #21A6019FMCC cast iron timing gear cover installed with new polished stainless steel bolts and lock washers using Loctite and torqued to 15 ft-lb. Gasket installed using silicone sealant. Inside of timing cover painted with Glyptal #G-1228A medium grey gloss enamel and outside painted with Endura #EX-2C black 160 hi-gloss polyurethane.	$100.00
New Speedway Motors #916-15201 exhaust baffles installed.	$34.95
New Fel-Pro #1055 and #1056 copper "sandwiched" cylinder head gaskets, 0.062″ thickness, 14 cc. compressed volume, installed using Permatex copper spray-a-gasket. New Edelbrock #1115 polished 356T-6 "finned" aluminum cylinder heads, 9.1:1 compression ratio, installed with new grade "8" cylinder head bolts, 150,000 psi, and new Manley Performance Parts #42102 heat-treated head bolt washers, 7/16″ i.d., using Permatex aviation form-a-gasket and torqued to 40 ft-lb. New J.C. Whitney & Company #38BB2776R chrome acorn nut covers, 5/8″ head size, installed.	$740.00
1949-50 Ford #8BA-8592-A2 water outlet elbows installed using silicone sealant on gaskets. New polished stainless steel bolts and lock washers installed using Permatex aviation form-a-gasket and torqued to 15 ft-lb. New Speedway Motors #910-15802, thermostats, 180 degree F, installed. Water outlet elbows painted with Endura #EX-2C black 160 hi-gloss polyurethane.	$80.00
CAMSHAFT AND CYLINDER HEAD TOTAL:	**$1,645.10**

CHAPTER 6
INTAKE SYSTEM

Carburetors

There are two types of carburetors normally used on the Ford flathead V-8 engine These are the Stromberg 97 and the Holley 94. I prefer the Holley 94 carburetor because it is a simple carburetor, easy to work on, and does not have any delicate parts such as emulsion tubes. The main jets and power valves are available from any Holley parts outlet, and the tune-up kits are available from most automotive supply stores. The best tune-up kit I have encountered for the Holley 94 is the Niehoff #CK-302A. Speedway Motors and Vintage Speed sell tune-up kits for the Stromberg 97.

These days it is common to hear people refer to the Holley 94 carburetor as the "poor man's Stromberg" or the Stromberg 97 as "the true nostalgia carburetor." I think these concepts were invented by New York advertising executives who had inherited a garage load of Stromberg 97 carbs and wanted to drive the price through the roof. If you look at the prices being asked for Stromberg 97 carbs on the eBay website, they succeeded!

The Stromberg 97 carburetor was used on the larger Ford flathead V-8 engines from 1936 to 1938. In 1938 Chandler-Groves introduced a carburetor designed to replace the Stromberg 97 on the flathead engine due to problems Ford was having with the Stromberg 97. In 1939 Holley starting producing this carburetor, and they produced all the two-barrel carburetors for the Ford V-8 until 1957. The Holley 94 carburetor has been around almost as long as the Stromberg 97 carburetor, so I would say this makes the Holley 94 as nostalgic as the Stromberg 97. If you look through hot rod magazines from the 1950s and the 1960s, there appear to have been as many engines equipped with Holley 94 carburetors as engines equipped with Stromberg 97 carburetors. So there!

The one problem that is encountered when running multi-carb setups with Holley 94 carburetors is the power valve. This single power valve was designed to feed engines of up to approximately 250 cubic inches. If you have two to four Holley 94 carburetors on an engine and they all have power valves, it is obvious why the spark plugs are easily fouled. This problem is solved by blocking off the power valves in the end carburetors when three or four carburetors are installed. This is one of the reasons I prefer to run only a three-carburetor setup on a Ford flathead V-8 engine. Each Holley 94 carburetor is rated at approximately 160 cfm. The type of carburetors and the quantity used are entirely up to the owner of a flathead engine.

One item should be noted regarding the Holley #26-36 power valve plug: the gasket supplied with the plug is much larger than the power-valve seat in the Holley 94 carburetor. Use the stock Holley 94 power valve plug gasket. You may have to double up the power valve gaskets to ensure the power valve plug is leak-proof due to a slight "shoulder" on the Holley #26-26 power valve plug.

This is the usual condition of the Holley 94 cores that I am asked to rebuild. Sometimes I feel like quitting before I even get started!

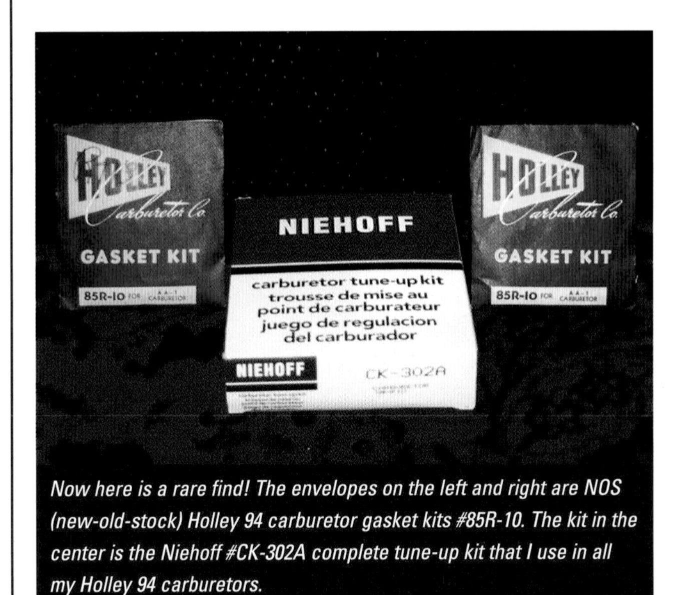

Now here is a rare find! The envelopes on the left and right are NOS (new-old-stock) Holley 94 carburetor gasket kits #85R-10. The kit in the center is the Niehoff #CK-302A complete tune-up kit that I use in all my Holley 94 carburetors.

If a three-carburetor setup with the Holley 94s are used, then you have two options. You can block off the power valve in the end carburetors using the Holley #26-36 power valve plug. Then replace the idle adjustment screws with button head socket screws, 10-32 x ⅜" length (I use polished stainless steel). Only the center carburetor will now operate at idle, and the other two carburetors will start to operate at whatever part-throttle you want. This is the beauty of using progressive linkage with a three-carburetor

This shows the condition of the Holley 94 carburetors when I set out to build a four-carb intake system. Anyone else would have just packed it in and joined the French Foreign Legion!

setup. The linkage can be adjusted to have the end carburetors start to function at 50%, 60%, 70%, or whatever throttle opening position desired. You will now have an engine that will deliver economy at lower speeds and still have throttle response when you want it.

The second option is to fabricate two block-off plates out of thin sheet metal or aluminum, and place them beneath the two end carburetors. Make the plates the same outline as the carburetor base and not the outline of the carburetor mounting pad on the intake manifold. Only the center carburetor will function. Even though you will not be using the end carburetors, you should still install the tune-up kits in them. Each carburetor kit costs about $20 and you will now have two spare carburetors. You will have to install extended throttle shafts in all the carburetors in order to attach the progressive linkage. Do not forget to plug the fuel line fittings, in the fuel block, that feed the two blocked-off end carburetors.

Detailing

I have built dozens of Holley 94 carburetors over the past few years. I start off with the complete disassembly of the carburetor. Next, I cold tank all the parts, glass bead the bodies, and re-surface the gasket mating areas. I use the services of "Tim the polishing guy" for all my buffing and polishing work. This fellow has even polished the inside of two Hilborn fuel injection scoops, and, as a result, I am not certain whether he should be institutionalized or not! His work is excellent. I have him buff the carburetor bodies and then I coat them with Eastwood Company #10200Z "Diamond Clear" gloss finish or V.H.T. #SP-115 clear

Things are starting to look up and maybe life isn't so bad after all! This is how the carburetors look after being cold tanked and glass beaded. Two of the "little devils" have a beveled top that was used to fit an oil-bath air cleaner on Ford trucks. The solution for this dilemma is to use a lathe and remove the bevel to the same diameter as the tops of the regular carburetors.

Here is one of my Holley 94 carburetors that has been glass beaded, polished, and coated. An extended throttle shaft, torsion base spring, and complete tune-up kit have been installed.

high-temperature coating. This helps prevent the polished carburetor bodies from tarnishing.

The bases are glass beaded and painted the same color as the engine block. Extended oversize throttle shafts are installed allowing for 0.002″ clearance, and I install throttle base torsion return springs. The installation of these springs permits each carburetor throttle shaft to close without the use of one great big ugly spring. These parts are available from Vintage Speed, parts #H-39C for extended throttle shafts (0.005″ oversize) and #CL-35 for torsion base springs. The carburetors are assembled using complete tune-up kits, and all the fasteners are polished stainless

An army of Holley 94 carburetors waits for marching orders. They have been coated with Eastwood Company #10200Z "diamond clear" gloss finish. This picture was taken in the recreation room of my house. Sometimes it helps to have an understanding family!

steel. I install all the screws using anti-seize compound in order to prevent the threads from galling. Do not remove the choke assembly from the carburetor, as this aids the direction of the airflow. I initially install the stock (at sea level) Holley 0.051″ main jets. You might want to change these a few sizes up or down depending on your particular engine application and altitude. The float level is set at 1$\frac{11}{32}$″ and the float drop is set at 1$\frac{7}{16}$″.

It is very important to ensure the throttle shaft butterflies fit snugly in the throttle bores when using multi-carb setups. You do not want the butterflies to jam, but you should barely see any light through the throttle bores when you hold the base up to a bright light.

Intake Manifold

You as a flathead owner are going to have to make a decision as to what type of carburetion you are going to install on the engine. Is it going to be 1 x 2 barrel, 2 x 2 barrel, 3 x 2 barrel, 4 x 2 barrel, or 1 x 4 barrel carburetors?

A single Holley 94 carburetor with the 1949-53 Ford #6519 single two-barrel carburetor aluminum intake manifold will work very well on the street for stock engines. The intake runner design is excellent and should provide good fuel economy, but it is not really suitable for a street performance flathead with a large displacement.

The Offenhauser #1078 (1949-53) and the Offenhauser #1079 (1939-48) single-carburetor four-throat intake manifolds are still being produced. Combined with a Holley model 4160, 390-cfm four-barrel carburetor, this setup performs well on the street although it is not very nostalgic looking. The Edelbrock #452 quad-jet manifold (1949-53), the Edelbrock #452X (1939-48), and the single four-barrel intake manifold manufactured by Sharp (1949-53) occasionally surface on the eBay website or at swap meets. Another carburetor option is the Edelbrock #1404 "performer" 500-cfm carburetor, which is about $100 cheaper than the Holley 390-cfm model. If fuel economy is not important and you would rather stand up and be counted, install a Holley 600-cfm double-pumper carburetor. The #0-4776C is the "classic look" model, and the #0-4776S is the "silver finish" model. This is total overkill but a lot of fun! A Trans-Dapt #2064 carburetor adapter is required to mount the Edelbrock or the Holley carburetors on the Offenhauser, Edelbrock, and Sharp four-barrel intake manifolds.

A lot of flatheads driven on the street use a 2 x 2-barrel carburetor setup. Many owners swear this setup works well, but I do not believe the fuel economy is all that great. If

Here is a 1939-48 Evans intake manifold that has been meticulously buffed by "Tim the polishing guy" and modified by Luke's Custom Machine & Design so three of my Holley 94 carburetors will fit.

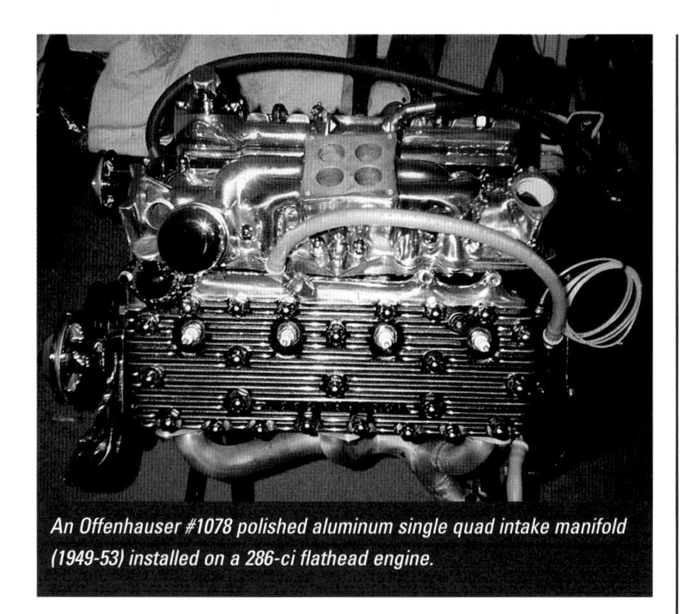

An Offenhauser #1078 polished aluminum single quad intake manifold (1949-53) installed on a 286-ci flathead engine.

This shows a "show" polished Offenhauser #1090 regular dual-carb intake manifold (1939-48) with two Stromberg 97 carburetors and Edmunds cast aluminum replica air cleaners. The Stromberg 97 were only used on the 1936-38 Fords.

you are going to use a dual-carb manifold, I recommend using the "super" dual ones. The carburetors are better situated over the intake ports for more equal fuel distribution.

If you are going to use 3 x Holley 94 carburetors, you will have to locate a used Sharp or Edelbrock #1030 intake manifold, Model SU-349, for the 1949-53 Ford flathead V-8 engine.

The Edelbrock #1050, Model SU-359, three-carb intake manifold for a 1939-48 flathead will work if the later model is not available. It should be noted the pre-1949 intake manifold does not have the two openings for the road draft/breather tube and the crankcase breather/oil filler tube. A 1939-48 Ford #9415 fuel pump stand/crankcase breather housing will have to be used. The used Edelbrock three-carb intake manifolds are getting harder to find; therefore, their price is going up. Be prepared!

The Offenhauser #1077 (1949-53) and the Offenhauser #1074 (1939-48) three-carburetor intake manifolds are still being manufactured. However, the Holley 94 carburetors will not fit. The spacing on the Offenhauser intake manifolds is designed for the slightly narrower Stromberg 97. Weiand and Evans used to manufacture a three-carb intake manifold with the same problem. Some flathead owners in the past have cut off the front flange and screw of the Holley 94 in order to make them fit those intake manifolds. People who do this should be banished to a Siberian gulag for the remainder of their lives!

Spacers can be built of whatever desired height between the carburetors and the Offenhauser, Weiand, or Evans intake manifolds. The end spacers are then machined so they tilt slightly outward. Only the spacer should tilt and the carburetor should not. The outline for the spacers should be taken from the carburetor mounting pad on the intake manifold and not the carburetor base. Luke's Custom Machine & Design fabricates spacers, usually 2¾" tall, for intake manifolds. Some flathead owners use these spacers simply because they look impressive on the engine.

Another method of solving the problem of Holley 94s on the Offenhauser, Weiand, or Evans intake manifolds is to add additional material to the front of the forward carburetor mounting pad and rear of the end carburetor mounting pad. This material is milled flat and new carburetor mounting stud holes are drilled and tapped. The bores

Here are three more carburetors I built. The intake manifold is a polished Edelbrock #1030, Model SU-349, for a 1949-53 Ford. The carburetors are Holley 94s fully assembled and chomping at the bit to go!

This rare Evans intake manifold has had the front mounting pad moved ahead and the rear mounting pad moved back in order to mount three Holley 94 carburetors. You would never know it!

in the intake manifold for the front carburetor are angled very slightly forward, and the bores in the intake manifold for the rear carburetor are angled very slightly backward.

The four-carburetor Weiand or Edelbrock #1025 intake manifold (1939-48) is not a practical setup for a Ford flathead V-8 street engine due to the design of the intake runners along with the location of the carburetors on the intake manifold. If an engine owner is determined to use this intake manifold, then the best approach is to block off the power valves (Holley 94) in the two end carburetors and install standard in-line linkage. This intake manifold was originally designed for high-rpm, all-out race applications.

The left front of the intake manifold for a 1949-53 flathead has two large holes in it. The front hole is for the Ford #6762 and #8502 road draft/crankcase breather tubes that snake down the front and under the engine. The road draft tube actually works in removing the pressure from the crankcase. If you do not want the road draft tube, fabricate an aluminum plug to block off the hole in the intake manifold. The second hole is for a crankcase breather/oil filler tube. Speedway Motors sells a very nice stainless steel tube with a chrome breather cap, part #910-17443. Buy one, because they are bargain priced!

The underside of this intake manifold is painted with V.H.T. #SP-101 flat white high-temperature coating. The theory behind this practice is the white will reflect some of the engine heat off the underside of the intake manifold, thereby keeping the air/fuel mixture cooler.

The intake manifold gasket used as a template to scribe around the intake ports in the engine block should be used as a template for the intake manifold to gasket-match the ports. Any casting flash in the ports of the intake manifold should be ground off.

Fuel Lines and Progressive Linkage

Mooneyes USA manufactures polished cast aluminum "finned" fuel blocks for two-carbs, part #MP1010; for three-carbs, #MP1011; and for four-carbs, #MP1012. Speedway Motors offers chrome "T-style" fuel blocks for two-carbs, #550-6150; for three-carbs, #550-6151; and for four-carbs, #550-6152. The Offenhauser #1081 polished aluminum fuel block is for a three-carb setup but can be used for dual carbs. Luke's fabricates polished aluminum or polished stainless steel mounting brackets for the fuel blocks. The brackets mount the fuel block over the intake manifold next to the cylinder head with the outlet fuel line fittings in the vertical position. They look great!

About the only place I know of that supplies the original Eelco fuel line fittings for the carburetors and the fuel blocks is Vintage Speed. The only alternative for the fuel line fittings are those manufactured by Weatherhead or Fairview.

I like the look of the old red fuel lines on the flathead motors. The original plastic fuel lines produced in the 1950s used to harden, crack, and discolor. The fuel line available today is of a high-quality vinyl and does not do this. The "ruby red" fuel line is available from Speedway Motors, part #910-11450 (3/8" i.d. in red only); Vintage Speed, part #FL-H-R (5/16" i.d. or 3/8" i.d. in red, green, blue, yellow, or clear); or Mooneyes, part #AF4215 (5/16" i.d. in red only) and #AF4216 (3/8" i.d. in red only). A Fairview #NSI-127-55 fitting is required for the Holley 94 in order to use the 5/16" i.d. hose.

Gibson stainless steel double annealed tubing can be used to fabricate the fuel lines. It is easy to work with and polishes up beautifully. This is definitely not nostalgic! Vintage Speed supplies stainless steel fuel lines, or the Gibson stainless steel fuel line can be purchased from Summit Racing Equipment, part #SUM-220238 for 3/8" i.d. and #SUM-220256 for 5/16" i.d. This is only available in 20-foot lengths.

If you use stainless steel 3/8" i.d. fuel lines, you will need a Weatherhead #7915 brass carburetor fitting for the Holley 94 carburetor. The end of this fitting will have to be

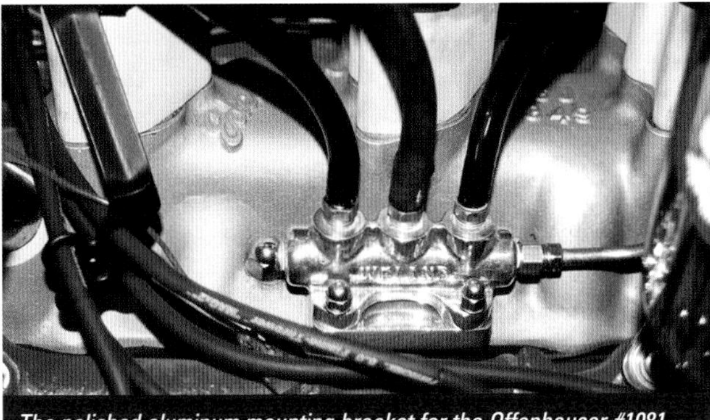

The polished aluminum mounting bracket for the Offenhauser #1081 polished aluminum fuel block is manufactured by Luke's Custom Machine & Design. This model bolts to the left-hand center of the intake manifold. The unpolished carburetor spacers are visible in the background.

This is a photograph of the Weatherhead #7915 brass fuel inlet fitting for the Holley 94 carburetor when using 3/8"-i.d. stainless steel fuel line. The one on the right has been machined to a cone shape in order to properly fit the carburetor.

machined on a lathe in order to have the oval shape that will mate with the opening in the Holley 94 fuel inlet hole. This is a simple procedure. For added insurance against fuel leaks, install a "crush" washer between the fuel inlet fitting and the carburetor opening. Once you have installed this fitting in the carburetor, double-flare the tubing and install it using inverted flare nuts. This is a very neat-looking and leak-proof assembly. The tubing should be buffed before it is bent and then re-buffed after bending.

One last item concerning fuel lines: Never, and I repeat never, use copper fuel lines or brake lines in an automobile. Copper fatigues very easily and will crack. If this happens with a fuel line, your vehicle will most likely go up in flames and possibly even you with it!

The Offenhauser #6271 progressive linkage for three-carburetors is a good-quality item. Offenhauser also manufactures a regular dual-carb standard in-line linkage, part #2864; super dual-carb standard in-line linkage, #2865;

This is the completed 4 x Holley 94 setup I built. The intake manifold is a polished Edelbrock #1025 (1939-48 Ford). The scoops are for show, and if they were to be used, they should face the rear. Use proper air filters for any engine that is going to be driven on the street. It is hard to believe, but those are the four carburetors I started out with at the beginning of this chapter.

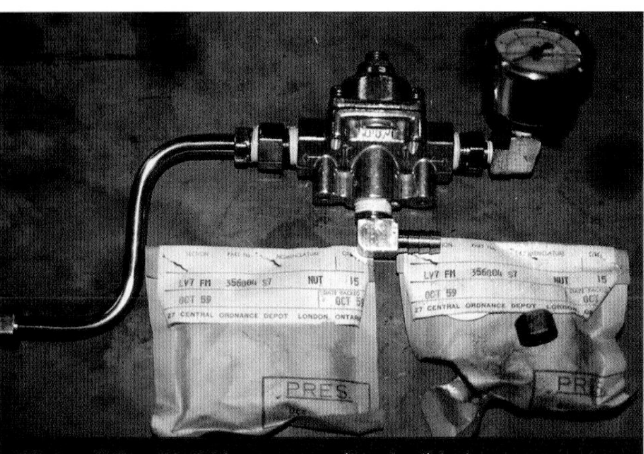

This is a Holley #12-804 low pressure (1 to 4 psi) fuel pressure regulator setup that attaches to the fuel block. The fuel line is Gibson polished stainless steel, and the liquid-filled fuel pressure gauge is a Spectre #2515. The really interesting part of this picture is the NOS (new-old-stock) Ford connecting rod nuts in the two packages. These were supplied to the Canadian Military, and the packages say: "Central Ordnance Depot; London, Ontario; Oct. '59." Each package contained 15 nuts. Why not a complete set of 16 nuts?

The K & N #E-3120 air filter is the best of the best and is guaranteed for a million miles. Happy driving! Throw those cheesy paper filters away that come with the chrome air cleaners.

and three-carb standard in-line linkage, #2866. I polish all the carburetor linkage arms and use polished stainless steel cotter pins, washers, and linkage rods on my own engines.

Fuel Pressure Regulator

If you are using more than one Holley 94 or Stromberg 97 carburetor on your engine, you will have to install an electric fuel pump. Install it as near to the gas tank as possible in order to push the fuel and not pull it. The old Ford flathead mechanical fuel pump will not provide enough fuel for multi-carb applications. You will require a fuel pump stand block-off plate for the rear of the 1949-53 intake manifold if you are using the road draft/crankcase vent and oil filler/crankcase vent tubes. Vintage Vendors #235FPBP (Tatom Custom Engines) sells a finned aluminum fuel pump stand block-off plate. If you are using a 1939-48 intake manifold with multi-carbs, a fuel pump block-off plate will be required. The Offenhauser #5265 aluminum fuel pump block-off plate is a suitable candidate.

As a result of using an electric fuel pump, you will have to install a fuel pressure regulator. The fuel pressure should not exceed 3 psi for Holley 94 or Stromberg 97 carburetors. A good unit to use is the Holley #12-804 fuel pressure regulator, 1to 4 psi, which is usually factory preset at 3 psi. This unit has an almost chrome-like finish to it or it can be buffed. Holley parts are available from Speedway Motors, Summit Racing Equipment, or your local high-performance automotive outlet. The fuel pressure regulator is attached directly to the fuel block using a 3/8″ N.P.T. connector. You can easily adapt a small mechanical fuel pressure gauge to the fuel pressure regulator on the outlet side. I use the V.D.O. #153-002 model, 0 to 15 psi, with a 1 1/2″-diameter face.

Air Cleaners

The most common air cleaners used on the Ford flathead engine with multi-carbs are the velocity stack, scoop, louvered, and helmet designs. It is up to the owner of the engine to decide which air cleaner to use. Just make certain that it has a proper air filter in it. You should not be driving a flathead on the street without a proper air filter installed. The helmet and louvered air cleaners come equipped with a ridiculous paper air filter, which is why the price of these items is so low. Buy the K & N #E-3120 (3.875″ diameter x 2″ height) air filters and allow your engine the proper breathing it deserves.

Bolts

The stock flathead intake manifold bolts are a good quality item and therefore can be reused. If you do not have a set of the stock bolts, purchase a new set of Grade "8" (150,000 psi) or stainless steel bolts. You will require 14 pieces of 3/8″ N.C. x 1 1/2″ length bolts and 14 pieces of 3/8″ AN flat washers. That quantity is for the 1949-53 Edelbrock #1030 intake manifold. Speedway Motors sells the chrome acorn nut covers for the 9/16″ head size intake manifold bolts, part #910-10125. During your stainless steel buying spree, you should purchase 5/16″ N.F. nuts with 5/16″ lock washers, for securing the carburetors to the intake manifold. Each carburetor uses three nuts and lock washers.

Intake System Summary

Edelbrock #1030, Model SU-349 (1949-53) polished aluminum three-carburetor intake manifold installed using silicone sealant on gasket and bolts, with bolts torqued to 25 ft-lb. New stainless steel intake manifold bolts and AN flat washers installed with new Speedway Motors #910-10125 chrome acorn nut covers, for 9/16″ head. New stainless steel nuts & lock washers installed on carburetor studs using anti-seize compound. 1939-48 Ford #9415 polished fuel pump stand/crankcase breather housing installed with new polished stainless steel bolts and lock washers using silicone sealant on gasket. New Speedway Motors #910-15195 crankcase breather/oil filler cap, for 1939-48 Ford, painted with Endura #EX-2C black 160 hi-gloss polyurethane. Luke's new polished aluminum road draft/crankcase breather and crankcase breather/oil filler tube plugs and fuel pump block-off plate installed. $435.97

3 x 2-barrel Holley 94 polished carburetors, 94/100″ (15/16″) venturi, 160 C.F.M. (approximate), installed. $670.00

New Offenhauser #6271 polished three-carburetor progressive linkage installed using anti-seize compound. New Speedway Motors #910-11005 chrome louvered air cleaners installed with new K & N #E-3120 high-flow air filters, 3.875″ diameter x 2″ high. $145.80

New Holley #12-804 polished fuel pressure regulator, adjustable from 1-4 psi, installed with new Fairview #KA06-04MB90 polished brass 90-degree elbow, 1/2″ N.P.T. to 3/8″ i.d. hose, and new Weatherhead #3320-6-4 polished brass reducer, 3/8″ N.P.T. to 1/2″ N.P.T. (inlet line); new Weatherhead #3325-6 polished brass coupling, 3/8″ N.P.T. (outlet line), and new polished stainless 3/8″ N.P.T. plug installed. New Offenhauser #1081 polished aluminum three-carburetor fuel block installed with Luke's new polished stainless steel mounting bracket using new polished stainless steel bolts and lock washers with anti-seize compound. New Weatherhead #3220-6-2 polished brass reducer, 3/8″ N.P.T. to 1/8″ N.P.T.; new Weatherhead #3400-2 polished brass 90-degree elbow, 1/8″ N.P.T. (outlet to fuel pressure gauge); and new Spectre #2515 stainless steel mechanical fuel pressure gauge, 0-15 psi, 1½″-diameter face, installed. New Weatherhead #7915 polished brass carburetor fuel inlet fittings, 3/8″ i.d. tube, installed. New Weatherhead #202-6-6 polished brass adapter, 3/8″ N.P.T. to 3/8″ tube (carburetor lines), and new Weatherhead #100-6 polished brass inverted flare nuts installed with new Summit Racing Equipment #220238 polished stainless steel fuel line, 3/8″ x 0.028″ wall, double annealed, 5′ length. $180.00

INTAKE SYSTEM TOTAL: $1,431.77

CHAPTER 7 IGNITION SYSTEM

Distributor

The original 1949-53 Ford flathead V-8 distributor was not a very classy unit. I am convinced it was designed by a Ford engineer while attending the Munich Beer Festival for the entire week! In order to remove one's self from the "Dark Ages," the use of an electronic distributor is the only means to guarantee an efficient and reliable ignition system.

There are two excellent manufacturers of aftermarket electronic distributors for the 1949-53 Ford flathead V-8. The first is Mallory, which produces the #3727501 Unilite model with full mechanical (centrifugal) advance. They also produce the Mallory #5027501 magnetic breakerless unit with full mechanical (centrifugal) advance. The 1951-53 Ford #OBA-6059-A aluminum timing gear cover or the 1949-50 Ford #8BA-6059 cast iron timing gear cover can be used with either of those distributors if the stock 1951-53 Ford #12390 distributor gear or the 1949-50 Ford #12390-C distributor gear is installed. The two gears are the same. Speedway Motors sells a replacement distributor gear, part #910-12701. The 1949-53 Ford #12270 distributor hold-down clamp can be used with the Mallory distributors. Mallory products are available from your local Mr. Gasket dealer.

The second choice is the MSD #8574 Pro-Billet aluminum electronic distributor. This distributor, if fitted with the MSD drive gear, will require the use of the 1949-50 Ford #8BA-6059 cast iron timing gear cover. If that distributor is purchased without the MSD drive gear and the 1951-53 Ford #12390 distributor gear or the 1949-50 Ford #12390-C distributor gear is installed, then the 1951-53 Ford #OBA-6059-A aluminum timing gear cover can be used. The 1949-53 Ford #12270 distributor hold-down clamp will not work with the MSD distributor due to the bulkier size of that unit. Luke's Custom Machine & Design fabricates an aluminum clamp for the MSD distributor. The MSD products are available from your local performance equipment outlet.

There have been articles written in the past on how to convert a Chevrolet distributor for use in a Ford flathead V-8 engine. This can be done, but it is strictly a task for an experienced machine shop. The use of a lathe is required to trim the Chevrolet housing and shaft. A Pertronix Performance Products #1181 breakerless ignition conversion can be added to make this a very good unit. A Standard Motor Products #DR429 black distributor cap and #VC160 vacuum advance fits the Chevrolet distributor housing. Luke's builds these converted Chevrolet distributors and sells them at a competitive price. The 1949-53 Ford #12270 distributor hold-down clamp is used in conjunction with a Luke's aluminum distributor clamp to secure the Chevrolet distributor.

Although unrelated to the engines being described in this book, this interesting part is an adapter to use a 1942-48 distributor with a pre-1942 camshaft.

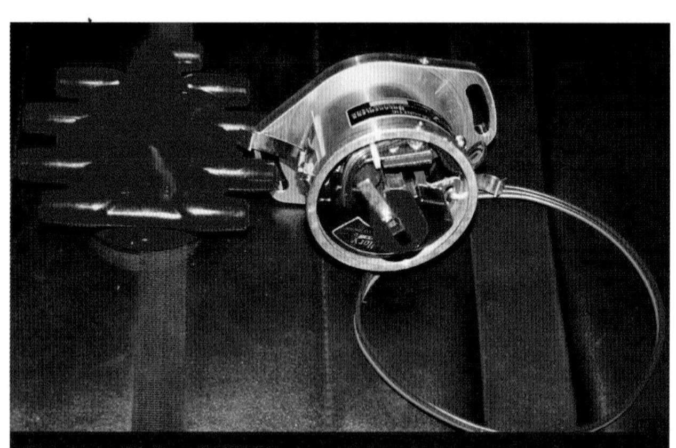

This is the Mallory #5072001 magnetic breakerless crab-style centrifugal (mechanical) advance distributor, for the 1942-48 Ford, which will be used in the engine built for this section. An electronic distributor is the only way to go in the new millennium for an efficient ignition system.

Another alternative for a distributor is to use a Mallory #3772001 Unilite or the Mallory #5072001 magnetic breaker less crab-style unit for the 1942-48 Ford, available from Speedway Motors, part #500-507-1501. The use of this centrifugal (mechanical) advance distributor in a 1949-53 Ford flathead V-8 engine requires a 1946-48 camshaft, crankshaft and camshaft gears, and timing cover. This distributor will be used in the engine described in this section. Note: All the distributors described in this chapter are 12-volt, negative ground.

Coil and Ignition Control

The MSD #8200 Blaster 2 chrome ignition coil with an output of 45,000 volts is very good. The engine featured in this section is going to be equipped with a multiple spark discharge ignition control box, and not all ignition

The MSD #8200 Blaster 2 ignition coil puts out 45,000 volts and is compatible with multiple-spark-discharge ignition-control boxes.

coils are compatible with this type of unit. The MSD Blaster 2 ignition coil is compatible with that box and has the same outward appearance as the stock ignition coil, except for the chrome finish.

The MSD Ignition #6A, model 6200, or #6AL, model 6420, are excellent multiple-spark-discharge ignition-control boxes to install. The model 6420 is equipped with rpm limiter modules, while the model 6200 is not. The use of an electronic distributor, good coil, and ignition control will provide the reliable spark the flathead requires. The Mallory #6852M Hyfire VI-A microprocessor-controlled

There are a lot of great parts, and a story, in this photograph. This is a stock 1950 Ford motor in a 1950 Meteor (Canadian Ford) belonging to Luke Balogh. The car and the engine were left for more than 10 years to rot in a field and never touched. I changed the oil, which looked like black tar, cleaned up the carburetor, fuelled up the car, and succeeded in starting the engine. Simply amazing; flatheads will run forever! In the picture there are an offset coil bracket, 2¾"" carburetor spacers (unpolished), and a Chevrolet distributor machined to fit the flathead timing cover. The spark plug wires are Pertronix Flame Throwers. The three-carb setup is for looks only; the two end carburetors are blocked off. The linkage was made from sweepings off of the shop floor! There is a GM chrome alternator on the front of the intake manifold.

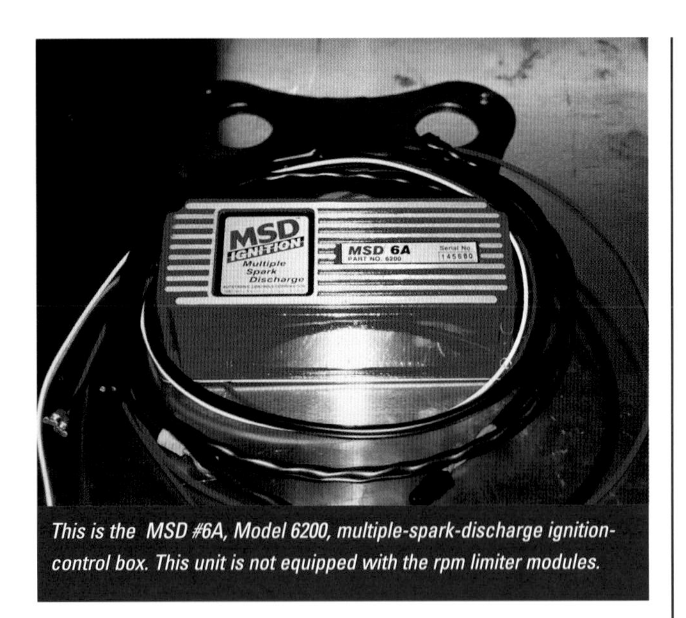

This is the MSD #6A, Model 6200, multiple-spark-discharge ignition-control box. This unit is not equipped with the rpm limiter modules.

CD ignition system or the Mallory #685 Hyfire VI multi-strike CD ignition system with multi-stage rev limiting are excellent ignition control boxes as well.

An offset coil bracket will be required, as well as the stock 1949-53 Ford #12043 coil bracket, when installing the MSD, Mallory, or the Chevrolet distributor in a 1949-53 flathead V-8 engine. The MSD, Mallory, and Chevrolet distributors are slightly bulkier than the stock Ford unit, and this results in little or no room for the coil in the stock mounting position. Luke's makes a polished aluminum offset coil bracket to solve this problem.

Spark Plug Wires and Plugs

A good spark plug wire to install is the Pertronix Performance Products #808290 Flame Thrower with high-performance, 8 mm black 90-degree boots. I prefer this spark plug wire because the boots for the spark plugs are very similar in size to the original flathead boots, and they are not the massive type most commonly found on high performance OHV engines. The Spectre #4245 chrome wire separators are low cost and look good. Spectre components are available from your local speed shop.

The spark plugs that are designed for use in the flathead are the Champion #H-10, the Autolite #216, and the NGK #B-6L. The spark plug gap should be 0.050″ when using an electronic ignition system, such as the MSD or Mallory described above. Always coat the threads on the spark plugs with anti-seize compound when they are being installed in aluminum cylinder heads, as this will help to prevent the threads from galling.

Alternator

Use a new style alternator on your flathead. The old Ford generator was a 6-volt bulky object that should be put out to pasture. A decent chrome GM 12-volt alternator, 63 amp, internally regulated, is available from Speedway Motors as part #913-67163 or from Summit Racing Equipment, part #PRO-66445. This is an affordable item.

An alternator bracket is required to mount the alternator on the front of the 1939-53 Ford flathead V-8 intake manifolds. Speedway Motors supplies a very good chrome "slingshot" bracket for the GM alternator, part #916-67909

This is a nicely chromed GM internally regulated 63 amp. alternator installed on a Speedway Motors #916-67909 (1946-53 Ford) chrome "slingshot" alternator mounting bracket. I love the crankcase breather/oil filler cap. It has a horseshoe with the number "13" on it! That is a three-carb Edelbrock intake manifold.

This is a 1961-89 Chrysler alternator mounted on the lower part of a 1949-53 Ford flathead V-8 #8BA10153C passenger car generator mounting bracket. The Chrysler unit is much more compact than the GM alternator. Now there is lots of clearance for the front carburetor on a three-carb setup.

This photo, taken from the right side of the engine, shows the Chrysler alternator mounted on a part of the flathead generator bracket. There is now enough room between the alternator and the front carburetor to drive the Borax 20-mule wagon train through!

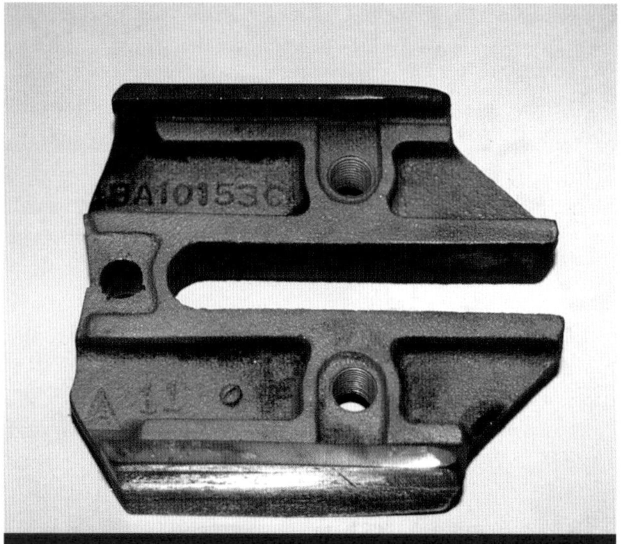

The 1949-53 flathead generator mounting bracket should look like this after it has been cut, trimmed, ground smooth, and drilled.

The Powermaster #17509 chrome 1961-89 Chrysler 75 amp. alternator requires an external regulator.

(1946-53 Ford), at a reasonable price. This alternator bracket, with the GM alternator, will only fit the 1939-53 flathead regular dual-carb intake manifolds. If a three-carb intake manifold is going to be used, then carburetor spacers of at least 2½" height must be installed in order for the front carburetor to clear the GM alternator. If a super-dual or four-carb intake manifold is used, the alternator will have to be mounted on the left cylinder head. Luke's fabricates a stainless steel mounting bracket for this purpose, or a steel cylinder head mounting bracket can be purchased from Speedway Motors, part #916-67915.

Aftermarket aluminum offset generator brackets are available for the 1949-53 flathead intake manifolds. However, I am not a great enthusiast of those brackets because they place a lot of stress on the front of the intake manifold, which is the reason you see many used intake manifolds with a broken generator mounting flange.

Another method to mount an alternator on the front of a 1939-53 flathead intake manifold is to use a Powermaster #17509 chrome 1961-89 Chrysler alternator, 75 amp, and part of the stock 1949-53 Ford #8BA10153C passenger car generator mounting bracket. There is one slight drawback when using the Chrysler alternator: an external regulator is required. The Chrysler alternator is available from Summit Racing Equipment, part #PMW-17509.

To mount the Chrysler alternator, cut off the bottom 4½″ of the stock 1949-53 Ford #8BA10153C generator bracket. Trim the edges and grind them smooth. There is a locating pin at the top of the bracket that you must cut off as well. Drill a ⅜″ hole in the center of the upper part of the generator bracket, approximately ¾″ from the top. The generator bracket is then chromed or painted. A steel spacer, 1½″ length x ⅜″ i.d., is required for the front of the alternator. A bolt is passed through the Chrysler alternator, then through the spacer, and finally into the hole in the bracket. This is the bottom mount for the alternator. The Chrysler alternator fits securely in the bracket, eliminating the need for any upper braces. The modified generator bracket is bolted to the intake manifold in the normal fashion and the Chrysler alternator is then bolted to the bracket. You can still bolt the stock 1949-53 Ford flathead V-8 fan assembly to the front of the generator mounting bracket.

Starting Motor

Some flathead owners use the stock 1949-53 Ford flathead V-8 starting motor for their engines. Even though that starting motor operated on 6 volts, it will not be harmed using 12 volts as long as it is used for regular starting. If the engine is being continually started, the 6 volt starting motor will not last.

The Powermaster #9507 hi-torque 12-volt mini-starter.

I recommend that you avoid this outdated practice and procure a new Powermaster #9507 hi-torque 12-volt mini-starter. This is a much more compact unit, and it will be trouble-free operating on 12 volts. Powermaster products are available from your local speed equipment shop at a reasonable price.

Ignition System Summary

Item	Price
New Mallory #5072001 magnetic breakerless crab-style distributor (for the 1942-48 Ford), full centrifugal (mechanical) advance, 34 degrees advance @ 3,000 rpm, installed with NOS (new-old-stock) 1942-48 Ford #48-12148 distributor bolts using anti-seize compound. New MSD #6200, Model 6A, multiple spark discharge ignition control and new MSD #8200 Blaster 2 chrome ignition coil, 45,000 volts, installed with 1949-53 Ford #12043 coil bracket. Coil bracket painted with Endura #EX-2C black 160 hi-gloss polyurethane.	$548.18
New Pertronix Performance Products #808290 FlameThrower high-performance 8 mm spark plug wires, black 90 degree boots, installed with new Spectre #4245 chrome professional wire separators. New NGK #B-6L spark plugs installed with 0.050″ gap and torqued to 15 ft-lb using anti-seize compound.	$70.00
New Powermaster #17509 chrome 1961-89 Chrysler alternator, 75 amp, externally regulated, installed with 1949-53 Ford flathead V-8 #8BA10153C generator mounting bracket. Generator mounting bracket painted with Endura #EX-2C black 160 hi-gloss polyurethane and installed with new polished stainless steel bolts, flat washers, and lock washers using anti-seize compound. Luke's new polished aluminum alternator pulley installed.	$184.95
New Powermaster #9507 hi-torque starting motor installed.	$189.95
IGNITION SYSTEM TOTAL:	**$993.08**

CHAPTER 8
COOLING SYSTEM AND MISCELLANEOUS

Water Pumps

In the past, there has been a lot of controversy about the Ford flathead V-8 cooling system. There have been conversion kits available to mount the water pump from a Chevrolet 348/409-ci engine on a flathead motor. There is really nothing wrong with the stock Ford flathead V-8 cooling system. You should not encounter any cooling problems provided you have a good, clean engine block and radiator, mechanical or electric fan, and water pumps in good working order. A fan shroud is an item that is often overlooked; however, it is an integral part of the cooling system and will aid in engine cooling.

The 1949-53 Ford passenger car water pumps #8BA-8503-D and #8BA-8504-D and the double groove crankshaft pulley #8BA-6372-C2, 7" diameter. These pulleys are the "narrow" (⅜") type. Notice the angle of the motor mount pads on the water pumps.

Here are the 1949 Mercury passenger car water pumps on the front of a legendary Ardun engine. The horizontal motor mount flange is located higher up on the water pump body than the 1949-53 Ford Truck models.

The 1949 Mercury #OCM-8503 and #OCM-8504 chrome water pumps and the double-groove crankshaft pulley #8BA-6372-A2, 7" diameter. These pulleys are the "wide" (⅝") type. Notice the motor mount pads are horizontal, which allows this motor to be adapted to almost any type of chassis.

Another important item to remember is to use as little antifreeze as possible, or none at all, in the summer months or hot climates. Antifreeze traps the heat in the engine cooling system and does not allow this heat to dissipate as quickly as it should, which results in a much higher engine temperature than normal during hot days. A minimal amount of antifreeze, or a substitute, should be used in order to lubricate the water pumps.

The best water pumps to use on the flathead motor are from the 1949-53 Ford Truck model. These water pumps have a horizontal motor mount flange cast into them. The fact that this flange is horizontal makes these pumps ideal for installing the flathead engine in just about any type of automobile frame. The 1949 Mercury #OCM-8503 and #OCM-8504 passenger car water pumps are almost the same, except the horizontal motor mount flange is located higher up on the water pump body.

You might encounter some difficulty in locating these particular water pumps, and even if you do, they may be badly corroded. It is getting harder to find new impellers and shafts for the flathead water pumps in order to rebuild them. The answer to this dilemma is Speedway Motors, which is now selling brand-new water pumps in four different versions. These pumps consist of new castings, shafts and bearings, impellers, and seals, all at a very reasonable price. Use stainless steel bolts for attaching the water pumps to the engine block. You will require six pieces of ⅜" N.C. x 1" length and two pieces of ⅜" N.C. x 2" length, as well as eight pieces of ⅜" lock washers.

Use a new fan belt of good quality, such as that provided by Gates. The fan belt length will vary with each engine due to the different diameters of the alternator, water pump, and

This picture is of a 1949-53 Ford Truck #8RT-8504-B water pump. The motor mount flange is lower than the flange on the 1949 Mercury water pumps. This pump is in dire need of a professional rebuild.

crankshaft pulleys and the height of the alternator on the engine. Fabricate an aluminum alternator pulley to accommodate the wide (5/8″) belt used with the 1949-53 Ford Truck water pumps and crankshaft pulley. Luke's Custom Machine & Design fabricates alternator pulleys.

An easy method to determine the fan belt length is to cut an old fan belt of sufficient length in half, wrap this belt around all the pulleys, remove it, and measure the length.

Labor

The cost of the labor for checking clearances, gapping piston rings, degree camshaft, painting and detailing, trial assembly of the motor, final assembly of the motor, and the initial start-up of the engine is not included in the summaries at the end of each chapter. I include that cost here.

Cooling System and Miscellaneous Summary

1949-53 Ford Truck #8RT-8503-B and #8RT-8504-B water pumps rebuilt by Luke's and installed with new polished stainless steel bolts and lock washers using silicone sealant on gaskets and torqued to 25 ft-lb. New Gates #3560 water pump/alternator/crankshaft V-belt, Truflex (21/32″ x 56″ length) installed. Water pumps painted with Endura #EX-2C black 160 hi-gloss polyurethane.	$205.13
Labor for checking bearing clearances, gapping piston rings, degreeing camshaft, painting and detailing, trial engine assembly, final engine assembly, and initial engine start-up.	$1,040.00
COOLING SYSTEM AND MISCELLANEOUS TOTAL:	**$1,245.13**

NOTE: The estimated output of this engine is: 221 hp @ 5,000 rpm and 286 ft-lb torque @ 3,000 rpm (See the Dyno Printouts section).

Performance Street Engine Total

Engine block	$1,494.73
Crankshaft	$922.98
Connecting rods and pistons	$1,181.40
Lubrication system	$597.23
Camshaft and cylinder head	$1,645.10
Intake system	$1,431.77
Ignition system	$993.08
Cooling system and miscellaneous	$1,245.13
TOTAL	**$9,511.42 (U.S.)**

CHAPTER 9
MISSING PARTS

Exhaust Manifolds

I have not included the exhaust manifolds in the description of the engines in this book because the type of header will depend on the construction of the frame the engine will be installed in. Speedway Motors offers three different types of good-quality headers. They sell the original Fenton cast iron manifolds, a high-temperature coated (H.T.C.) center-dump header, and a more conventional economy header. Use stainless steel header bolts and torque them to 25 ft-lb using Loctite.

The steel tube header is from Speedway Motors #910-13606. A Walker #31807 exhaust flange is welded to the header because these headers do not come with a flange attached. Speedway Motors #910-44084 Cermakrome high-temperature coating was sprayed and baked on the header. These headers fit 1937-41 Ford cars with Vega steering and 1942-53 Ford cars with stock steering.

Here is a Vintage Vendors #227ELT equal-length exhaust header. These headers should be high-temperature coated after they are port matched.

This very rare cast iron exhaust manifold for a flathead motor has "Alhambra Calif" (possibly a Belond model) in raised letters on the side. It was discovered in the rafters of Luke's Custom Machine & Design along with Judge Crater! The right side of the engine has a 1939 Ford flathead V-8 exhaust manifold attached. The two exhaust manifolds make for a nice, almost stock looking, dual-exhaust system.

Tatom Custom Engines sells a very nice 14-gauge steel equal-length set of exhaust headers with ⅜″ thickness flanges. The headers for 1932 and later models are Vintage Vendors #227ELT. After these headers are port matched, they should receive a high temperature coating. One important item regarding these headers: the right header must have the end tube (#4 cylinder) modified in order to clear the Powermaster #9507 starting motor.

Flywheel and Flexplate

If a standard transmission is to be installed, you will require the 1949-53 Ford #6375 flywheel, heat-treated steel, 14.20″ diameter, 146 teeth, weight: 32 lbs. The flywheel can be machined down to approximately 23 lbs. In addition, you need: Ford #350816-S flywheel bolt washer plate; Ford #20350-S flywheel bolts (4); Ford #6387 crankshaft dowels (2); and Ford #7600 bronze pilot bearing. The flywheel bolts should be torqued to 80 ft-lb using Loctite. The clutch disc pressure plate requires the Ford #350433-S pressure plate bolts (6) and the Ford #34846-S lock washers (6). The pressure plate bolts should be torqued to 35 ft-lb using Loctite.

Now for a few words about aluminum flywheels. The lighter the flywheel, the faster the engine will accelerate or slow down, and the clutch will probably have to be slipped more in order to prevent the engine from stalling. A lighter

Here is a 1949-53 Ford #6375 flywheel that originally weighed 32 lbs. and now weighs 23 lbs. after being machined.

One of Gene Benson's Flat-O Products flexplates for use with the Ford C-4 automatic transmission. The pilot bearing adapter and ARP flexplate bolts are pictured in the center of the flexplate.

flywheel should be used in a vehicle that is being used to accelerate and decelerate frequently. However, for normal street driving, the stock Ford flathead flywheel should prove to be quite satisfactory. If you use an aluminum flywheel for normal street driving, make certain it has a steel or bronze friction surface. Without this friction surface, the flywheel will wear excessively fast.

A 1949-53 Ford Truck #8RT-6392 bellhousing adapter (for use with 1949-53 Ford blocks to pre-1949 Ford transmissions) is available from Speedway Motors, part #910-28950. This bellhousing adapter should be torqued to 30 ft-lb using Loctite on the bolts. The 1949-53 Ford Truck #8RT-6366 starting motor plate bolts to this bellhousing adapter. Use the Ford #6411 rubber dust seal (if available) with the starting motor plate.

Three different types of starting motor plates were used on the Ford flathead V-8 engines. The 1949-53 Ford Truck #8RT-6366 plate had the center section pushed out toward the front of the motor. The 1949-53 Ford #8BA-6366 plate was pushed out at the bottom toward the front

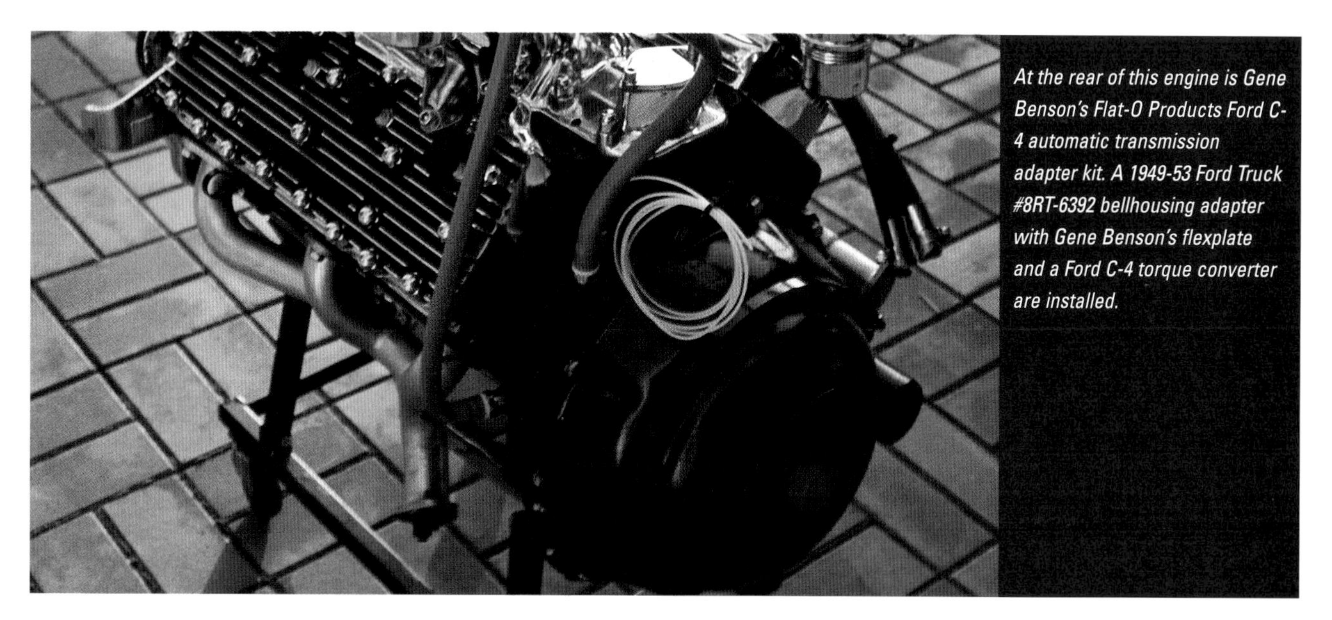
At the rear of this engine is Gene Benson's Flat-O Products Ford C-4 automatic transmission adapter kit. A 1949-53 Ford Truck #8RT-6392 bellhousing adapter with Gene Benson's flexplate and a Ford C-4 torque converter are installed.

Here is the complete engine prior to its first start-up. The header is a Vintage Vendor #227ELT equal-length model that has not been high-temperature coated. The engine is another example of the superb quality of workmanship turned out by Luke's.

of the motor and had a horizontal rib pressed in it. The 1949-50 Mercury #8CM-6366-C plate was flat. The one used will depend on the type of oil pan and bellhousing on the engine.

If you decide to install an automatic transmission, you can obtain a complete Ford flathead V-8 to Ford C-4 transmission kit from Benson's Flat-O Products. Speedway Motors also manufactures a kit for this type of conversion, part #910-28905. Both suppliers provide complete kits or the basic hardware to which you add your own transmission. A number of years ago I purchased one of the basic kits from Benson's Flat-O Products (in those days it was called "Flat-O-Matic"), and I found it to be an excellent product.

Fan

I have not included the stock 1949-53 Ford #8602 fan and #8603 hub assembly. The owner of the engine will decide whether to use a stock unit, a stock fan hub assembly with an aftermarket fan, or an electric fan attached to the radiator.

A polished stainless steel 18"-diameter flexfan.

CHAPTER 10

ASSEMBLY

ASSEMBLY

The clearances and torque settings I have indicated in this book are the ones I use in my own engines, and I know they work. It is up to the engine builder to ensure the engine is assembled using the proper clearances and torque settings. An accomplished engine builder will follow the clearances specified by the *Ford Motor Company of Canada Master Repair Manual* and those recommended by the aftermarket equipment manufacturers.

The engine block was thoroughly cleaned prior to the exterior paint being applied. This being the case, assembly of the Ford flathead V-8 engine commenced.

Engine Block

Clean the camshaft bearings with clean solvent using a clean, lint-free cloth. Install the camshaft bearings dry in

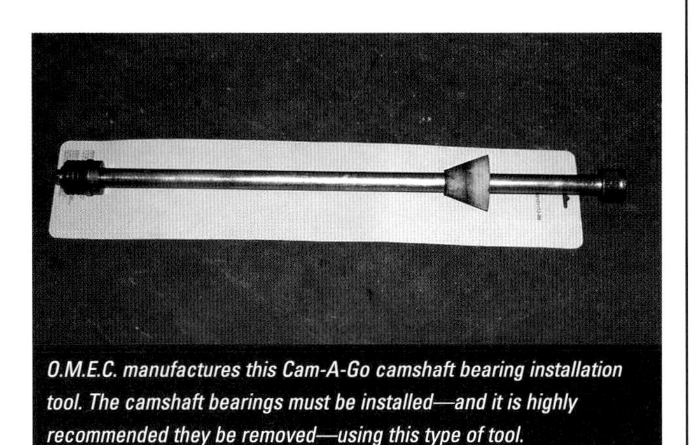

O.M.E.C. manufactures this Cam-A-Go camshaft bearing installation tool. The camshaft bearings must be installed—and it is highly recommended they be removed—using this type of tool.

This photograph shows the installed oil-pump idler gear. The opening next to it is for the gear on the end of the camshaft.

There is a new stainless steel oil-line plug is installed behind the camshaft timing gear. Use Permatex aviation form-a-gasket or pipe thread sealant on the plug.

the engine block using a camshaft bearing installation tool (this is a must!), taking special care to line up the oil holes in the camshaft bearings with the oil holes in the engine block. Do not lubricate the camshaft bosses.

Lubricate the oil pump idler gear bushing and the oil pump idler gear shaft with motor oil. Then install this assembly in the rear of the engine block by gently tapping the oil pump idler gear shaft into position using a brass drift and hammer. The smaller side of the oil pump idler gear faces outward.

Install a new stainless steel pipe plug, ⅜" N.P.T., in the oil line at the face of the engine block (behind the camshaft

The fuel pump pushrod bushing installed.

The camshaft timing gear installed on the camshaft. The vise had aluminum plates over the jaws to protect the camshaft gear. Use aluminum or plastic protector plates when doing this job.

This photograph shows the stainless steel connecting rod journal oil line plugs. Always use Loctite when installing these plugs.

timing gear) using Permatex aviation form-a-gasket. Install a new stainless steel pipe plug, ⅛ N.P.T., in the stock oil return line hole at the bottom of the block on the left side near the oil pan rail using Permatex aviation form-a-gasket.

Apply some motor oil to the fuel pump pushrod bushing and insert it in the rear of the valve lifter gallery. Gently tap it into position using a brass drift and hammer.

Install the camshaft gear on the camshaft using Loctite on the bolts and torque the bolts to 20 ft-lb. Bend the camshaft locking plate tabs over the camshaft bolts.

Lubricate the face of the camshaft bearings and the camshaft bearing journals with Clevite 77 Bearing Guard and generously apply the camshaft assembly lube, provided by the camshaft manufacturer, on the lobes of the camshaft. Gently slide the camshaft into the block, taking care not to nick the camshaft bearings.

Crankshaft

Install the stainless steel connecting rod journal oil line plugs using Loctite. Place the crankshaft gear woodruff key in the crankshaft key slot using anti-seize compound and gently tap the woodruff key into position with a hammer. Apply anti-seize compound to the crankshaft snout and then slide the crankshaft gear on the snout as far as it will go by hand. The side with a dot or line on a tooth of the crankshaft gear faces outward. Line up the crankshaft gear with the crankshaft gear woodruff key and gently tap the gear into position using a piece of steel pipe a little larger than the diameter of the crankshaft snout. Slide the crankshaft oil slinger on the crankshaft snout.

This crankshaft oil slinger, installed, is painted with Glyptal #G-1228A medium grey gloss enamel.

Install the rear main bearing oil seal retainer in the block using silicone sealant and gently tap it into position with a rubber hammer. Install the rear upper cord material oil seal in the retainer by rolling it in place with a large socket, or use the head of a large ball peen hammer and tap the head of the hammer with another hammer.

Clean the main bearings in clean solvent and wipe them dry with a clean lint-free cloth. Line up the locking tang (tab) on the main bearings with the notch in the engine block and install the main bearings dry in the engine block. Do not lubricate the main bearing saddles in the engine

The timing marks on the crankshaft gear and the camshaft gear are lined up.

The main bearing bolts are in the final stage of being torqued to 105 ft-lb.

block. Use Clevite 77 Bearing Guard to lubricate the face of the main bearings after they are installed in the engine block. Apply the same procedure to the main bearing caps when inserting the main bearings in the caps. Do not lubricate the faces of the main bearing caps. Use Clevite 77 Bearing Guard to lubricate the face of the main bearings after they are installed in the main bearing caps.

Gently lower the crankshaft into the main bearing saddles, taking special care not to nick the main bearing inserts. Make certain to line up the timing marks on the camshaft and crankshaft gears. The camshaft gear has a line or dot and the crankshaft gear has a line or a dot. These marks should be vertically in line with each other. The main bearing caps are placed in their correct order in the engine block with the tang (tab) in the engine block and the main bearing cap tang on the same side. Lubricate the main bearing cap bolts with Molykote. Torque the main bearing cap bolts to 105 ft-lb in incremental steps, torquing

The crankshaft has been installed and torqued, and it spins freely. It is a great feeling when you get something right, for a change!

the bolts to 75 ft-lb, then 90 ft-lb, then 105 ft-lb. The crankshaft should now turn freely in the engine block.

Connecting Rods and Pistons

Remove the wrist pins from the pistons and coat them and the wrist pin bushings in the connecting rods with motor oil. Some cast pistons (not Ross's forged pistons) have an arrow on the piston head to indicate they are to be installed with the arrow facing the front of the engine block. Other cast pistons (again, not Ross's forged pistons) have an "F" cast into one side to indicate which side faces the front of the engine block. The cylinder numbers stamped on the side of the connecting rods always face outward from the crankshaft. These numbers are on the same side of the connecting rod as the tang for the connecting rod bearings. Assemble the

A piston ring expander tool is being used to install the piston rings on the piston.

A connecting rod/piston assembly is being installed with a piston ring compressor tool.

The plastic protectors on the connecting rod studs prevent any nicks to the connecting rod journals.

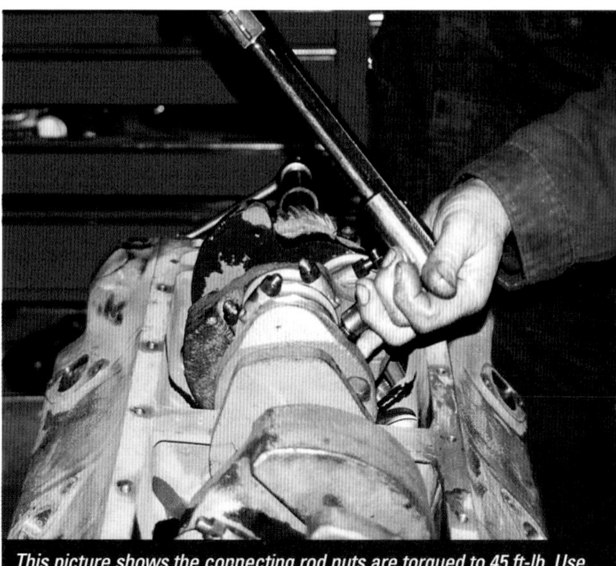

This picture shows the connecting rod nuts are torqued to 45 ft-lb. Use Loctite on the connecting rod stud threads prior to installing the nuts.

rods and pistons and install the Spiro Lox retainers by spreading the retainer, inserting one end into the wrist-pin hole, and gently but evenly spinning the retainer into the wrist-pin hole with the aid of a screwdriver.

Install the piston rings on the pistons using a piston ring expander, and rotate each of the piston rings on the pistons so they are within the manufacturer's recommended arc, also known as the preferred ring gap location.

Clean the connecting rod bearings with clean solvent and wipe them dry with a clean lint-free cloth. Install the connecting rod bearings dry in the connecting rods and

The side clearance, per pair of connecting rods, is being checked. The clearance for this engine was 0.014". That is within the Ford Motor Company of Canada Master Repair Manual *specifications.*

This photograph shows the ¼" N.P.T. plug installed inside the horizontal pressure-out oil line hole.

the connecting rod caps. Line up the locking tang on the bearing shell with the notch in the connecting rod, and do the same with the connecting rod cap. Use Clevite 77 Bearing Guard to lubricate the faces of the connecting rod bearings. Place plastic connecting rod bolt protectors on the connecting rod studs.

Apply motor oil to the inside of the piston ring compressor and place the piston ring compressor around the piston. Tighten the piston ring compressor and insert the connecting rod into the cylinder, with the cylinder numbers and connecting rod bearing tang facing outward from the crankshaft, and gently tap the piston down into the cylinder using a rubber hammer or piece of wood. Guide the connecting rod studs over the crankshaft journal as the piston is being pushed down. After the connecting rod is on the crankshaft journal, install the connecting rod cap with the tang on the same side as the tang on the connecting rod. Install the connecting rod nuts using Loctite. Torque the connecting rods to 45 ft-lb.

Install the crankshaft bolt in the crankshaft and turn the crankshaft. The rotating assembly should turn over smoothly.

Use a feeler gauge to check the final side clearance per pair of connecting rods.

Lubrication System

Install a new ¼" N.P.T. stainless steel socket head plug inside the horizontal pressure-out oil line hole using pipe thread sealant.

Lubricate the oil pump drive gear with motor oil and install the oil pump assembly in the engine block. Install the oil pump bolt and lock washer using Loctite and torque the bolt to 15 ft-lb.

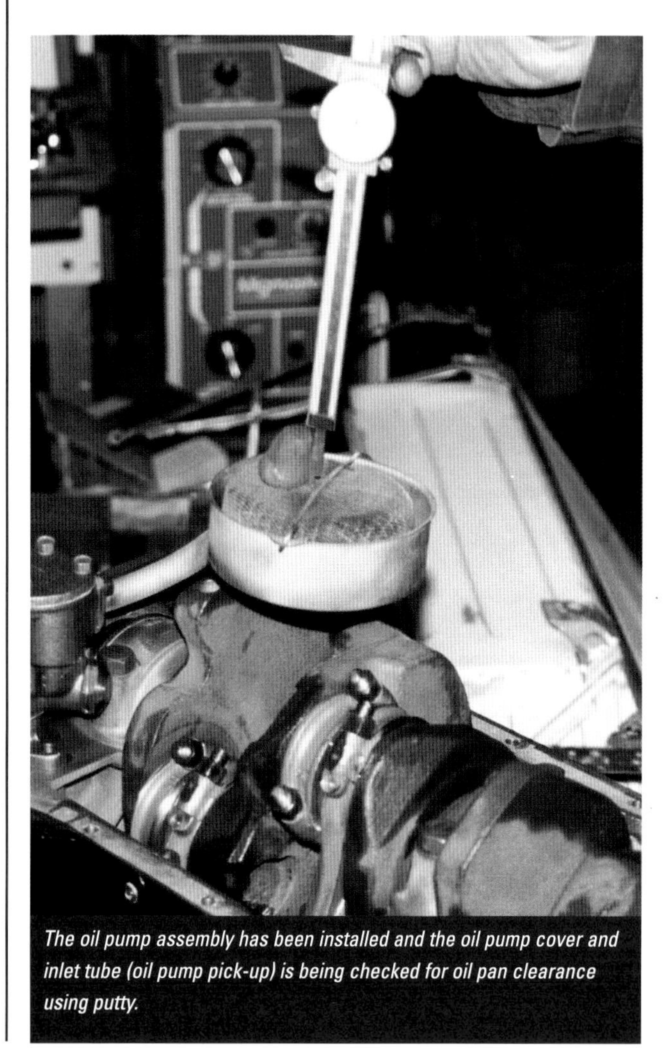
The oil pump assembly has been installed and the oil pump cover and inlet tube (oil pump pick-up) is being checked for oil pan clearance using putty.

The oil pump idler gear cover is installed with the stainless steel safety wire through the bolt heads.

Install the oil pump idler gear cover using silicone sealant on the gasket. Install the oil pump idler gear cover bolts and lock washers using Loctite and torque to 15 ft-lb. Install the stainless steel safety wire through the oil pump idler gear cover bolts if so equipped.

The timing gear cover has been installed with the one-piece oil seal and the Luke's Custom Machine & Design crankshaft oil seal sleeve.

The oil gallery breather tube has been installed and painted with Glyptal #G-1228A medium grey gloss enamel. Those are Iskenderian #185-G single valve springs with the Speedway Motors #450-F8502 "Johnson" adjustable lifters.

Camshaft and Cylinder Heads

Install the intake and exhaust valve camshaft lifters (tappets) for the #1 cylinder and degree the camshaft. If all the results of this exercise are in accordance with the camshaft manufacturer's specification card (timing tag), then continue on with the engine assembly. If they are not, you had better find out why before proceeding any further.

Install the one-piece oil seal and the crankshaft oil seal sleeve on the crankshaft by gently tapping it into position with a piece of pipe and a hammer. Install the timing gear cover using silicone sealant on the gasket and around the oil seal. Install the timing cover bolts using Loctite and torque to 15 ft-lb.

Install the cord material rear oil seal in the oil pan by rolling it in place with a large socket or using the head of a large ball peen hammer and tapping the head of the hammer with another hammer. Place some putty on the oil pump pick-up screen and position the oil pan on the engine block without the oil pan gaskets. Push down firmly on the oil pan and then remove the oil pan from the engine. Measure the putty for compressed thickness. The proper oil pan-to-oil pump pick-up clearance should be ¾″ to 1″. If the compressed thickness is correct, carry on. If it is not, adjust the oil pump pick-up arm until the correct clearance is obtained. Install the oil pan on the engine block using silicone sealant on the gaskets. Install the oil pan bolts using Loctite and

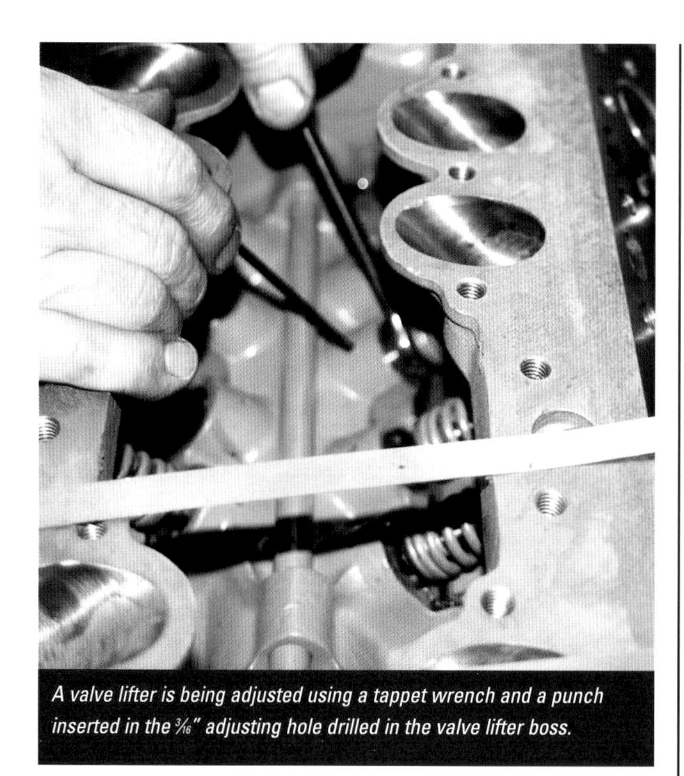
A valve lifter is being adjusted using a tappet wrench and a punch inserted in the 3⁄16" adjusting hole drilled in the valve lifter boss.

The cooling system hole, just below the exhaust baffle stud, shows the irontite plug that was installed through the exhaust port into the exhaust baffle in order to prevent the exhaust baffle from ever slipping out of position.

torque them to 165 in-lb. Screw the dipstick tube into the oil pan using silicone sealant and install the dipstick.

Install the camshaft lifters using motor oil on the camshaft lifter bosses and coat the face (bottom) of the camshaft lifters liberally with the camshaft assembly lube provided by the camshaft manufacturer.

Assemble the valves with the valve guide bushings, springs, retainers, and locks. Install the intake valve guide bushing O-rings. Coat everything with motor oil as you assemble it. Install the assemblies into the engine block. Use a valve guide removal tool to compress the valve springs, allowing the crow's foot valve guide bushing retainers to be installed. Insert the chuck end of a 3⁄16" drill, or a punch, into the hole drilled in the valve lifter boss, and adjust the valves according to the camshaft manufacturer's specifications. Rotate the crankshaft until the exhaust valve for a cylinder starts to open, and adjust the intake valve for that cylinder. Rotate the crankshaft until the intake valve

The smaller fork-end of the valve spring compressor is being inserted through the valve spring into the groove at the bottom of the valve guide bushing. The valve guide bushing is then pulled downward and the crow's foot valve guide bushing retainer is installed.

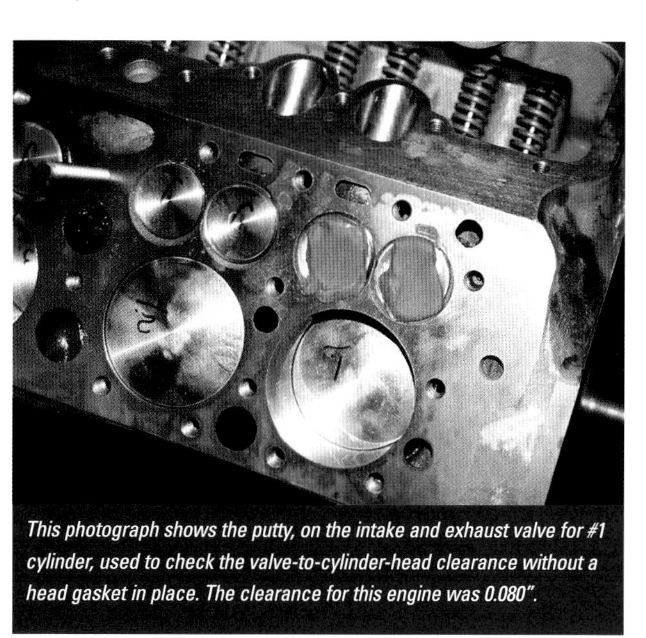
This photograph shows the putty, on the intake and exhaust valve for #1 cylinder, used to check the valve-to-cylinder-head clearance without a head gasket in place. The clearance for this engine was 0.080".

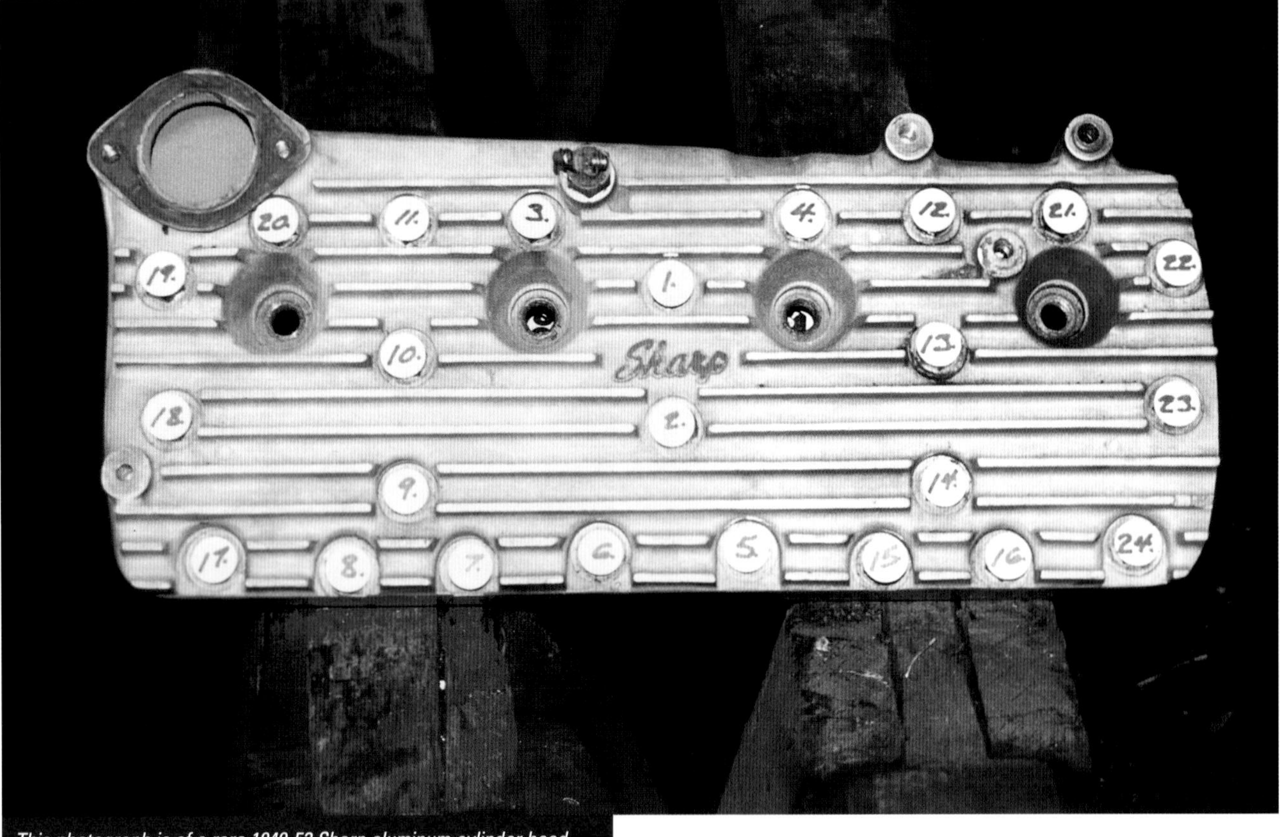

This photograph is of a rare 1949-53 Sharp aluminum cylinder head with the head bolts numbered in the correct order they are to be torqued, as specified by the Ford Motor Company of Canada Master Repair Manual. This cylinder head is in dire straits and requires the personal attention of "Tim the polishing guy."

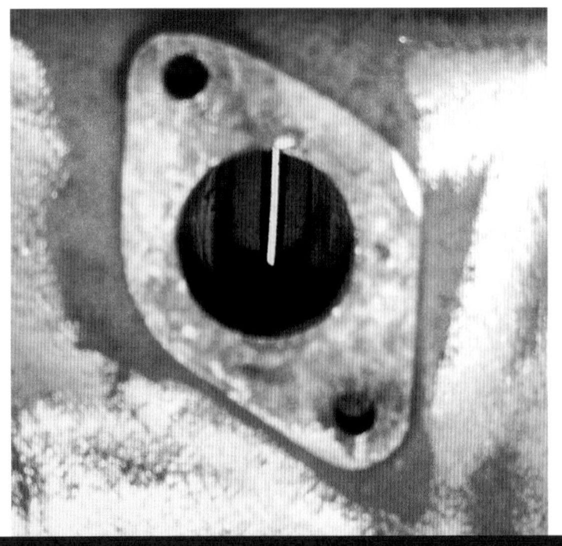

The Speedway Motors #916-15201 exhaust baffle has been installed in the center exhaust port.

for that cylinder starts to close, then adjust the exhaust valve for that cylinder. Adjust all the valves for each cylinder in the same manner. Install the valve lifter gallery crankcase breather tube by gently tapping it into position with a rubber hammer. Install the two valve-lifter gallery oil return hole baffles by snapping them into position.

Install the exhaust port baffles and install an irontite plug in each baffle (drilled through the exhaust port) using Loctite as additional insurance against the possibility of the baffle shifting.

Put some putty on any intake and exhaust valve in the same cylinder, and then place the cylinder head on the engine block and lightly tighten the cylinder head down with two bolts. Do not use the cylinder head gasket. Turn the crankshaft through 360 degrees. Remove the cylinder head and measure the height of the putty. This measurement will indicate the valve-to-cylinder-head clearance, the minimum of which should be 0.040".

Spray the head gaskets with Permatex copper form-a-gasket. Install the cylinder head gaskets and the cylinder heads using the head bolts and head bolt washers. Apply Permatex aviation form-a-gasket on the threads of the bolts and torque the bolts to 40 ft-lb using the factory-approved torque pattern. Do not install the chrome acorn nut covers until after the engine has been initially started and the cylinder heads are re-torqued.

Install the thermostats in the cylinder heads using silicone sealant on the water outlet elbow gaskets and bolts, and install the water outlet elbows. Torque the water outlet elbow bolts to 15 ft-lb.

Intake System

It is much easier to install the carburetors on the intake manifold and the linkage on the carburetors before installing the intake manifold on the engine. You can do this at your workbench or sit comfortably at your oak dining room table, if you are single!

Place the carburetor gaskets on the intake manifold and install the carburetors on the intake manifold using antiseize compound on the carburetor studs. Tighten the carburetor nuts snugly; do not overtighten them. Install the carburetor linkage on the extended throttle shafts and adjust the linkage. Install the air cleaners on the carburetors.

Trace the intake manifold outline on the intake manifold gasket and trim the intake manifold gasket accordingly. Install the intake manifold gasket using silicone sealant. Install the intake manifold and torque the bolts to 25 ft-lb using the factory-approved torque pattern.

Here is a great photograph of the Edelbrock 3-carb setup with the Holley 94 carburetors installed, which I built for the engine featured in Section I of this book.

This picture shows the progressive linkage installed for a three-carb setup.

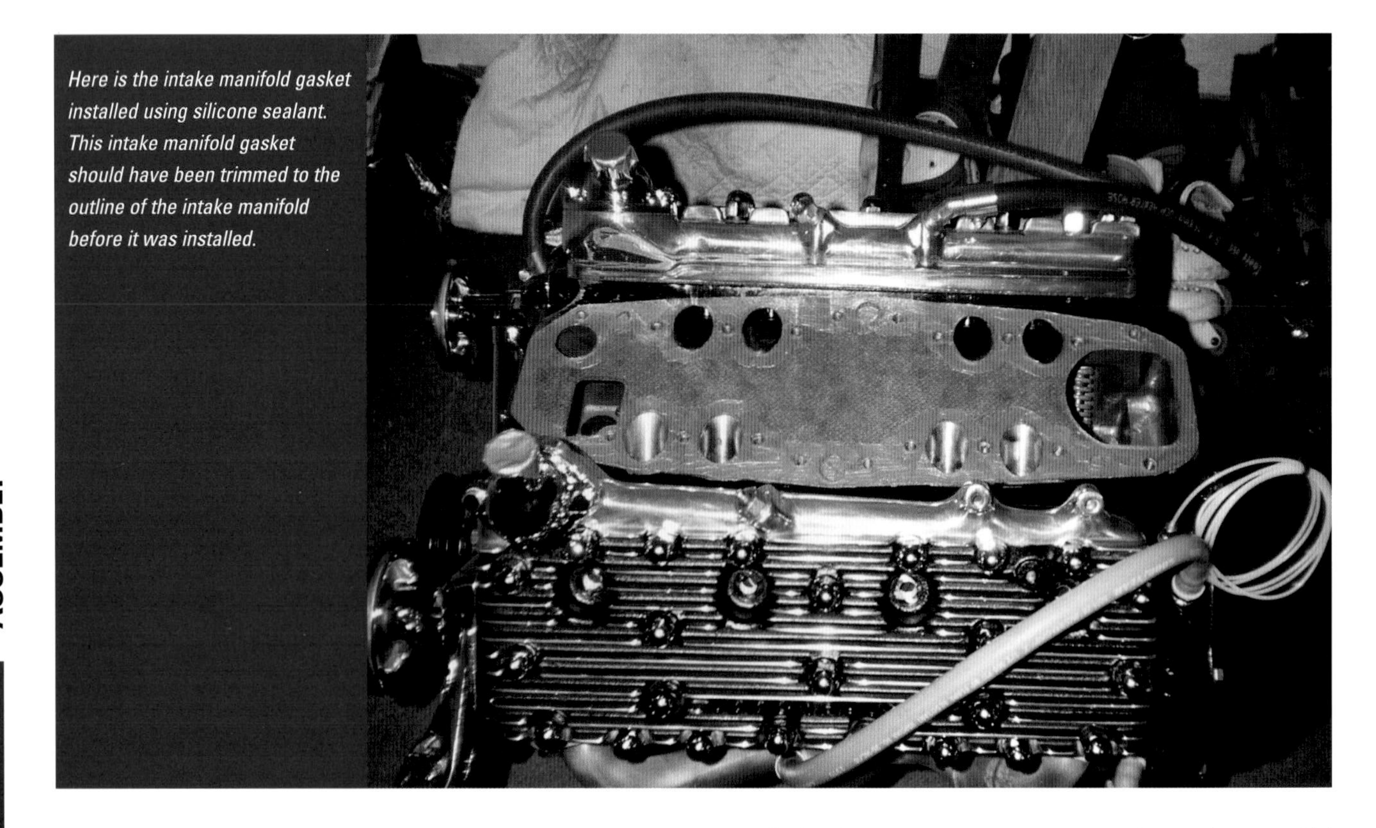
Here is the intake manifold gasket installed using silicone sealant. This intake manifold gasket should have been trimmed to the outline of the intake manifold before it was installed.

The intake manifold has been installed. The crankcase breather/oil filler tube at the rear of the intake manifold has been rotated 180 degrees in order to have the fuel pump block-off plate face the firewall. The Chrysler alternator is on the front of the intake manifold. The water outlet elbows on this engine were painted black to give the engine some contrast.

Install the chrome acorn nut covers on the intake manifold bolts. Install the road draft/crankcase vent tube and the crankcase vent/oil filler tube plugs (if a 1949-53 intake manifold is used) in the intake manifold. Install the fuel pump stand/crankcase breather housing (if the road draft/crankcase vent and crankcase vent/oil filler holes are blocked off) using silicone sealant on the gasket and anti-seize compound on the studs. Torque the nuts to 15 ft-lb.

This photograph shows the proper sequence to torque the intake manifold bolts. The intake manifold is an Edelbrock #1030, Model SU-349, for the 1949-53 Ford. Some of the Edelbrock intake manifolds require 12 bolts to secure them, others require 14 bolts.

Here are a Summit Racing Equipment #900310 double flaring tool and a Performance Tool #W80675 precision tubing bender tool. All metal fuel line tubing **must** be double flared.

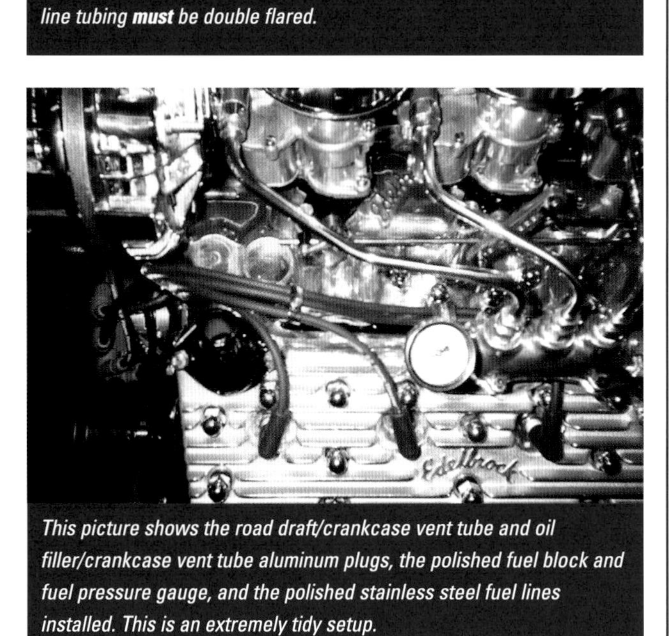

This picture shows the road draft/crankcase vent tube and oil filler/crankcase vent tube aluminum plugs, the polished fuel block and fuel pressure gauge, and the polished stainless steel fuel lines installed. This is an extremely tidy setup.

Install the fuel block mounting bracket and the fuel block, with the fuel pressure regulator attached. Fabricate the fuel lines from the fuel block to the carburetors using a tubing bender tool and a double flaring tool, then install the fuel lines.

Attach the oil line from the outboard pressure-out hole in the engine block to the inlet side of the remote oil filter, and attach the oil line from the inboard drain-back hole in the engine block to the outlet side of the remote oil filter. Use teflon tape or pipe thread sealant on the oil line fittings.

Fill the oil filter with oil and install it on the remote oil filter bracket. Pour the required amount of motor oil in the engine. Install a temporary oil pressure gauge.

This photograph shows the remote oil filter hook up. The bottom hose is the pressure-out line and the top hose is the drain-back line. A 1949-53 Ford Truck #6392 bellhousing adapter has been installed along with a Benson's Flat-O Products flexplate.

The Mallory #5072001 magnetic breakerless distributor has been installed with the polished stainless steel timing pointer. The 1949-53 Ford Truck crankshaft pulley has been machined to 4 ¾" diameter in order to clear the distributor.

This is a close-up of a polished aluminum mounting bracket for the fuel block/fuel pressure gauge/fuel pressure regulator assembly. This unit, fabricated by Luke's, bolts to the cylinder head where the stock oil filter was mounted.

Ignition System

Install the crankshaft pulley woodruff key in the crankshaft slot using anti-seize compound and gently tap the key into position with a hammer. Apply some anti-seize compound to the snout of the crankshaft and install the crankshaft pulley. The pulley should have a snug fit, but it should not require the use of a harmonic balancer installation tool. Gently tap the crankshaft pulley onto the crankshaft using a piece of wood and a hammer. Install the crankshaft pulley bolt and washer using Loctite and torque the crankshaft bolt to 50 ft-lb.

Rotate the crankshaft until the engine is set with the #1 piston at 10 degrees before TDC (top dead center) and insert the distributor into the timing gear cover with the distributor rotor at the #1 spark plug lead position. Clamp the distributor down.

Gap the spark plugs at 0.050″ and install them using anti-seize compound. Torque the spark plugs to 15 ft-lb. Lay out the spark plug wires and cut them to length for each cylinder. The cylinders on the right or passenger's side of the engine are numbered 1, 2, 3, and 4 from the front and the cylinders on the left side of the engine are numbered 5, 6, 7, and 8 from the front. The firing order is: 1, 5, 4, 8, 6, 3, 7, 2. Install the wires on the spark plugs and in the distributor cap. Install the ignition coil and coil bracket on the right cylinder head using anti-seize compound on the bolts. Connect the coil wire to the distributor.

Bolt the alternator to the alternator mounting bracket and install the complete unit on the front of the intake manifold using anti-seize compound on the bolts.

You must install a flywheel or flexplate in order to start the engine. Install the flywheel or flexplate bolts with Loctite

Of this pair of 1949-53 Ford Truck water pumps, one is being rebuilt with a new shaft/bearing assembly, and the other one has been rebuilt and is now complete.

Here is a great photo of the front of the engine. The crankshaft/water pumps/alternator V-belt has been installed along with everything else.

and torque them to 80 ft-lb. A bellhousing and starting motor mounting plate will have to be installed to mount the starting motor.

Install the starting motor using anti-seize compound on the bolts.

Cooling System and Miscellaneous

Apply silicone sealant to the water pump gaskets and bolts. Install the water pumps and torque the bolts to 25 ft-lb.

Install the water pumps/alternator/crankshaft V-belt allowing for approximately ½″ to 1″ slack.

Hook up some headers and mufflers, a radiator with some water in it, and the ignition system with a battery and starter switch. Start the engine and adjust the timing and the carburetor. Allow the engine to run at approximately 2,000 rpm for 30 minutes in order to break in the camshaft. After the engine is at full operating temperature, shut it off. Allow the engine to cool, and re-torque the cylinder heads using the factory-approved torque pattern. Install the chrome acorn nut covers on the cylinder head bolts. Now, go find a vehicle in which to install this thing of beauty!

This street performance engine is a little gem. It was completed by Luke's Custom Machine & Design for a customer at the end of March 2002. The computer-generated dyno sheets show a nice torque curve from 2,000 rpm through 4,500 rpm. This clearly indicates that the correct camshaft was chosen for that engine. About the maximum that a street performance flathead will achieve is 5,000 to 5,500 rpm. Besides, you are not going to be driving your car through town at 5,000 rpm!

SECTION 2: BLOWN PERFORMANCE STREET ENGINE

It is now time to move on and get started with one of the most interesting and powerful of all Ford flathead V-8 engines, and that is the "blown" version. The technical term for this is supercharging. That word is too long, so I shall use blown!

The engine in this section is a 265-ci Ford flathead V-8 equipped with a GMC 4-71 "Roots" type blower. This blower was named after the designers, the Roots brothers (circa 1850s). Although this blower is quite simple in design and very few parts are used in the construction, the clearances and assembly must be performed by an expert blower builder. This is not a job for the home engine builder or even the average mechanic. I have seen blowers that were so poorly assembled they had little or no boost, and the owner was left wondering why the vehicle did not meet performance expectations. The owner of this engine is going to install it in his daily-driven 1936 Ford five-window coupe.

Since many of the procedures described in the first section apply to this section, certain subheadings in the following chapters refer the reader back to Section I. Consult the corresponding topic there for a full explanation. I will add to the chapters anything new and applicable to the blown engine as well as a complete summary and build up list along with the prices.

The engine I am about to describe was completed in December 2001 by Luke's for a customer. The engine started and ran beautifully. At idle, a cup full of coffee was placed on the blower and the coffee hardly stirred! The computer-generated dyno sheets in Chapter 31 for this engine indicate a good torque curve from 2,500 to 5,000 rpm (see the Dyno Printouts section). Once again, this shows the right camshaft was chosen for this particular engine. It's more evidence that what I am describing will work.

Purchase and Magnaflux

The engine in this section is going to be bored 0.060″ (3.2475″) oversize. Thus, if you want the same engine, you should locate a block that has been previously bored to a maximum of 0.030″ (3.2175") oversize. However, this is not critical because the blower pistons for this engine are going to be custom-made by Ross Racing Pistons and they can be made for almost any bore size (see Section II, Chapter 13).

One of the end exhaust ports has been ported to a "D" shape.

A nice job was done porting and polishing the exhaust ports, which resulted in a "D" shape for the end ports on both sides of the block. The exterior surface of the block has been sanded and is now ready for paint.

This picture shows a cylinder-head bolt hole being re-tapped. Run a tap through every threaded hole in the engine block to ensure all the threads are clean and in good working order.

For cleaning, and porting and polishing, refer to Section I.

In addition, if you are going to port and polish the end exhaust ports in a flathead block so they result in a "D" shape, do not buy your exhaust headers with high-temperature coating already on them. The end flanges of the headers will have to be modified in order to match the "D" shape exhaust ports. After this is done, you can have the headers high-temperature coated.

For detailing the block and drilling valve lifter bosses; full-flow oiling; relieving the block; and heat risers, refer to Section I.

Re-Tap and Chamfer Bolt Holes

Re-tapping all the bolt holes in the engine block will ensure accurate torque readings are obtained when the engine is reassembled.

For redi-stripping the block, Glyptal application, and machining, refer to Section I.

Cylinder Boring

The engine block described in this section will be bored and the cylinders honed and de-glazed, resulting in a final bore of 3.2475″. You should purchase the pistons beforehand and deliver them to the machine shop with the block. The machine shop will then measure each piston with a micrometer and bore the block accordingly to ensure there is 0.008″ piston-to-bore clearance (after cylinder honing), measured below the bottom of the wrist pin perpendicular to the wrist pin. This is the piston clearance Ross Racing Pistons recommends. The engine block is usually bored to within 0.003″ to 0.004″ of the final bore and then honed and de-glazed, resulting in the final cylinder bore.

This picture shows a cylinder-head bolt hole being chamfered using a drill with a countersink bit. This process will help to prevent the threads from being "pulled" when the cylinder head is torqued.

The final stage of the boring operation is the cylinder honing and de-glazing. This is a very important step and must be carried out correctly in order to ensure the proper seating of the piston rings. This procedure is undertaken using a Sunnen automatic cylinder re-sizing machine, Model CK-10, or similar type of equipment. This machine is used to remove the last 0.003″ to 0.004″ of material from the cylinder walls using Sunnen 800-series 400-grit stones (for moly rings). The final result is the finished bore. The finish on the cylinder walls will be a cross-hatch pattern.

The installation of a blower on an engine will result in increased cylinder pressure and temperature. As a result of this, the piston-to-bore clearance must be increased to 0.008″.

Align Bore and Hone

The flathead engine in this section will be blown, and as a result, there will be a lot of additional stress placed on the front and center of the crankshaft. The #1 and #2 main bearing caps will have to be beefed up. Luke's Custom Machine & Design fabricates 1045 steel #1 and #2 main bearing caps. The #3 main bearing cap is wide and strong enough to handle the rigors of a blower on a street performance flathead. Although the stock main bearing bolts are ½″ diameter, they are replaced with aircraft-quality ½″ diameter socket head bolts of at least 180,000 psi strength.

The engine block will have to be align bored in order to match the new main bearing caps with the crankshaft bores

This is an excellent picture of the #1 and #2 main bearing caps fabricated by Luke's Custom Machine & Design. The block has been redi-stripped and has just arrived back from being align bored.

This is a close-up of the #2 main bearing cap that was fabricated by Luke's for a blown flathead engine. Those are aircraft-quality ½"-diameter main bearing cap bolts countersunk in the cap.

This is a photograph of the Sunnen align bore attachment, Model PLB-100, which replaces the honing bar attachment on the Sunnen horizontal hone, Model CH-100, align honing machine.

On this flathead engine block, the main bearing caps have been milled flat. This is the first step in equipping this block with main bearing cap support bridges. The pressure-out fitting for the race version of the full-flow oil system is also pictured.

and ensure they are exactly parallel to the centerline of the crankshaft. This is a very critical process and it should only be done at a machine shop that specializes in high-performance engine building. The estimated cost to align bore a flathead block is $200.

The use of larger main bearing caps in a blown flathead will result in the oil pan having to be modified to clear those bulkier caps. The engine block must be align bored when new custom-made main bearing caps are supplied or

This photograph shows the main bearing cap support bridges installed. They were fabricated by Luke's. This flathead engine block was originally being built for use with a blower, but those plans went out the window when the customer could not find his wallet!

This photograph shows the results of a Serdi-machined multi-angle blueprint valve grind. The valve seats are beautifully blended into the ports.

occasionally when stock main bearing caps other than the original main bearing caps are being used. The diameter of the main bearing housing bores should be 2.670″ to 2.671″. Part of the align boring procedure requires material to be milled off the mating surface of the main bearing caps.

This is the engine block used in Section II. This block has been expertly masked off and painted with red polyurethane. The valve lifter gallery and the front of the block have been painted with Glyptal #G-1228A medium grey gloss enamel.

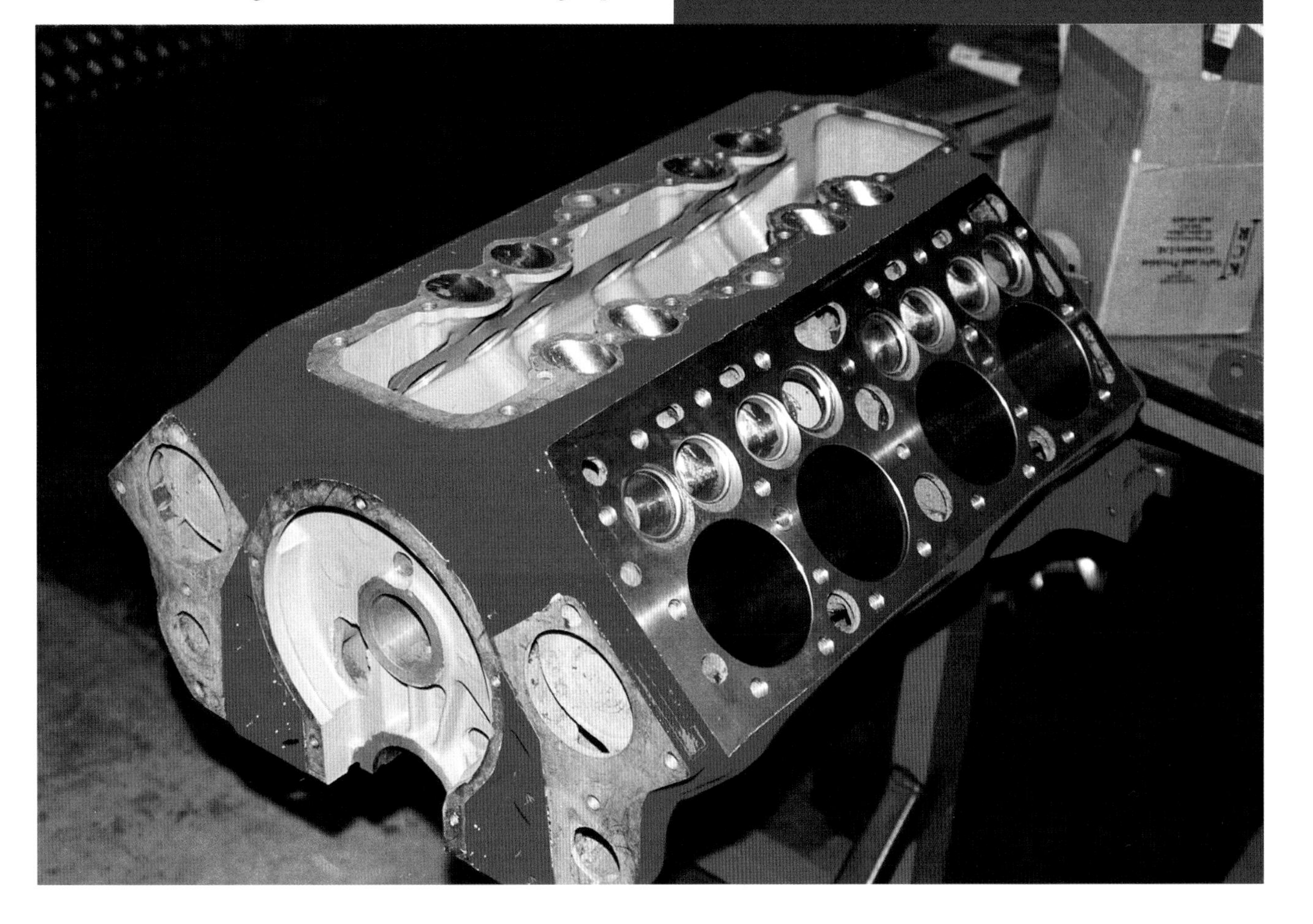

After the align boring is completed, the main bearing bores and caps are align honed to the specified diameter.

The same Sunnen horizontal hone, model CH-100 align honing machine is used for the align boring and align honing. One bar is used for the boring and another bar is used for the honing.

There is another method of strengthening the main bearing caps in a flathead street engine that is going to be equipped with a blower. This involves the use of main bearing cap support bridges. The tops of the main bearing caps are milled flat and 1045 steel support bridges fabricated to fit on top of the main bearing caps. The support bridges fabricated by Luke's are ¾″ thick and the same length and width of all the main bearing caps. Longer main bearing cap bolts are required, so all the main bearing cap bolts are replaced with aircraft quality ½″ socket head bolts having a minimum strength of 180,000 psi. The use of main bearing cap support bridges does not usually require any oil pan modifications for clearance purposes.

For information on parallel decking and shot peening, refer to Section I.

Valve Seat Inserts

The engine block in this section had hardened exhaust valve seat inserts, all of which were in good condition. As a result, no new valve seat inserts were required.

For information on valve grinding, de-glazing, cracks, and cleaning and painting, refer to Section I.

Engine Block Summary

1950 Canadian Ford 239.4-ci L-head V-8 engine block; Casting Number C8BA; 2-bolt main bearing caps; 24 stud block; Stock Bore: 3³⁄₁₆″ (3.1875″); Stock Stroke: 3¾″; Stock Compression Ratio: 6.8:1; 100 H.P. @ 3,600 rpm and 181 ft-lb torque @ 2,000 rpm. Engine block weight (bare): 200 lbs.	$200.00
Engine block hot tanked and redi-stripped. Engine block, main bearing caps, and main bearing cap bolts Magnafluxed.	$205.00
All threads re-tapped; main bearing caps and main bearing cap bolts shot peened; cylinder head bolt holes chamfered; valve lifter bosses de-glazed allowing for 0.0015″ valve lifter clearance; valve lifter bosses drilled with ³⁄₁₆″ (0.1875″) hole for valve lifter adjustment. Exterior surface of engine block sanded and detailed. Valve lifter gallery and front of engine block painted with Glyptal #G-1228A medium grey gloss enamel. Exterior surface of engine block painted with RM #79666 signal red hi-gloss polyurethane.	$373.06
Engine block converted to full-flow oil system.	$65.00
Engine block bored 0.060″ oversize and cylinders honed and de-glazed using Sunnen 800-series 400-grit stones, final bore: 3.2475″. Piston-to-bore clearance: 0.008″ measured below bottom of wrist pin perpendicular to wrist pin.	$125.00
Engine block parallel decked to 0.010″ average, below deck.	$110.00
Serdi-machined multi-angle blueprint valve grind performed.	$200.00
Engine block aligned bored and honed.	$200.00
New 1045 steel #1 and #2 main bearing caps installed with new aircraft-quality main bearing cap socket head bolts, ½″ diameter, 180,000 psi.	$370.00
Intake and exhaust ports fully ported and polished and gasket matched.	$216.67
ENGINE BLOCK TOTAL:	**$2,064.73**

CHAPTER 12
CRANKSHAFT

Purchase

The 1949-53 Mercury cast alloy steel crankshaft is a very good quality item and is entirely adequate for use in a blown street Ford flathead V-8 engine. Crower Cams & Equipment offers billet steel crankshafts in just about any stroke for the flathead, but they are expensive. This option could be considered for a blown race engine or where the owner wants a wild flathead engine with over 300 cubic inches. In the latter case, I would question whether the owner had "crossed the line!"

For Magnafluxing; shot peening and plug removal; and straightening, chamfering, and polishing, refer to Section I.

The 1949-53 Mercury 4"-stroke cast alloy steel crankshaft used in the engine built for this section has been Magnafluxed, shot peened, and aligned. The main and connecting rod journals have been ground 0.010" undersize. The oil holes have been chamfered and the journals polished. The crankshaft has been balanced. The whole nine yards! This crankshaft has been sitting around for so long there is some minor surface rust that will be easily wiped off.

Re-Grinding and Cleaning

An old mechanic's trick to check if the crankshaft journals require re-grinding is to rub a penny lengthwise on a journal. If copper appears on the journal, then the crankshaft needs to be re-ground. This is far from scientific and should not be relied on.

Main Bearings

Clevite 77 (Michigan Bearings) is presently offering the main bearings in 0.010″ oversize and 0.020″ oversize only for the 1949-53 Ford flathead V-8 engines. Sealed Power (Federal Mogul) is presently offering the main bearings in standard size, 0.010″ oversize, 0.020″ oversize, and 0.030″ oversize for the same year engines.

Crankshaft Gear and Pulley

The engine featured in this section will be using the stock 1949-53 distributor location. A 1949-53 camshaft will be installed, which requires the use of the 1949-53 Ford #6306 crankshaft gear. If the Ford gear is not available, use a Melling #2701 crankshaft gear (1949-53 Ford) with the same 22 teeth.

You will not be using the stock Ford flathead V-8 crankshaft pulley because a blower pulley must be mounted on the front of the crankshaft pulley and 1949-53 Ford Truck water pumps will be installed (more about water pumps later). A single V-belt pulley will be required; since Ford did not produce a crankshaft pulley like that, one will have to be fabricated or purchased.

Luke's manufactures an excellent aluminum single V-belt crankshaft pulley that is 6½″ diameter with the timing adjustment degrees notched in the outer edge. Polishing is optional.

This picture shows the 6½"-diameter crankshaft pulley and the crankshaft/blower drive pulley fabricated by Luke's.

CRANKSHAFT

Crankshaft Summary

1949-53 Mercury #6303 cast alloy steel crankshaft; Model CM; Casting Number: 61402; main journal diameter: 2.498-2.499"; connecting rod journal diameter: 2.138"-2.139"; non-floating connecting rod bearings; Stock Stroke: 4.00". Crankshaft weight: 67 lbs.	$400.00
Crankshaft Magnafluxed, aligned, and shot peened; main journals ground 0.010" undersize; connecting rod journals ground 0.010" undersize; oil holes chamfered; journals polished; and crankshaft balanced. Factory crankshaft connecting rod journal oil plugs removed and new stainless steel ⅛" N.P.T. plugs installed using Loctite.	$270.00
New Clevite 77 #MS-109P-10 main bearings, 0.010" oversize, installed allowing for 0.002" clearance and 0.004" crankshaft end play. Main bearing cap bolts torqued to 105 ft-lb using Molykote.	$117.11
1949-53 Ford #6303 cast iron helical crankshaft gear, 22 teeth, and Ford #6310 oil slinger installed with Ford #357654-S crankshaft gear woodruff key. Luke's new crankshaft sleeve and polished aluminum crankshaft pulley, 6½" diameter, single belt, installed with Ford #74153-S crankshaft pulley woodruff key and Ford #351590-S crankshaft pulley bolt washer with Ford #20639-S crankshaft pulley bolt. Crankshaft pulley bolt installed using Loctite and torqued to 50 ft-lb. Oil slinger painted with Glyptal #G-1228A medium grey gloss enamel.	$239.04
CRANKSHAFT TOTAL:	**$1,026.15**

CHAPTER 13
CONNECTING RODS AND PISTONS

For purchasing; Magnafluxing and shot peening; and aligning and re-sizing, refer to Section I.

De-Beam and Box

The Ford flathead connecting rods will have to be reinforced in order to deal with the added stress of a blower. Luke's builds boxed connecting rods for the blown flathead. The connecting rods are the 1949-53 Ford forged steel "I" beam connecting rod, casting #8BA6205A. These connecting rods are shot peened to remove any stress and Magnafluxed to ensure there are no hidden flaws.

Weld an insert made from 4130 chrome moly steel plate, 0.080″ thickness, to both sides of the face of the connecting rod. As soon as you complete the welding on each connecting rod, place them in an oven pre-heated to 400 degrees F for approximately eight hours. Then turn off the oven and allow the connecting rods to cool down overnight to room temperature. This process assists with removing stress from the connecting rods.

The owner of Luke's Custom Machine & Design, Luke Balogh, gives his personal attention to the alignment of a boxed connecting rod. This is what I call service! That is a Sunnen connecting rod alignment tool he is using.

Luke tries out his "breakfast of champions" by straightening a boxed connecting rod! The connecting rod is being held in a connecting rod vise. Do not clamp connecting rods in anything but a connecting rod vise.

A 1949-53 Ford connecting rod, casting number 8BA6205A, is being boxed at Luke's. An insert of 4130 chrome moly steel, 0.080″ thickness, is welded to both sides of the face of the connecting rod.

The boxing process of this connecting rod is partially completed.

I refuse to make any stupid "oven" jokes! These are the boxed connecting rods. As soon as the welding is completed on the rods, they are placed in an oven that is pre-heated to 400 degrees F, baked for eight hours, and then allowed to cool overnight to room temperature. This process aids in removing stress from the rods.

De-beam the connecting rods by grinding the welds and the sides as smooth as possible, and then finish-sand them. Any grinding or sanding should be done from top to bottom in order to stay with the "flow" of the grain in the connecting rod. Do not grind across the sides of the connecting rods! Then, align and re-size the connecting rods and fit new wrist pin bushings to them. Finally, balance the connecting rods and install new connecting rod nuts. The completed product is a fine-looking piece.

Boxing the connecting rods, as described above, is probably the most economical method of obtaining strong rods for a blown Ford flathead V-8 engine. The other alternative is to have connecting rods custom-made for the flathead.

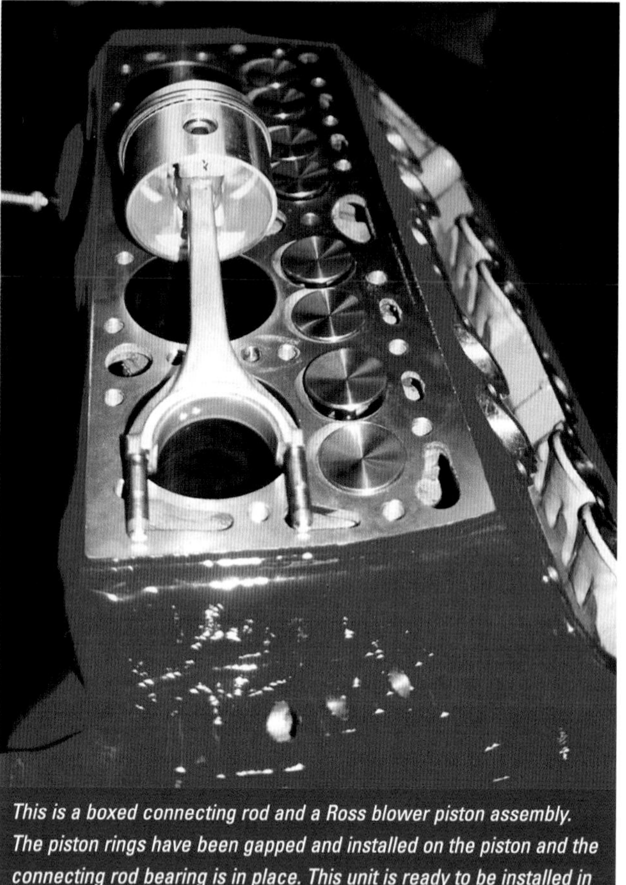
This is a boxed connecting rod and a Ross blower piston assembly. The piston rings have been gapped and installed on the piston and the connecting rod bearing is in place. This unit is ready to be installed in the engine.

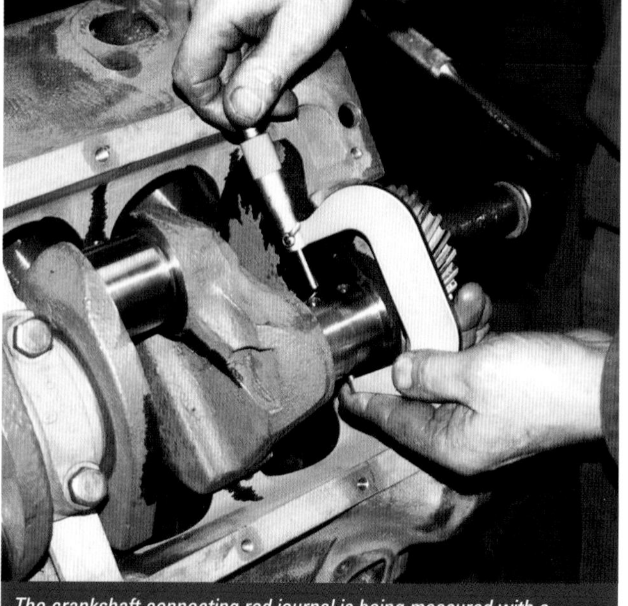
The crankshaft connecting rod journal is being measured with a micrometer to check the connecting rod bearing clearance.

The big end (crankshaft end) of a connecting rod is being measured with a dial indicator. The bearings have been installed and the nuts torqued to 45 ft-lb. Notice the use of a connecting rod vise; this is a must!

This is a Ross forged aluminum blower piston for a Ford flathead block that has been bored 0.060″ oversize. These top-quality pistons are to be fitted with the Ross #R3251 ductile moly top ring piston ring set. Those are not the connecting rods that will be used with the blown motor.

The connecting rod and piston assemblies are laid out for installation in the engine block. Three of the assemblies have already been installed. These assemblies consist of Ross Racing Pistons blower pistons and moly rings, Luke's boxed connecting rods, and Clevite 77 connecting rod bearings. This is a great setup for a blown flathead street performance engine.

Crower Cams & Equipment and Cunningham Rods manufacture superb connecting rods for the flathead, but they are expensive.

Connecting Rod Bearings

Clevite 77 (Michigan Bearings) is currently offering the nonfloating connecting rod bearings for the 1949-53 Ford flathead V-8 in standard size, 0.010″ oversize, 0.020″ oversize, 0.030″ oversize, 0.040″ oversize, 0.050″ oversize, and 0.060″ oversize. Sealed Power (Federal Mogul) is currently offering the nonfloating connecting rod bearings for the 1949-53 Ford flathead V-8 in standard size, 0.010″ oversize, 0.020″ oversize, 0.030″ oversize, and 0.040″ oversize.

Pistons

If a Ford flathead V-8 engine is going to be equipped with a blower, then forged aluminum blower pistons should be used. Blower pistons have a thicker "crown" area than regular forged aluminum pistons, in order to handle higher operating temperatures and cylinder pressures. The top compression ring should be at least 0.250″ below the top of the piston.

The blower pistons used in this engine are manufactured by Ross Racing Pistons using forged 2618 T-61 aluminum, with a flat top. The pistons are the three-ring design and weigh 350 grams. The wrist pins are full-floating chrome moly steel straight-wall. Spiro Lox retainers (the best) are supplied with the pistons. The price for a set of blower pistons, wrist pins, and piston rings is very reasonable.

The blower pistons used in this engine were custom-made by Ross Racing Pistons. The engine will have an 8.0:1

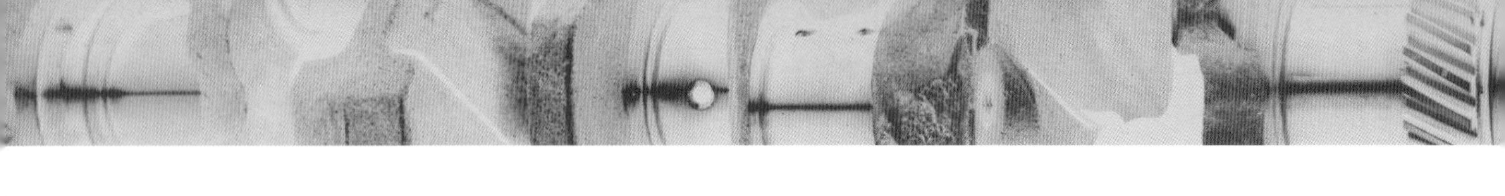

compression ratio with the Ross pistons and the Edelbrock #1115 aluminum cylinder heads, as they came out of the box. These pistons have thicker ring lands, bigger wrist-pin bosses, and large internal radii to withstand additional cylinder pressure.

The pistons are for a blown flathead with a 3.2475″ bore and 4.00″ stroke. The rings supplied are the moly top ring, ductile iron second ring, and oil ring. These are very high-quality pistons, and they handle anything a blown street flathead can throw at them. Ross Racing Pistons can manufacture the flathead blower pistons for just about any bore size and stroke combination imaginable.

Moly rings should be used with a blown street flathead engine due to the higher operating temperatures and boost. The moly rings are much more flexible than cast iron rings. The Ross Racing Piston rings should be gapped according to their instructions. For this particular engine, the top ring gap is 0.019″, the second ring 0.022″, and oil ring 0.016″.

The top piston rings are ductile SG iron- and molybdenum-inlaid. They are barrel-lapped, which ensures quick seating, and coated with zinc phosphate, which adds corrosion resistance. The second rings are cast iron and also zinc phosphate coated. The oil rings consist of a stainless steel expander and chromium-plated carbon steel rails. Ross Racing Pistons has these metric piston rings made exclusively for their pistons. The top piston ring groove width is 1.5 mm, the second piston ring groove width is 1.5 mm, and the oil ring groove width is 3.0 mm.

For balancing, refer to Section I.

Gaskets

Fel-Pro produces a complete gasket set for the 1949-53 Ford or Mercury flathead V-8 engine. This kit is available from Speedway Motors or your local automotive parts dealer. This is a good package with all the gaskets required.

Having said that, you will need good head gaskets for the blown flathead. The head gaskets supplied with the Fel-Pro flathead set are not suitable for this application. Fel-Pro manufactures copper sandwiched cylinder-head gaskets, which are excellent for the blown flathead. These are the #1055 (right side) and the #1056 (left side) for the 1949-53 Ford. The Fel-Pro head gaskets are available from your local speed equipment dealer or from Speedway Motors, part #910-15895 (1949-53). The copper sandwiched head gaskets are not cheap but are entirely necessary.

Connecting Rods and Pistons Summary

Item	Cost
1949-53 Ford #6200 forged steel connecting rods; Model Number: 8BA; Casting Number: 8BA6205A; non-floating connecting rod bearings. Connecting rod length: 7.00″. Connecting rod ratio: 1.75 (with 4″ stroke crankshaft).	$80.00
Connecting rods Magnafluxed, shot peened, aligned, re-sized, boxed, and balanced. New Sealed Power (Federal Mogul) #9024VA wrist pin bushings, 0.8125″ o.d., installed allowing for 0.002″ clearance. New Pioneer #CRN-731 connecting rod nuts installed using Loctite and torqued to 45 ft-lb.	$720.18
New Clevite 77 #CB-15P-10, connecting rod bearings, 0.010″ oversize, installed allowing for 0.002″ connecting rod clearance and 0.014″-0.018″ side clearance per pair of connecting rods.	$160.00
New Ross Racing Pistons forged 2618T-61 aluminum "blower" pistons; 8.0:1 compression ratio; 0.060″ oversize; flat tops; piston weight: 350 grams, each. Full-floating heat treated and case hardened 4340 chrome moly steel straight-wall wrist pins with new Ross Racing Pistons #4004J Spiro Lox retainers. Wrist pin diameter: 0.750″; wrist pin length: 2.770″; wrist pin weight: 120 grams. Piston grooves: top ring: 1.5 mm; 2nd ring: 1.5 mm; and oil ring: 3.0 mm. New Ross Racing Pistons #R3251 ductile moly top ring piston ring set, 0.060″ oversize, installed within manufacturer's recommended arc. Top ring gap: 0.019″; 2nd ring gap: 0.022″; oil ring gap: 0.016″.	$646.80
Complete V-8 engine balance.	$190.00
New Fel-Pro #FS7525B gasket set installed (valve guide O-rings included).	$54.95
CONNECTING RODS AND PISTONS TOTAL:	**$1,851.93**

CHAPTER 14

LUBRICATION SYSTEM

For purchase, refer to Section I.

Oil Pan and Pick-Up

The best oil pans to use for a street performance blown flathead are the 1949-53 Mercury passenger car and the 1949-53 Ford Truck models with four-quart capacity (five quarts with the large filter). These oil pans have the sump at the rear. The Mercury model has a built-in oil baffle. Try to locate one of these oil pans with the matching oil pump pick-up and screen.

Luke's modifies the truck oil pan so that it has a longer length sump in order to clear the new main bearing caps. The modified oil pan will have a seven-quart capacity including the oil filter. The original Ford Truck #6615 oil pump pick-up tube and screen is still used. The additional-capacity oil pan is considered good insurance for a blown flathead engine.

This is a 1949-53 Mercury #6615 oil pump pick-up tube and screen, with the attached baffle. This particular model is not that easy to come by. The oil pump pick-up is attached to a Melling #M-19 standard volume oil pump. This is another good example of Luke's #1 and #2 main bearing caps.

This is a good photograph of the 1949-53 Ford Truck #6675 oil pan that has been modified by Luke's. The modified oil pan now holds six quarts of oil, or seven quarts with the large oil filter.

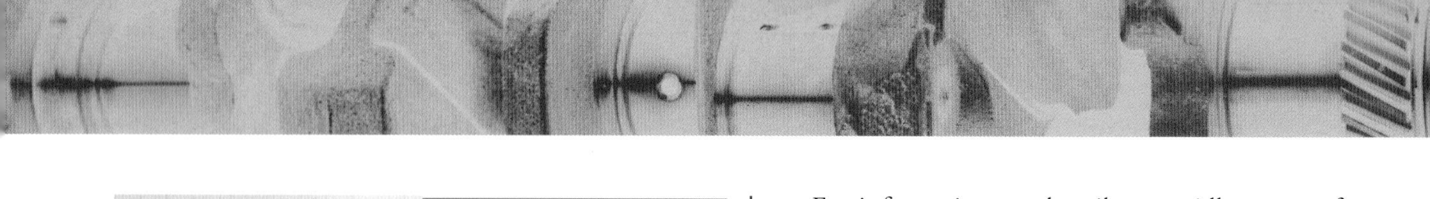

This is the fuel pump pushrod bushing with a drill bit used to indicate the location of the lubrication hole. This hole must be brazed closed; otherwise, there will be a loss of oil pressure.

For information on the oil pump idler gear, refer to Section I.

Fuel Pump Pushrod Bushing

The fuel pump pushrod bushing was removed prior to the engine block being hot tanked. The fuel pump pushrod bushing has a hole in it that lines up with a hole in the block that feeds oil to the bushing in order to lubricate it. If the pushrod is removed and the hole is not plugged, there

This is a photograph of the valve lifter gallery oil return hole baffles installed. They have been glass beaded and painted with Glyptal #G-1228A medium grey gloss enamel.

Although this engine is not a blown flathead, this is a good photo of the pressure-out line (lower hose) and the drain-back line (upper hose) used for the full-flow oil system. A plastic oil pressure gauge line is seen attached and coiled.

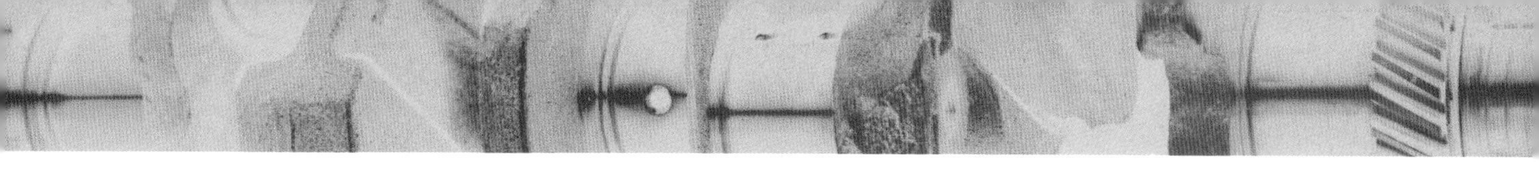

will be a loss of oil pressure. Braze the hole closed and then reinstall the fuel pump pushrod bushing in the block.

The engine built for this section will have a single Holley double-pumper carburetor and will therefore require an electric fuel pump. The stock flathead fuel pump is not suitable for use with a 650-cfm carburetor.

For information on the baffles and breather tube, refer to Section I.

Oil Filter

The engine built for this section was not fitted with a remote oil filter on the left cylinder head. A Trans-Dapt #1045 remote oil filter bracket was attached to the firewall of the vehicle and the oil lines were plumbed from there to the engine block.

Lubrication System Summary

Item	Cost
New stainless steel ⅜″ N.P.T. plug (Ford #6026) front of oil gallery line, installed using Permatex aviation form-a-gasket. Ford #6025 fuel pump pushrod bushing oil hole brazed closed. Ford #6657 oil pump idler gear bushing installed with Ford #6655 oil pump idler gear, and Ford #6656 oil pump idler gear shaft allowing for 0.002″ clearance. Ford #6658 oil pump idler gear cover installed with Ford #22507 oil pump idler gear cover bolts and lock washers using Loctite and torqued to 80 in-lb, with stainless steel safety wire. Oil pump idler gear cover gasket installed using silicone sealant. Inside of oil pump idler gear cover, Ford #6756 valve lifter gallery crankcase breather tube, and Ford #6524 valve lifter gallery oil return hole baffles (2), painted with Glyptal #G-1228A medium grey gloss enamel.	$153.43
New Melling #M-19 standard volume oil pump (for 1949-53 Ford) installed with 1949-53 Mercury #6615 oil pump cover and inlet tube, Ford #6623 oil pump cover screen, and Ford #6628 oil pump cover screen spring retainer. Oil pump end clearance: 0.00025″. Oil pump cover and inlet tube gasket installed using silicone sealant and bolts torqued to 80 in-lb using Loctite. 1949-53 Ford #8BA-6335 rear upper oil seal retainer installed. Rear oil seal packings (Ford #6700) soaked in SAE 30 Wt. motor oil and installed. New Speedway Motors #912-S12853 front one-piece oil seal installed using silicone sealant.	$162.90
1949-53 Ford Truck #6675 oil pan, six-quart (originally four-quart) capacity, modified by Luke's and installed with new stainless steel bolts, lock washers, and AN flat washers using Loctite and torqued to 15 ft-lb. Gaskets installed using silicone sealant. Ford #6754 dipstick tube and Ford #6750 dipstick installed. Oil pan, dipstick tube, and dipstick redi-stripped and painted with RM #79666 signal red hi-gloss polyurethane. Engine lubricated with seven quarts Penzoil HD-30 Wt. motor oil.	$409.10
New Trans-Dapt #1045 remote oil filter bracket with horizontal inlet/outlet; new Moroso #22400 chrome oil filter; and new Trans-Dapt #1032 neoprene rubber hoses, 2′ length x ½″ N.P.T. New Weatherhead #3200-8-6 polished brass reducers, ½″ N.P.T. to ⅜″ N.P.T.; new Weatherhead #3328-6 polished brass extension, ⅜″ N.P.T.; new Weatherhead #3300-6 polished brass coupling, ⅜″ N.P.T.; and new Weatherhead #3400-6 polished brass 90 degree elbow, ⅜″ N.P.T., installed using teflon tape. Hoses covered with new Spectre #3001A black nylabraid and new Spectre #3308B chrome champclamps.	$75.00
LUBRICATION SYSTEM TOTAL:	**$800.43**

CHAPTER 15
CAMSHAFT AND CYLINDER HEADS

Camshaft

The specifications for a camshaft used in a street performance blown flathead engine are different from the specifications of a camshaft used in a normally aspirated engine. As far as I know (which means nothing), none of the large camshaft manufacturers have an off-the-shelf street performance blower camshaft for the Ford flathead V-8. This means you will have to have one ground. This is actually a good thing, because now the camshaft will be perfectly suited for your individual engine.

A street performance flathead blower camshaft must have a larger lobe separation angle, somewhere between 112 and 115 degrees. A camshaft with long duration and big overlap (remember all these terms from Section I?) is not recommended.

The camshaft Crower Cams & Equipment recommends for a blown street performance 1949-53 Ford flathead V-8 similar to the engine being built for this section is the #SPL8BA "blower grind." The advertised duration is 264 degrees intake and exhaust. Duration @ 0.050″ lift is 238 degrees intake and exhaust; there is 0.350″/0.348″ net intake and exhaust valve lift. Lobe separation angle is 112 degrees. This is an excellent camshaft for a blown street engine, and it is competitively priced. Their price is outright with no core exchange.

For information on camshaft bearings and interchange, and degreeing the camshaft, refer to Section I.

The Crower Cams & Equipment #SPL8BA "blower grind" camshaft for the 1949-53 Ford flathead V-8 engine really works well in a blown street motor. The advertised duration is 264 degrees intake and exhaust; duration @ 0.050″ lift is 238 degrees intake and exhaust. The lobe separation angle is 112 degrees, and net valve lift is 0.350″/0.348″ intake and exhaust. The motor idles beautifully with this camshaft, and there is instant response when the throttle is hit!

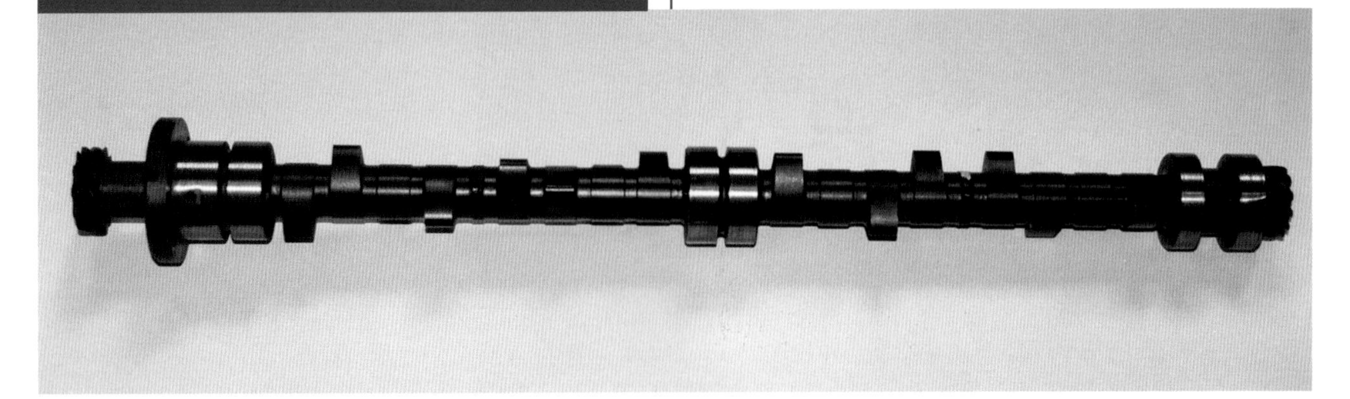

Valve Lifters

I shall mention a point regarding adjustable valve lifters. Luke's Custom Machine & Design recently discovered in an engine a set of adjustable lifters that looked exactly the same as any other set of adjustable lifters, except the head

An Iskenderian #4005 dual-valve spring is being measured at High Performance Engines on a Rinck-McIlwaine 0-500 lbs. precision valve spring tester.

This photograph is of he Iskenderian #4005 dual-valve springs installed in the engine in this section. It has 1.61″-diameter stainless steel intake and exhaust valves, Ross blower pistons, and intake and exhaust ports fully ported and polished. The valve lifter gallery has been painted with Glyptal #G-1228A medium grey gloss enamel and the outside of the block painted with red polyurethane.

on the adjusting bolt was thicker. The head thickness of the adjusting bolt in most adjustable lifters is 0.150″ and the head thickness of the adjusting bolt in these lifters was 0.225″. There was a stock camshaft in the engine, and it was impossible to lower the adjusting bolt in the lifter enough to permit the correct valve lash. The length of the actual body of most adjustable lifters, whether hollow or not, is 1.50″ and these goofy lifters were the same. No wonder the owner could not get his engine to run properly! These lifters would not be a problem with a higher lift aftermarket camshaft.

For valves and valve guide bushings, refer to Section I.

Valve Springs

The valve springs used in a blown street flathead must have sufficient spring tension to withstand the higher cylinder pressure when the engine is under boost, which tries to pull the intake valves off the valve seat inserts. If this happens, there will be a backfire, resulting in a disaster of major proportions for the internal components of the engine as well as your cash reserves!

In order to ensure there are no problems in the valve spring department, you should use the Iskenderian #4005 dual-valve springs. According to Iskenderian Racing Cams, the installed height is 60 lbs. @ 1.90625″ (1$\frac{29}{32}$″). The spring seat pressure (when the valve is closed) of the valve spring can be increased to 82 lbs. @ 1.8125″ by shimming the valve springs, which will result in 170 lbs. @ 0.1.4625″ (0.350″ lift).

A brand-new set of the Iskenderian Racing Cams #185-G single valve springs and the #4005 dual springs were measured at High Performance Engines by Dave Child. These measurements are in Section I, Chapter 5.

For valve spring retainers and locks, refer to Section I.

Camshaft Gear and Timing Cover

The distributor for the engine in this section will be in the stock location of the 1949-53 Ford passenger cars. The stock 1949-53 Ford fiber camshaft timing gear should not be installed in a street performance blown flathead engine, because it will not withstand the increased stress caused by the aftermarket performance valvetrain. A new aluminum camshaft timing gear should be purchased. A Melling #2702 aluminum camshaft timing gear is available from your local automotive parts outlet or from Speedway Motors, part #910-14625L.

One-Piece Oil Seal and Sleeve

One thing that is missing with the one-piece oil seal is the crankshaft sleeve. The stock 1949-53 Ford flathead V-8 crankshaft sleeve is not designed to work with a one-piece oil seal as a result of the spiral grooves in the sleeve. The

The Speedway Motors #912-S12853 one-piece oil seal, a super item, can be seen just ahead of the 1949-53 Ford #6306 crankshaft gear. This is a good photograph of the #1 and #2 main bearing caps fabricated by Luke's as well as a good side view of the boxed connecting rods.

stock diameter of the crankshaft snout is 1.625". The only place I know that manufactures the correct crankshaft sleeve is Luke's. This is a very low-cost item.

Cylinder Heads

A Ford flathead V-8 engine, similar to the one in this section, equipped with a GMC 4-71 blower, should have a maximum compression ratio of 8.0:1 for use with today's highest octane unleaded gasoline. This will be explained in greater detail in Section II, Chapter 16.

Cylinder-head bolts are completely adequate for use with aluminum cylinder heads on a blown street flathead engine. If the engine was to be used for all-out racing or the blower boost was to exceed 10 lbs., then cylinder-head studs should be used.

For cylinder head gaskets, refer to Section I.

Water Outlets

The 1949-53 flathead cylinder heads were designed so that a water outlet elbow was bolted onto each head. The water outlet elbows are cast iron and the neck is vertical with the engine. These water outlets are fine when used with most carburetor-equipped Ford flathead V-8 engines. However, when a GMC 4-71 blower is installed and the radiator hose is attached to the water outlet elbow on the left cylinder head, it will not clear the blower casing.

The Offenhauser #3496 aluminum "straight" water outlet elbows are available from your local speed equipment vendor or from Speedway Motors as part #560-3496. The Offenhauser water outlet elbow neck is in a vertical position from the cylinder head—not the engine. The stock Ford flathead water outlet elbow could be used on the right side of the engine and the Offenhauser unit on the left side of the engine, which would result in each of the radiator hoses sticking out at a different angle. That is

Here is a photograph of the Manley #42102 heat-treated head-bolt washers. Aluminum cylinder heads should only be installed with hardened head-bolt washers.

something a person would do just before being admitted to the Betty Ford Clinic!

In order to clear the blower housing, the proper solution is to cut the necks off of two Offenhauser straight water outlet elbows, and then re-weld them in the 45-degree position from the cylinder head—not the engine. Have the aluminum units buffed after the welding. This will give the engine that "uptown look" it deserves!

For exhaust baffles, refer to Section I.

This is the Fel-Pro #1056 (left side) copper sandwiched cylinder head gasket. The pistons are painted with V.H.T. #SP-101 flat white high temperature coating, which makes them show up very well in photographs, if nothing else!

This is the polished aluminum water outlet elbow modified by Luke's Custom Machine & Design. The water outlet elbow on the left cylinder head matches this one and they both clear the GMC 4-71 blower case.

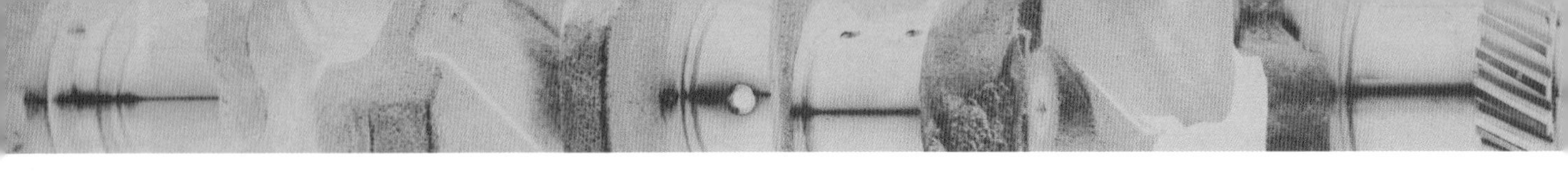

Camshaft and Cylinder Heads Summary

Item	Cost
New Clevite 77 #SH-21S camshaft bearings installed allowing for 0.002″ camshaft clearance and 0.007″ end play.	$26.12
New Crower Cams & Equipment #SPL8BA blower-grind cast iron alloy solid lifter camshaft with advertised duration: 264 degrees intake and exhaust; duration @ 0.050″ lift: 238 degrees intake exhaust; net valve lift: 0.350″/0.348″ intake and exhaust; lobe separation angle: 112 degrees; valve lash (hot): 0.020″ intake and 0.022″ exhaust. Camshaft degreed. Camshaft journal diameter: 1.7965″-1.7970″.	$256.22
New Speedway Motors #450-F8502 Johnson hardenable iron solid adjustable lifters, stock 1.00″ diameter. Solid body lifter weight: 114 grams, each.	$139.95
New Iskenderian Racing Cams #4005 aircraft-quality racing dual-helical coil valve springs, oil tempered, shot peened, silicon chrome. Installed height: 82 lbs. @ 1.8125″ valves closed and 170 lbs. @ 1.4625″ (0.350″ lift) valves open; 1.240″ o.d. and 0.925″/0.690″ i.d.; coil bind: 0.960″; color: grey. 1949-53 Ford #6514 valve spring retainers installed with new Iskenderian Racing Cams #87-F dual valve spring retainers and new Iskenderian Racing Cams #VL-11/32 standard, 7 degree, stamped steel, heat treated, valve stem locks, 11/32″ stem diameter. New Speedway Motors #910-15315 heat treated one-piece valve guide bushings installed with 0.0015″ valve guide boss clearance and 0.0015″ valve stem clearance. 1949-53 Ford #6512 valve guide bushing retainers installed.	$239.02
New Dale Wilch's R.P.M. Catalog #40961 small block Chevrolet stainless steel 1.61″ diameter intake and exhaust valves, hardened tips, swirl polished, 11/32″ stem diameter, stock length. Valves installed with Serdi-machined multi-angle blueprint valve grind.	$100.00
New Speedway Motors #910-14625L aluminum camshaft helical timing gear, 44 teeth, installed with Ford #6258 lock washer plate and Ford #350400 camshaft gear bolts using Loctite and torqued to 20 ft-lb. 1949-50 Ford #8BA-6059 cast iron timing gear cover installed with new polished stainless steel bolts and lock washers using Loctite and torqued to 15 ft-lb. Timing gear cover gasket installed using silicone sealant. Inside of timing gear cover painted with Glyptal #G-1228A medium grey gloss enamel and outside painted with RM #79666 signal red hi-gloss polyurethane.	$100.00
New Speedway Motors #916-15201 exhaust baffles installed.	$34.95
New Fel-Pro #1055 and #1056 copper sandwiched cylinder head gaskets, 0.062″ thickness, 14 cc compressed volume, installed using Permatex copper spray-a-gasket. New Edelbrock #1115 polished 356T-6 finned aluminum cylinder heads, 8.0:1 compression ratio, installed with 1949-53 Ford #6065 and #6066 cylinder head bolts and new Manley #42102 heat-treated head bolt washers, 7/16″ i.d., using Permatex aviation form-a-gasket and torqued to 40 ft-lb. New Speedway Motors #910-10115 chrome acorn nut covers, 11/16″ head size, installed.	$740.00
New Offenhauser #3496 "straight" polished aluminum water outlet elbows modified by Luke's. Gaskets installed using silicone sealant. New polished stainless steel bolts and lock washers installed using silicone sealant and torqued to 15 ft-lb. New Speedway Motors #910-15802, thermostats, 180 degrees F, installed.	$145.00
CAMSHAFT AND CYLINDER HEADS TOTAL:	**$1,781.26**

Intake Manifold

As far as I know, Barney Navarro was the only manufacturer of an off-the-shelf GMC 4-71 blower intake manifold for the Ford flathead V-8 engine. In the past, Luke's has taken a used Fenton #DM11 dual-carb intake manifold for the 1949-53 flathead, and modified it for blower use.

The top of the Fenton intake manifold is cut off at the forward end of the intake runner nearest the front of the manifold and after the end of the intake runner nearest to the back of the manifold. The cut is made at the top of the intake runners across the manifold. A rectangular aluminum "box" is then welded to the intake manifold. The box is a V-shape that fits the bottom of the GMC 4-71 blower case and has lips on each side in order to attach the blower case to the manifold. This process involves a tremendous amount of milling machine work and aluminum welding. The end result is an excellent flathead blower intake manifold.

Luke's has now started to have their own blower intake manifolds cast out of high-grade aluminum. These units are being cast in the United States and they sell for $550 completely "show" polished. The intake runner layout is an excellent design that should ensure equal air/fuel distribution. The manifold does not have the openings for the road draft/crankcase breather or the crankcase breather/oil filler tube, so a 1939-48 Ford #9415 fuel pump stand/crankcase breather must be installed. This is a top-quality product and looks great when polished. The cost of this new blower intake manifold is less than converting the old Fenton intake manifold. Ford flathead V-8 blower intake manifolds are expensive due to the limited quantities that are cast in a single order.

Luke's Custom Machine & Design converts Fenton #DM11 aluminum dual-carburetor intake manifolds for the 1949-53 Ford into blower manifolds. This is the first step in the process.

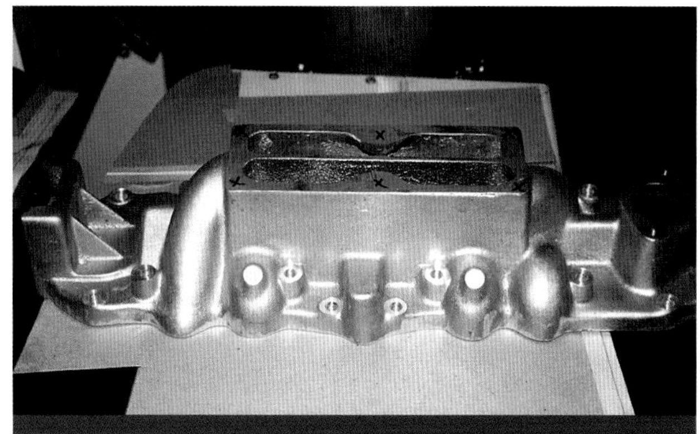

This is the new model of Luke's blower intake manifold for the flathead engine. The manifolds are cast in the United States of very high quality aluminum and look fantastic when polished. There is still a lot of fabrication and aluminum welding to do to the top of the manifold in order to mount the GMC 4-71 blower.

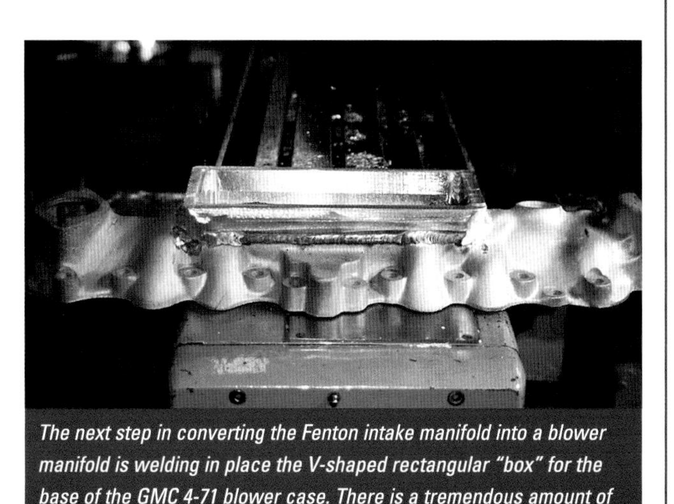

The next step in converting the Fenton intake manifold into a blower manifold is welding in place the V-shaped rectangular "box" for the base of the GMC 4-71 blower case. There is a tremendous amount of labor required to convert this piece into a flathead blower intake manifold.

GMC 4-71 Blower

Since the early 1990s there has been a resurgence in the popularity of the Ford flathead V-8 engine, and this popularity is growing. One item pertaining to this engine that is becoming more common is the use of a supercharger. Many people believe the addition of a blower is a new phenomenon, but that is not true. McCulloch offered blower kits in the 1930s, while the Italmeccanica/S.Co.T. and Frenzel blower kits were available in the very early 1950s. The use of the GMC 3-71 and GMC 4-71 blowers on Ford flathead V-8 engines was started in the late 1940s.

This is a photograph of a GMC 4-71 "Roots" type blower disassembled, showing the blower case, two rotors, two rotor gears, front and rear bearing plates, and front cover. The front and rear bearing plates have the bearings and seals installed.

This is a GMC 4-71 blower case undergoing major surgery on a milling machine at Luke's. The stock mounting flanges on the bottom of the blower case have been milled off, and the sides are being shaped. When this blower case is completed and buffed, it is an outstanding-looking piece of equipment. Just consider the amount of work that goes into this operation.

In the past few years I have seen the flathead engine equipped with "billet look" blowers that are mounted "in the sky." The alternator, power steering pump, and sometimes even an air conditioning pump are all sticking away from the engine in different directions. To top off this whole combination, there is a serpentine belt wrapped around everything. That is the perfect way to destroy the look of a beautiful old Ford flathead V-8 engine! In my opinion, if a blower is going to be installed on a street performance flathead engine, it should be the GMC 4-71 or an Italmeccanica/S.Co.T. model.

It is a common misperception that a blower is a highly complex mechanical unit found only on N.H.R.A. top fuel and funny cars or show cars. This is definitely not the case. First of all, a blower is not complicated, because only the two rotors turn internally in a blower such as the GMC 4-71. A blower forces a greater volume of the air/fuel mixture into the engine than in a normally aspirated engine. The blower creates "boost" only when it can get enough air, which is usually at wide open throttle (W.O.T.), when the engine is under load. The boost should only be measured at W.O.T., and this measurement is in pounds (lbs./sq. in.). It is seldom that a street performance blown flathead will experience boost. The boost effectively raises the compression ratio of an engine, but it also raises the cylinder and exhaust temperatures along with cylinder pressure. The blower is basically a very efficient and trouble-free mechanical device when it is set up properly.

A GMC 4-71 blower will be installed on the engine being described in this section, so I shall limit my brief explanation and description of a blower to that particular model. The GMC 4-71 blower is referred to as a "Roots" type and is fitted with two of the three-lobe helical rotors and gears, a front and rear bearing plate, a front cover, and of course the blower case. Although this blower consists of very few parts and is quite simple in design and construction, the proper clearances and assembly of this unit should be left strictly to an expert blower builder. If an amateur starts playing in the domain of an expert blower builder, disaster is guaranteed to strike!

Luke's builds complete GMC 4-71 blower setups for the Ford flathead V-8 engine. The cost of the GMC 4-71 blower setup is slightly more than the cost of the GMC 6-71 blower setup because it is now harder to locate the GMC 4-71 cores.

The blower consists of a GMC 4-71 core that is completely disassembled and all the parts carefully inspected for cracks, score marks, or other damage. The blower case, rotors, front cover, and bearing plates are then thoroughly cleaned and glass beaded. This is a lot of fun because years worth of diesel fuel and oil are glued to the case in the form of black slime. After cleaning one of these dirty beasts, I suggest you throw yourself in a hot tank for proper restoration! The case, front cover, and front and rear bearing plates are sent out for buffing. The rear bearing plate is machined for the installation of rear bearing support rings and caps.

All new front and rear bearings, bearing seals, gaskets, and stainless steel bolts are installed. A pressure relief valve, oil level sight gauge, oil filler plug, and oil drain plug are fitted in the front cover. The blower is expertly clearanced and the rotors are double-pinned.

Luke's places the GMC 4-71 blower case in a milling machine and removes the entire outer mounting flange on both sides of the case. The sides at the bottom of the case are then curved inward by milling, which results in the finished blower case looking somewhat similar to the early Italmeccanica/S.Co.T blowers of the 1950s. This is a one-of-a-kind custom blower case that no other company produces, and it is an outstanding-looking piece of equipment!

Snout

Luke's markets a beautiful sculptured blower snout housing made from billet 6061 T-6 aluminum. This snout looks absolutely gorgeous when buffed. The blower snout shaft and coupler are machined from 4140 chrome moly steel and incorporate the deepest splines presently available in the industry. The price of this item is very reasonable. The sculptured snouts measure 7.20″ from the front of the blower cover, where the snout bolts on, to the front of the flange on the snout coupler, where the drive pulley bolts on.

Luke's used to individually fabricate the sculptured blower snout and the snout shaft and coupler on a lathe, as they were ordered. Demand for this product soon meant there were not enough hours in a day to produce enough of these snouts to fill the orders. The sculptured snout and snout shaft and coupler are now produced by CNC machining.

These are the sculptured blower snouts with the snout shaft and coupler that Luke's now has CNC machined. A lot of blood, sweat, and tears go into producing one of these pieces on a lathe, which is how the job used to be done.

This is the left-side view of the sculptured blower snout, the GMC 4-71 blower, and the Fenton intake manifold. This is truly a work of art. The blower belt idler pulley bracket is bolted to the front of the intake manifold.

This is the right-side view of the sculptured blower snout, the GMC 4-71 blower, and the Fenton intake manifold. The oil level sight gauge can be seen installed in the front cover of the blower.

This picture shows the great-looking idler pulley bracket along with the blower belt idler pulley. This complete unit was machined by Luke's Custom Machine & Design from billet 6061 T-6 aluminum. The screws on the front of the idler pulley are for cosmetic purposes only, as the pulley consists of one piece.

Idler Pulley and Bracket

Luke's fabricates an aluminum blower drive idler pulley from billet 6061 T-6 aluminum. The idler pulley has a slight crown on the belt surface—as they are supposed to—in order to keep the belt(s) centered.

The idler pulley bracket is milled from aluminum and bolts to the front of the intake manifold, in the same position where the stock generator/fan assembly was attached.

Blower Drive Pulleys

The blown Ford flathead V-8 engine in this section was fitted with a V-belt blower drive system. The owner of the engine requested this in order to give his flathead a nostalgic appearance. Luke's machined the V-belt pulleys from aluminum. The crankshaft blower drive pulley was 5″ in diameter, the blower snout pulley was 5½″ in diameter, and four V-belts were used. The end result was a blower drive ratio of approximately 14.2% underdrive and a blower boost of approximately 6.18 lbs. This amount of blower boost works well on the street.

The boost for a street performance blown flathead engine should be in the 5 to 7 lbs. range. The blower drive ratio is adjusted by changing the size of the blower drive pulleys. A crankshaft drive pulley that is larger than the snout drive pulley will result in an overdrive ratio, and a crankshaft drive pulley that is smaller than the snout drive pulley will result in an underdrive ratio. A flathead engine of 265-ci displacement and 8.0:1 compression ratio actually has a compression ratio of approximately 11.0:1 when the engine experiences boost. For the street, anything higher than a 12.4:1 compression ratio when an engine experiences boost is totally unrealistic, especially with today's highest-octane unleaded gasoline. The Blower Drive Service catalog contains some very good blower information and the tables required for calculating the blower drive ratios and final compression ratio.

The pistons for the engine featured in this section were custom built for this particular engine, as are all of Ross

These are the blower drive V-belt pulleys, idler pulley and bracket, and the water pump pulleys that Luke's fabricated. This is a very compact and efficient design. The distributor is an MSD #8574 electronic unit. The polished coiled copper line on the front of the blower cover is in lieu of the usual pressure-relief valve. I know what I previously said about copper lines being used in a vehicle, but surely this is the exception!

Racing Pistons flathead blower pistons. Therefore, it is a fairly simple process to build a blown flathead engine with 7.5:1 or 8.0:1 compression ratio by supplying Ross Racing Pistons with all the necessary technical information relating to the engine (e.g., bore, stroke, camshaft specifications, cylinder heads, valve sizes, and carburetion) and having the pistons built accordingly.

If the owner of a blown flathead would rather have the usual ½"-pitch (Gilmer) blower drive belt and blower drive pulleys, then a 30-tooth pulley is required for the crankshaft and a 35-tooth pulley is required for the blower snout. This combination will give the same underdrive and "boost" as the engine in this section.

Blower Drive Service offers blower drive belts and blower drive pulleys in ½" pitch (Gilmer), 8 mm, 13.9 mm, and 14 mm sizes. The ½" pitch blower drive belts come in the widest range of lengths, and a multitude of sizes are offered for all the blower drive pulleys.

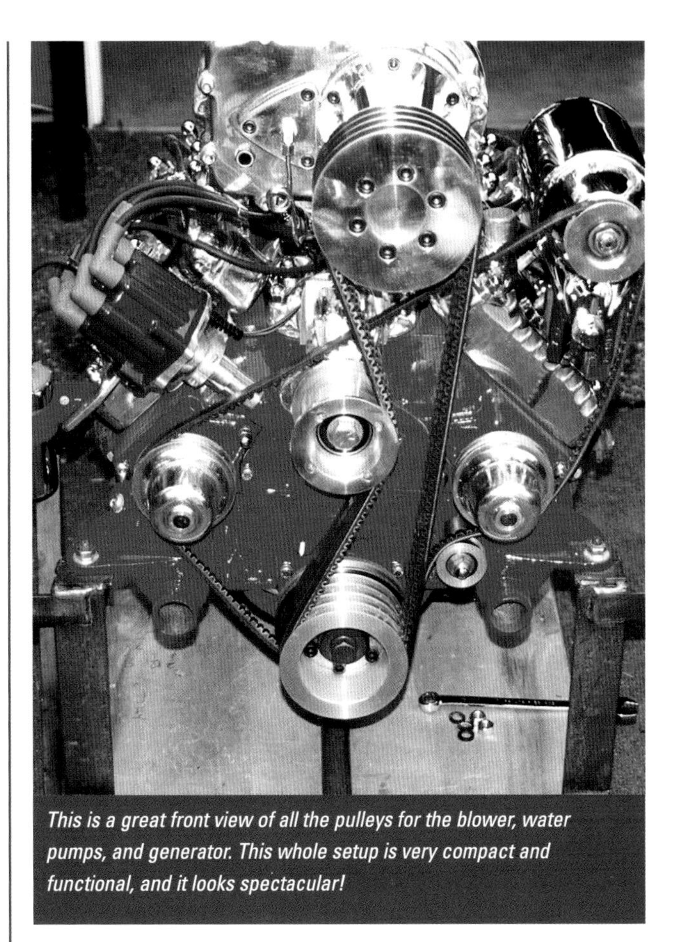
This is a great front view of all the pulleys for the blower, water pumps, and generator. This whole setup is very compact and functional, and it looks spectacular!

This flathead engine that Luke's built a number of years ago has been featured in hot rod magazines. The idler pulley bracket, which was attached to the blower snout, was the first design employed. The new system is much more compact and really shows off the sculptured snout. This blower is underdriven due to the larger blower drive pulley on the snout and the smaller blower drive pulley on the crankshaft.

Carburetion

Bruce Crower, the founder of Crower Cams & Equipment Company, is credited with being the first person to top-mount a GMC 6-71 blower on a "modern" V-8 engine. In 1954 he set a record of 157 mph at the Bonneville salt flats with his Chrysler "hemi" Hudson car. The blower was a GMC 6-71 and he had cast the five-belt blower pulleys in coffee cans using old pistons as the source of aluminum! Now here is the really interesting part: The four carburetors used on that engine were Dodge (Carter) two-barrel models. So much for the Stromberg 97 and the Holley 94, even in the 1950s!

A Holley #0-4777C "double pumper" of 650 cfm will be installed on the engine in this section. Luke's fabricates an aluminum adapter plate to mount the carburetor on the GMC 4-71 blower. You can order the Holley carburetor from your local high-performance merchant. The Holley #0-4777C double pumper carburetor is the "classic look" model. The Holley #0-4777S is the same cfm, but with the silver polish finish. The Holley double pumper carburetors are all equipped with manual chokes. Blower Drive Service also produces an adapter plate for a single Holley double pumper to a GMC 4-71 blower, part #14B4.

The formula for calculating the size of the carburetion required for an engine is:

$$\frac{\text{cubic inches} \times \text{maximum rpm}}{3456} = \text{carburetor cfm} \times 85\% \text{ (volumetric efficiency)}$$

An example would be a 276-ci engine operating at a maximum of 5,000 rpm. Based on the above formula, the cfm requirement would be 399.3 at 100% volumetric efficiency. At 85% volumetric efficiency, which is used for high performance engines, the actual requirement would be 339.4 cfm.

Now, some automotive wizards might argue that a 650-cfm carburetor is too much carburetion for a 265-ci flathead. If they applied the standard formula for calculating the required cfm for an engine of this displacement, they might be theoretically correct. However, it is best to run on the richer side with a blown motor. If a blown motor ever leans-out and backfires, the whole show is over. Besides, when you "hammer" a double-pumper carburetor on a blown engine and your teeth and eyeballs almost come out the back of your head, you will know you have done the right thing!

I do not believe carburetors that are over 60 years old in design, such as the Stromberg 97 or the Holley 94, are the route to go for the fuel system on a blown street Ford flathead V-8 engine being built today. You will have spent a lot of money to build an engine, and to risk everything on some vintage carburetors is not a wise decision. A modern four-barrel carburetor will outperform any three- or four-carburetor combination of antique two-barrel carburetors and offer proper fuel economy to boot! Consider using the smallest Holley double-pumper models or the smaller Edelbrock "performer" series four-barrel carburetors.

The plugs for the road draft/crankcase vent tube and the crankcase vent/oil filler tube were fabricated by Luke's from aluminum. The oil filler plug has a fitting installed to connect the copper line, which acts in lieu of the usual pressure relief valve. Pretty sneaky!

Fuel Pressure Regulator and Fuel Line

In your wildest dreams, the old Ford flathead fuel pump would not be able to feed a Holley 650-cfm double pumper carburetor. You will have to use an electric fuel pump. You should mount this as close as possible to the gas tank in order to push the fuel and not pull it.

This photograph shows the Mr. Gasket #1552 chrome dual-inlet fuel line for the Holley 650-cfm double-pumper carburetor. The Holley #162-510 chrome in-line fuel filter (no longer available) is attached directly to the fuel line. This is a neat touch, but there really should be a fuel pressure regulator between the fuel filter and the fuel inlet line.

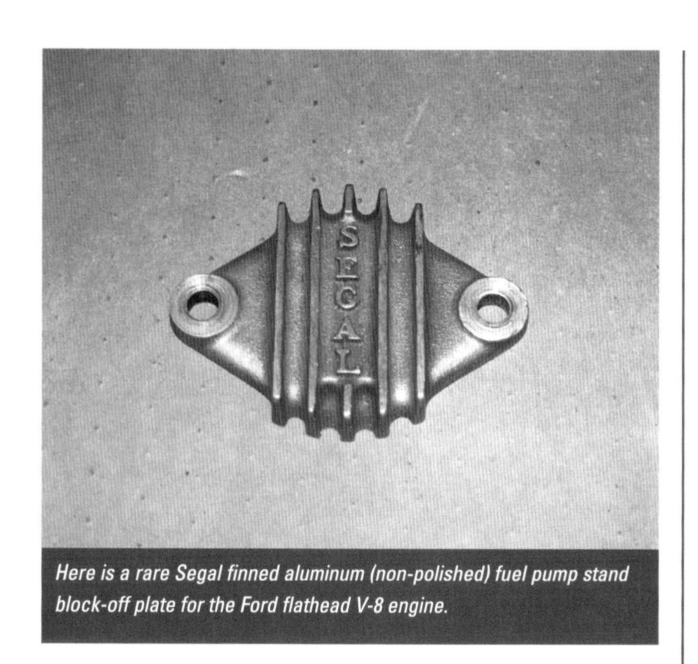

Here is a rare Segal finned aluminum (non-polished) fuel pump stand block-off plate for the Ford flathead V-8 engine.

A fuel pressure regulator should be used with a carburetor on a blown flathead engine. The fuel pressure regulator should be set at approximately 7 psi for a Holley double-pumper carburetor. The model to use with this particular engine is the Holley #12-803 fuel pressure regulator, adjustable from 4½ to 9 psi. This unit has an almost chrome-like finish to it, or it can be buffed. It is available from your local Holley dealer or Speedway Motors, part #427-12803.

The fuel line required for the Holley double-pumper carburetor is the Mr. Gasket #1552 chrome dual-inlet model. I like to attach the fuel pressure regulator directly to the inlet of the fuel line. The Mr. Gasket chrome fuel line is available from your local speed equipment outlet or Speedway Motors as part #910-11456.

A fuel pressure gauge should be installed at the fuel line inlet or from the fuel pressure regulator. A good gauge is the V.D.O. #153-002 model, 0 to 15 psi, with a 1½" diameter face. A vacuum/boost gauge such as the Auto Meter #4401 pro-comp model, 0-30 in.hg./0 to 20 psi, 2⅝" diameter face, should be installed below the blower. These gauges are available from your local speed equipment outlet.

Air Cleaner

I have not included an air cleaner with this engine because there are so many different types available for the Holley double-pumper carburetor. The owner of the engine will decide which model to chose.

The Speedway Motors #925-11902 "Mr. Roadster" polished aluminum single quad air cleaner assembly is a very nice unit and does not look out of place on a flathead engine. There is only the question of hood clearance, if you have one!

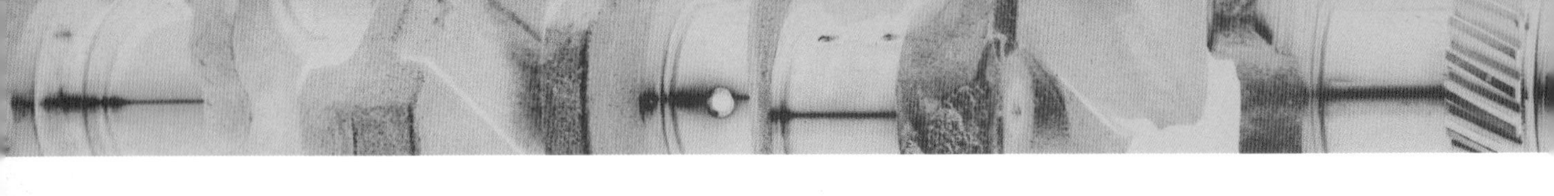

Intake System Summary

Luke's new polished aluminum Ford flathead V-8 blower intake manifold installed with new stainless steel bolts and AN flat washers using silicone sealant on gasket and torqued to 25 ft-lb. Luke's new polished aluminum road draft/crankcase vent tube and oil filler crankcase vent tube plugs installed using Permatex aviation form-a-gasket. New Speedway Motors #910-10125 chrome acorn nut covers for 9/16" head, installed.	$590.00
GMC #5114200 polished aluminum 4-71 supercharger; GM #5122363 polished front and rear bearing plates; new Blower Drive Service #671SL1 bearing seals; new MRC #5205 front bearings; new MRC #6205 rear bearings; and GM #51144442-M polished front cover assembled with new stainless steel bolts, lock washers, and AN flat washers. New Blower Drive Service #671-GK gasket kit installed using Permatex aviation form-a-gasket. New Blower Drive Service #555 pressure relief valve and #556 oil level sight gauge installed using silicone sealant. New stainless steel 3/8" N.P.T. oil filler and oil drain plugs installed using silicone sealant. Rear bearing plate machined for bearing supports. Polished aluminum rear bearing support caps installed with new stainless steel bolts using anti-seize compound. Blower case "shaped," rotors double-pinned, and blower clearanced. All machine work and assembly by Luke's.	$1,786.21
Luke's new #LS2000 polished 6061 T-6 aluminum sculptured blower drive snout; #LS2200 blower drive snout shaft, 4140 chrome moly heat treated steel; and #LS4100 blower drive snout coupler, 4140 chrome moly heat treated steel.	$500.00
Luke's new polished billet aluminum idler pulley and new polished aluminum idler pulley adjustment bracket.	$270.00
Luke's new polished aluminum V-belt crankshaft/blower drive pulley, 5" diameter, and blower/snout drive pulley, 5¾" diameter, installed with new polished stainless steel bolts and lock washers using Loctite and torqued to 25 ft-lb. New Gates #13A1370 blower V-belts (4), "Green Stripe XL" (7/16" x 54" length) installed. Blower drive ratio: 14.2% underdrive; Boost: 6.18 lbs.	$295.00
New Holley #0-4777C double-pumper 650-cfm carburetor installed with Luke's new polished aluminum carburetor to blower adapter, 1" thickness.	$460.00
New Mr. Gasket #1552 chrome dual-inlet fuel line, 9 5/16" center to center, installed. New Holley #12-803 fuel pressure regulator, adjustable from 4½-9 psi, installed with new Weatherhead #402-6-6 polished brass 90 degree elbow, 3/8" tube to 3/8" N.P.T. (inlet line); new Weatherhead #3325-6-4 polished brass reducer, 3/8" N.P.T. to ¼" N.P.T. (outlet line); and new stainless steel 3/8" N.P.T. plug. New V.D.O. #153-002 fuel pressure gauge, 1-15 psi, 1½" diameter face, installed in dual-inlet fuel line. New Auto Meter #4401 pro-comp ultra-lite vacuum/boost gauge, 0-30 in.hg./0-20 psi, 2 5/8" diameter face, installed with new Weatherhead #129F-4-4 polished brass hose fitting, 1/8" N.P.T. to ¼" i.d. hose.	$122.85
1939-48 Ford #9415 polished fuel pump stand/crankcase breather housing installed with new Speedway Motors #910-15195 crankcase breather/oil filler cap, for 1939-48 Ford. Luke's polished aluminum fuel pump block-off plate installed. Top of fuel pump stand/crankcase breather housing and top of crankcase breather/oil filler cap painted with RM #79666 signal red hi-gloss polyurethane.	$26.61
INTAKE SYSTEM TOTAL:	**$4,050.67**

CHAPTER 17

IGNITION SYSTEM

Distributor

A key part of a blown street performance Ford flathead V-8 engine is the ignition system. It is mandatory to have a top-of-the-line distributor in order to prevent any ignition failure when an engine is under boost. If this were to happen, the result would be some very serious and expensive internal engine damage. An electronic distributor is the only type of distributor to consider for a blown flathead.

One of the best electronic distributors manufactured for the 1949-53 Ford flathead V-8 is the MSD Pro-Billet model #8574 with full centrifugal (mechanical) advance. This distributor is machined from 6061 T-6 billet aluminum to + or – 1/1000th of an inch. There is an upper sealed ball bearing unit, and the shaft is polished and tuftrided. The distributor will operate through 10,000 rpm, something a street performance flathead won't see!

Mallory also produces excellent electronic distributors for the 1949-53 Ford flathead V-8 engine. The most popular model is the #3727501 Unilite. The other Mallory distributor is the #5027501 magnetic breakerless ignition mode. Both models, which feature full mechanical (centrifugal) advance, are machined from 6061 T-6 aluminum with an upper sealed ball bearing unit, and the shaft is heat treated and centerless ground. Both of the Mallory distributors will operate through 10,000 rpm.

This is the MSD #8574 billet aluminum electronic distributor installed with the Ford #8BA-6059 cast iron timing gear cover.

In most instances, the MSD #8574 and the Mallory #3727501 Unilite distributors can be installed in a Ford flathead V-8 engine the way they come out of the box, without any adjustments to the mechanical advance. The mechanical advance in the MSD distributor is adjusted by changing the color-coded springs. These springs are colored heavy silver, light silver, or light blue. The mechanical advance in the Mallory Unilite distributor is adjusted with the use of degree keys and springs.

Although the MSD and Mallory electronic distributors are fabricated from billet aluminum, they do not look out of place on a flathead engine. The MSD distributor is slightly larger in size than the Mallory units.

In the ignition chapter of Section I, it was mentioned there are two different 1949-53 Ford flathead V-8 distributor gears. The 1949-50 Ford #12390-C gear is secured on the distributor shaft with a rivet, Ford part #72837-S. The 1951-53 Ford #12390 gear is secured on the distributor shaft with a pin, Ford part #61465-S. Aside from this, both of those gears are the same. If you are going to use the 1951-53 Ford #OBA-6059-A aluminum timing gear cover, you must install the distributor gear at the correct height on the distributor shaft in order for the end of the distributor shaft to fit into the boss in that aluminum timing gear cover. The distributor has a flange on the upper housing that is used with the Ford #12270 distributor clamp to secure the distributor in position. The distance from the bottom of that flange to the bottom of the distributor gear must be exactly 8.00″ (+ or – 0.020″). The end play on the distributor shaft should be 0.002″ to 0.005″ after the gear is installed; shim accordingly. Use a polished stainless steel 5/16″ N.C. x 3/4″ length bolt and lock washer to hold the distributor clamp in place.

Coil and Ignition Control

A good ignition coil to use is the MSD #8200 Blaster 2 chrome model. The engine being built for this section of the book is going to be equipped with a multiple spark discharge ignition control box, and not all ignition coils are compatible with those units. The MSD Blaster 2 ignition coil is compatible and has the same outward appearance as a stock coil except for the chrome finish.

The MSD #6AL, model 6420, multiple spark discharge ignition control box is fitted with rpm-limiter modules. This model is highly recommended for use with a blown flathead engine in order to prevent over-revving the motor.

The Mallory #685 Hyfire VI microprocessor-controlled CD ignition system is fitted with rpm limiting. This unit and the MSD unit are both excellent ignition control boxes.

For spark plug wires and plugs, refer to Section I.

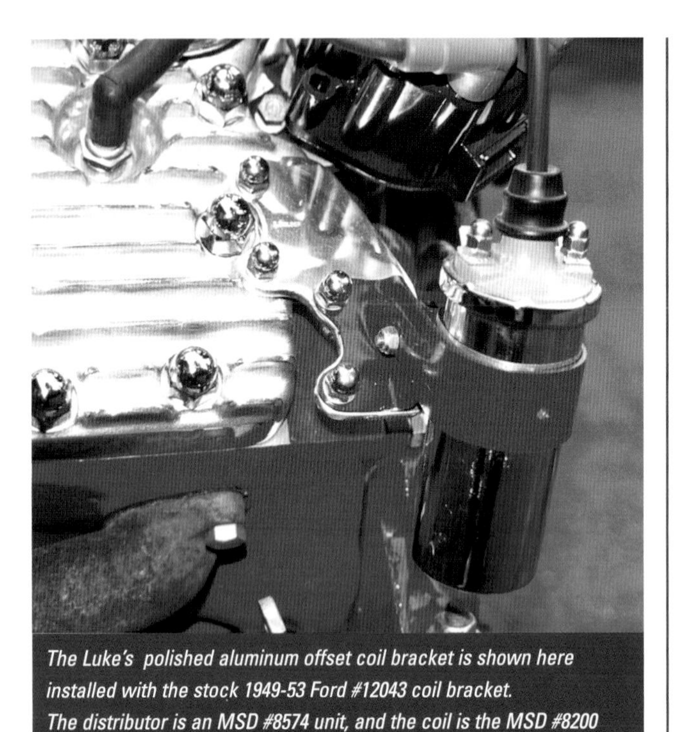

The Luke's polished aluminum offset coil bracket is shown here installed with the stock 1949-53 Ford #12043 coil bracket. The distributor is an MSD #8574 unit, and the coil is the MSD #8200 chrome model.

This is the generator installed on the left cylinder head using the Luke's polished stainless steel mounting bracket. Like everything else on this engine, this generator looks as if it belongs.

Alternator and Idler Adjustment Pulley

The owner of the engine being built for this section wanted to install the old-style 1939-48 Ford flathead V-8 generator, 6 volts, on his engine. The generator was upgraded to 12 volts by a local automotive electrical shop, and the housing was chromed. The result was a great looking piece of chrome that now functions on 12 volts and actually works! Most automotive electrical repair outlets can more than likely handle a straightforward generator conversion from 6 to 12 volts.

Luke's fabricated a polished stainless steel generator bracket with which to mount the generator on the front of the left cylinder head, and a polished aluminum pulley for the generator. The generator mounting bracket is the

This 1939-48 Ford flathead V-8 generator looks stock, except for the fine "show chrome," but is has been converted from 6 to 12 volts. The polished stainless steel generator mounting bracket on the left was fabricated by Luke's. This generator mounting bracket bolts to left cylinder head.

Here is the crankshaft/water pump/generator V-belt idler pulley produced by Luke's. This is a very ingenious design and solves the problem of belt contact with the water pump pulley.

adjustable design so that the generator belt tension can be fine-tuned. The generator had to be mounted on the lower part of the left cylinder head below the spark plugs in order to clear the blower housing and avoid clearance problems with the water outlet elbow and radiator hose. The generator mounting bracket was designed to install the generator in the vertical position and not at an angle, which is the result when using aftermarket generator mounting brackets. This stainless steel bracket gives the engine a cleaner look.

You must install an idler pulley for the V-belt connecting the crankshaft, water pumps, and the generator in order to have the belt make full contact with the left water pump pulley. The generator is mounted almost directly above the left water pump, which results in very little surface contact with the water pump pulley. Luke's manufacturers a polished aluminum idler pulley for this application. This idler pulley is approximately 2″ in diameter and bolts on the lower left side of the engine block, above the oil pan and next to the left-hand water pump housing.

For starting motor information, refer to Section I.

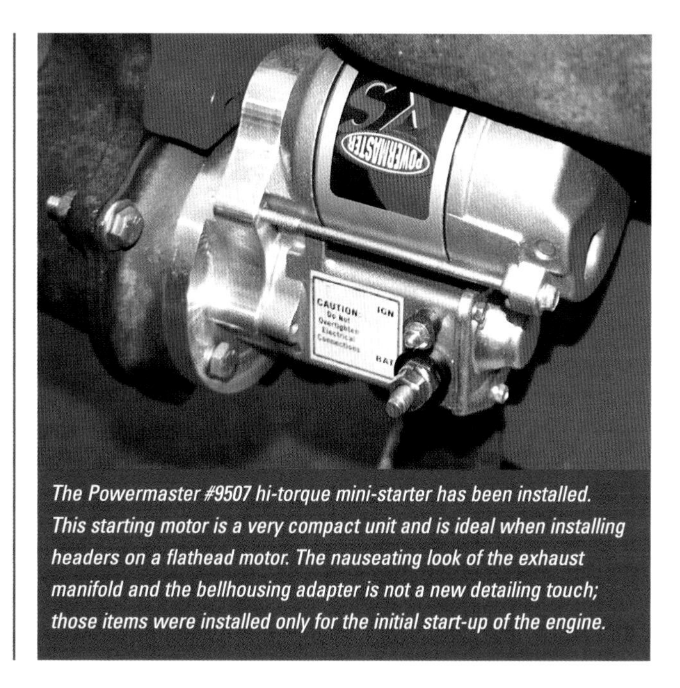

The Powermaster #9507 hi-torque mini-starter has been installed. This starting motor is a very compact unit and is ideal when installing headers on a flathead motor. The nauseating look of the exhaust manifold and the bellhousing adapter is not a new detailing touch; those items were installed only for the initial start-up of the engine.

Ignition System Summary

New MSD #8574 Pro-Billet T-6 aluminum Ford flathead CNC machined electronic distributor, with full centrifugal advance, installed with Luke's new aluminum distributor hold-down clamp. New MSD #6420, Model 6AL, multiple spark discharge ignition control, with rpm limiter modules, and new MSD #8200 "Blaster 2″ chrome ignition coil, 45,000 volts, installed with 1949-53 Ford #12043 coil bracket and Luke's new polished aluminum offset coil bracket using polished stainless steel bolts and lock washers. Ford coil bracket painted with RM #79666 signal red hi-gloss polyurethane.	$515.52
New Pertronix Performance Products #808290 "Flame Thrower" high-performance 8 mm spark plug wires, black 90-degree boots, installed with new Spectre #4245 chrome professional wire separators. New NGK #B-6L spark plugs installed with 0.050″ gap and torqued to 15 ft-lb using anti-seize compound.	$70.00
1939-48 Ford #P1A-10000-A generator, converted to 12 volts, installed with Luke's new polished stainless steel generator bracket and polished aluminum generator pulley. Generator bracket installed with new polished stainless steel bolts and lock washers using anti-seize compound. Luke's new polished aluminum idler pulley for water pumps/crankshaft/generator V-belt, installed with new polished stainless steel bolts and lock washer.	$375.00
New Powermaster #9507 hi-torque mini-starter, installed.	$189.95
IGNITION SYSTEM TOTAL:	**$1,150.47**

CHAPTER 18
COOLING SYSTEM AND MISCELLANEOUS

Water Pumps

The vehicle frame for the particular engine being built for this section dictated the use of the 1949-53 Ford Truck water pumps because of their horizontal motor-mount flanges. The owner of the engine requested that polished aluminum water-pump pulleys be fabricated by Luke's in order for those parts to look compatible with the rest of the pulleys on the motor.

The water pumps were rebuilt by Luke's using new Fag Bearing Limited #W2503 shafts and bearings.

Labor

The cost of the labor for checking clearances, gapping piston rings, painting and detailing, degree camshaft, blower setup, trial assembly of the motor, final assembly of the motor, and the initial start-up of the engine are not included in the final summary of each chapter. I include that at the end of this chapter.

Cooling System and Miscellaneous Summary

1949-53 Ford Truck #8RT-8503-B and #8RT-8504-B water pumps rebuilt by Luke's and installed with new polished stainless steel bolts and lock washers using silicone sealant on gaskets and torqued to 25 ft-lb. New Gates #13A1370 water pump/alternator/crankshaft V-belt, Green Stripe XL (7/16" x 54" length) installed. Luke's new polished aluminum water pump pulleys installed. Water pumps painted with RM #79666 signal red hi-gloss polyurethane.	$401.24
Labor for checking bearing clearances, gapping piston rings, degree camshaft, painting and detailing, blower assembly adjustments, trial engine assembly, final engine assembly, and initial engine start-up.	$1,733.33
COOLING SYSTEM AND MISCELLANEOUS TOTAL:	**$2,134.57**

The estimated output of this engine is: 307 hp @ 6,000 rpm and 312 ft-lb torque @ 4,500 rpm (See Chapter 31–Dyno Printouts section).

Blown Performance Street Engine Total

Engine block	$2,064.73
Crankshaft	$1,026.15
Connecting rods and pistons	$1,851.93
Lubrication system	$800.43
Camshaft and cylinder heads	$1,781.26
Intake system	$4,050.67
Ignition system	$1,150.47
Cooling system and miscellaneous	$2,134.57
TOTAL	**$14,860.21 (U.S.)**

CHAPTER 19
MISSING PARTS

For exhaust manifolds refer to Section I.

Flywheel and Flexplate

The standard Ford flathead V-8 transmissions are no match for any flathead engine that has been even slightly modified. On a number of occasions, Luke's Custom Machine & Design has adapted the 1985-93 Chevrolet S-10 Pick-up five-speed manual transmission to the Ford flathead V-8 engine. Luke's installs the 1949-53 Ford #6375 flywheel; the 1949-53 Ford #7563 long-style pressure plate, 10″ diameter; and the Tredex Automotive #TD4203 clutch disc (1985-93 Chevrolet S-10 Pickup), 14 splines, 9⅛″ diameter. That combination is fine for a mild flathead engine. If the engine is highly modified, then an 11″-diameter long-style pressure plate should be installed with the Tredex Automotive #TD4212 clutch disc from the 1985-91

This is a Fenton exhaust manifold that has been high temperature coated and installed on a 1950 Ford flathead V-8 engine. These are very good exhaust manifolds.

This is one combination for mating a 1985-93 Chevrolet S-10 Pickup five-speed manual transmission to a flathead engine. The flywheel is a 1949-53 Ford #6375. The 1949-53 Ford #7563 long-style pressure plate is a 10″-diameter model. The clutch disc is a Tredex Automotive #TD4203 with 14 splines and 9⅛″ diameter. The blue paint indicates the assembly has been balanced and is for alignment purposes.

This is another combination for mating a 1985-93 Chevrolet S-10 Pick-up 5-speed manual transmission to a flathead engine. The flywheel is a 1949-53 Ford #6375, the 1949-53 Ford #7563 "long style" pressure plate is an 11″-diameter model, and the clutch disc is a Tredex Automotive #TD4212 with 14 splines and 11″ diameter. The bronze pilot bushing is 1.575″ o.d. x 0.595″ i.d. The flywheel has been surfaced.

Chevrolet Astro Van, 14 splines, 11″ diameter. The bronze pilot bearing is fabricated by Luke's and is 1.575″ o.d. x 0.5.595″ i.d.

Fan

I have not included the stock 1949-53 Ford #8602 fan and #8603 fan hub assembly. There is no room to bolt the stock fan unit on the front of the motor because the blower belts are in the way. The owner will have to attach an electric fan unit to the radiator.

This is a photograph of the 1949-53 Ford Truck #8RT-6392 bellhousing adapter and the 1949-53 Ford #6375 flywheel installed. These items, along with the exhaust manifolds, were only in place for the initial engine start-up.

Any nostalgia addict would worship the finished product: a blown Ford flathead 265-ci V-8 performance street engine.

For engine block, connecting rod and piston, lubrication, and crankshaft assembly information, refer to Section I.

Camshaft and Cylinder Heads

The intake and exhaust valve-to-cylinder-head clearance for this engine, without the cylinder-head gasket installed, was 0.048″.

A connecting rod has been clamped in a connecting rod vise and the connecting rod nuts torqued to 45 ft-lb with the bearings installed in order to check the connecting rod bearing clearance.

Here is some more precious "loot." The lower boxes are NOS (new-old-stock) piston rings, parts #C99A-6T49-BR (0.005), #C91A-6149-DR (0.030), #C01A-6149-ER (0.045), and #C01A-6149-AR (std.). The upper boxes contain a camshaft gear, connecting rod bearings, pistons, and a bearing liner kit.

Intake System

Trace the intake manifold outline on the intake manifold gasket and trim that gasket accordingly. Install the intake manifold gasket using silicone sealant. Install the intake manifold and torque the bolts to 25 ft-lb using the factory-approved torque pattern. Install the chrome acorn nut covers on the intake manifold bolts. Install the fuel pump

Here is Luke Balogh torquing the cylinder head of the engine being described in this section. He did not pose for this picture, he is really torquing the cylinder head!

The 1939-48 Ford #9415 fuel pump stand/crankcase breather housing is shown with a NOS (new-old-stock) 1939-48 Ford #6766 crankcase breather/oil filler cap installed. This GMC 4-71 blower had a polished aluminum plate at the back of the rear bearing plate in order to cover up the rear rotor bearings.

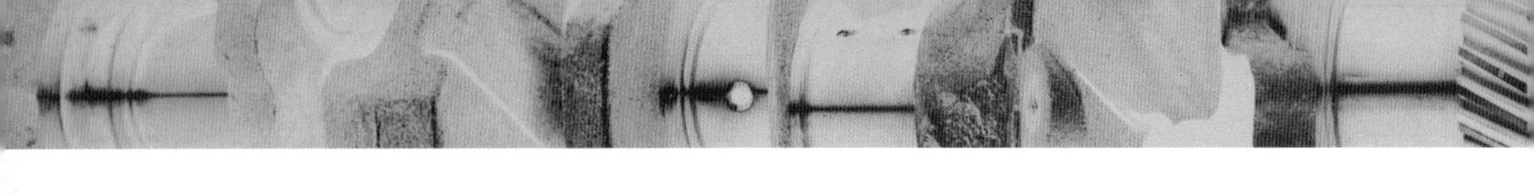

stand/crankcase breather housing using silicone sealant on the gasket and anti-seize compound on the bolts. Torque the bolts to 15 ft-lb.

Install the blower assembly on the intake manifold using silicone sealant on the intake manifold-to-blower gasket and torque the bolts to 25 ft-lb using anti-seize compound.

Install the carburetor/blower adapter using silicone sealant on the gasket and torque the bolts to 20 ft-lb using anti-seize compound. Install the carburetor on the adapter plate using anti-seize compound on the carburetor studs, and tighten the nuts snugly; do not over-tighten. Install the dual-inlet fuel line in the carburetor and the fuel pressure regulator in the end of the dual-inlet fuel line.

Attach the remote oil filter assembly oil line from the outboard pressure-out hole in the block to the inlet side of the remote oil filter, and attach the oil line from the inboard drain-in hole to the outlet side of the remote oil filter. Use teflon tape or pipe thread sealant on the oil line fittings.

Fill the oil filter with oil and install it on the remote oil filter bracket. Pour the required amount of motor oil in the engine. Install a temporary oil pressure gauge.

Ignition System

Install the crankshaft pulley woodruff key in the crankshaft using anti-seize compound, and gently tap the key into position with a hammer. Apply some anti-seize compound to the snout of the crankshaft and install the crankshaft pulley. The pulley should have a snug fit, but it should not require the use of a harmonic balancer installation tool. Gently tap the crankshaft pulley onto the crankshaft using a piece of wood and a hammer. Install the blower belt drive pulley on the crankshaft pulley and torque the bolts to 25 ft-lb using anti-seize compound. Install the crankshaft pulley bolt and washer using Loctite and torque the crankshaft bolt to 50 ft-lb. Install the blower snout drive pulley and torque the bolts to 25 ft-lb using anti-seize compound.

Rotate the crankshaft until the engine is set with the #1 piston at 10 degrees before TDC (top dead center) and insert the distributor into the timing gear cover with the distributor rotor at the #1 spark plug lead position. Clamp the distributor down.

Gap the spark plugs at 0.050″ and install them using anti-seize compound. Torque the spark plugs to 15 ft-lb. Lay out the spark plug wires and cut them to length for each cylinder. The cylinders on the right (passenger's) side of the engine are numbered 1, 2, 3, and 4 from the front, and the cylinders on the left side of the engine are numbered 5, 6, 7, and 8 from the front. The firing order is: 1, 5, 4, 8, 6, 3, 7, 2. Install the wires on the spark plugs and in the distributor cap. Install the ignition coil, the ignition coil bracket, and the offset ignition coil bracket on the right cylinder head using anti-seize compound on the bolts. Connect the coil wire to the distributor.

This photograph shows how the generator mounting bracket is secured to the left cylinder head using the three extended cylinder head studs.

Install the generator mounting bracket on the left cylinder head and torque the nuts to 40 ft-lb. Install the generator on the generator bracket using anti-seize compound on the bolts.

You will have to install a flywheel or flexplate in order to start the engine. Install the flywheel or flexplate bolts with Loctite and torque them to 80 ft-lb. You also must install a bellhousing and starting motor mounting plate to mount the starting motor.

Install the starting motor using anti-seize compound on the bolts.

Cooling System and Miscellaneous

Apply silicone sealant to the water pump gaskets and bolts. Install the water pumps and torque the bolts to 25 ft-lb.

Install the blower belt idler pulley bracket on the front of the intake manifold using anti-seize compound on the bolt. Install the blower belt idler pulley on the blower belt idler pulley bracket using anti-seize compound on the bolt.

Install the crankshaft/water pump/generator V-belt idler pulley and torque the bolt to 25 ft-lb using Locktite. Install the crankshaft/water pump/generator V-belt allowing for approximately ¾″ to 1″ slack. Install the blower drive pulleys V-belts (4) and adjust the idler pulley so there is approximately ¾″ slack.

Hook up some headers and mufflers, a radiator with some water in it, and the ignition system with a battery and starter switch. Start the engine and adjust the timing and the carburetor. Allow the engine to run at approximately 2,000 rpm for 30 minutes in order to break in the camshaft. After the engine is at full operating temperature, shut it off, allow the engine to cool, and re-torque the cylinder heads using the factory approved torque pattern. Install the chrome acorn nut covers on the cylinder head bolts. You are now the proud owner of some serious "rock and roll" stuff!

CHAPTER 21
ENGINE BLOCK

SECTION 3: ARDUN PERFORMANCE STREET ENGINE

I had almost completed writing this book when a once-in-a-lifetime opportunity came along that prompted me to add a third section. This section is about the Ardun engine.

Zora Arkus-Duntov (1909-96) and his brother, Yura Arkus-Duntov, designed the Ardun overhead-valve, hemispherical combustion chamber conversion kit for the Ford flathead V-8 engine (V-8-100) in 1947. The brothers were living in New York at the time, and their company was named the Ardun Engine Company. The name "Ardun" is derived from letters within their last name. Zora Arkus-Duntov went on to become one of the most influential forces in the development and refinement of the Corvette. The famous Duntov camshaft for the small block Chevrolet was named after him. The introduction of the Ardun cylinder heads revolutionized the American automotive engine industry.

The cylinder heads were cast in England of Alcoa 355 T-6 heat-treated aluminum alloy. It is my understanding only 200 sets were manufactured, although all the other parts in the conversion kit were produced in quantities large enough to service hundreds of sets of cylinder heads. Rumor has it that a number of these conversion kits ended up on engines installed in garbage trucks in England. How many of these cylinder heads remain today in working condition is unknown; after 50 years I am certain there cannot be many. Many drag race and salt flat speed records were set in the early 1950s with Ardun engines.

The Ardun conversion kits are being reproduced today in an improved version by Don Ferguson of Ardun Enterprises. These new cylinder heads are CNC machined using high-grade Alcoa 356 T-6 heat-treated aluminum. You had better be sitting down when you find out the price of this new kit!

In late May 2002, an Ardun owner contacted Luke Balogh, the proprietor of Luke's Custom Machine & Design, inquiring as to the possibility of having his Ardun engine rebuilt. Luke Balogh is one of a handful of Ardun specialists in the world today, and he rarely has the opportunity to work on those motors because there are so few of them still in existence. At the beginning of June 2002, the owner of the Ardun brought his engine from his home in Washington State to Luke's. The engine had been rebuilt in the late 1980s by Cotton Werksman, a legendary Ardun expert, but was now in a sad state of repair due to a number of unfortunate circumstances. Emergency aid was needed!

At that point I decided the situation was too good to pass up, and I thought of including the build up of this engine in my book. The last really informative and intensive article published about the Ardun that I am familiar with was the one written by Tom Senter in the May, June, and July 1971 issues of *Rod & Custom* magazine. Tom Senter was

This August 17, 1988, photograph shows Luke Balogh with the1927 Ford Model T Roadster, owned by Doug King, which set a new record of 143.799 mph in the XX/Street Roadster class at the Bonneville Salt Flats.

Here is Luke Balogh (on the right) with Tom Senter and Tom's blown Ardun engine. This picture was taken at Tom's house in 1982.

one of the foremost experts of the Ardun engine, and he referred to the Ardun as "the old days elephant motor."

I doubt very much that there will ever be a book published strictly about the Ardun engine due to the limited sales such a book would produce. There are not that many Ardun owners, so the interest in those engines is limited. Many avid hot rodders have never heard of the Ardun engine. However, the Ardun engine is a part of hot rod history, and something should be published about it today. There is room in my book!

On August 17, 1988, Luke Balogh set a new XX/Street Roadster record of 143.799 mph at the Bonneville Salt Flats with a 284-ci Hilborn-injected Ardun-powered 1927 Ford Model T Roadster owned by Doug King. Luke currently has an Ardun engine of his own that he is slowly picking away at, and when it is complete, he intends to race at Bonneville once again.

I should mention that Luke Balogh considered Tom Senter to be a good friend of his. Luke was very saddened when he learned of Tom's early demise in 1984. Out of respect for that relationship, I would like to dedicate this section to the fond memory of a fine gentleman, Tom Senter.

The basis for a street performance Ardun motor is the engine block, crankshaft, and connecting rods. These are the same items described in Section I, so I shall not rewrite everything about those items in this section. Certain subheadings in each chapter refer the reader back to the corresponding subheadings in Section I for a full explanation. However, I shall include everything new relating to the Ardun.

The owner of the Ardun engine is going to reinstall it in a 1932 Ford Roadster, an original 1950s-era hot rod: the perfect home for a perfect engine!

Even though readers may never own, or even see, a real Ardun engine, I am certain they will enjoy reading about and learning how to assemble one. Fasten your seat belts; we are going to launch off the starting line into the world of Arduns!

Engine Block

The specifications that were advertised for an Ardun #1000 V-8-175 OHV conversion kit for a 239.4-ci Ford flathead V-8 engine were 160 hp @ 4,000 rpm and 225 ft-lb torque @ 2,500 rpm. This information was based on a non-modified engine block, 7.0:1 compression ratio, standard Ford ignition and fuel pump, starting motor, generator, two-barrel carburetor, and 67-octane gasoline. Unbelievable fuel in those days! The maximum power was listed as 175 hp @ 5,200 rpm.

Purchase and Magnaflux

The engine block to locate for the foundation of an Ardun motor is the 1949-53 Ford or Mercury flathead V-8. This block will be bored to 3 5/16" (3.3125"), so you will have to find a block that has been previously bored to only 0.060" oversize, or 3.2475". The building of an Ardun engine is a very expensive proposition, so every effort should be made to locate an engine block in premium condition. If at all possible, do not purchase an engine block that has cracks in it.

The most important item concerning an engine block that is going to be used to build an Ardun is that the block cannot be relieved. It is impossible to seal the cylinder heads on an Ardun engine if the block has been relieved.

The original Ardun conversion kits were designed to fit the 1939-53 Ford or Mercury flathead V-8 non-relieved engine blocks (V-8-100). Pre-1949 transmissions were not designed to handle the horsepower produced by a well-tuned Ardun street performance engine, so it is best to use a 1949-53 block in order to easily adapt a late model transmission.

These are the six Ardun #1203 exhaust port block-off plates for the exhaust ports in the Ford flathead V-8 engine block. They have not yet been drilled and tapped for the oil drain fittings.

Shown here is the location where the oil line fittings for the full-flow oil system are attached on the Ardun engine in this section. The tapped hole on the left is for the pressure-out line, and the tapped hole nearest the center of the engine block is for the drain-back line. The horizontal hole just below the pressure-out hole will be used as a pressure-out oil line hole, in conjunction with the oil hole above it, for the oil lines to the cylinder heads and an oil pressure gauge. Notice how the block has been nicely sanded and detailed.

For cleaning, refer to Section I.

Porting and Polishing

The intake and exhaust ports in the Ford flathead V-8 engine block will not be ported and polished because they will not be used. The six Ardun #1203 exhaust manifold block-off plates (where the headers bolt on the block) will be installed.

Detailing the Block and Drilling Valve Lifter Bosses

It will not be necessary to drill holes in the valve lifter bosses to assist with the valve lifter adjustment. The valves in an Ardun engine are adjusted at the rocker arms.

For full-flow oiling, refer to Section I.

Relieving the Block

As previously mentioned, a relieved Ford flathead V-8 engine block cannot be used as the basis for an Ardun engine because it would be impossible to seal the cylinder heads.

Heat Risers

The heat riser passages in a Ford flathead V-8 engine blockwill not be used in an Ardun.

The stainless steel cylinder head bolt hole plugs for three of the four holes that must be plugged are just below the red on the deck surface. The fourth plug is underneath the reflection from the superior parallel decking job.

Re-Tap and Chamfer Bolt Holes

After re-tapping and chamfering the cylinder head bolt holes, and prior to the assembly of the engine, install four stainless steel socket head set screws (7/16″ N.C. x 1/2″ length) in the cylinder-head bolt holes on each side of the block using Permatex aviation form-a-gasket. The four holes are located on the top row of cylinder head bolt holes and they are: the first top hole from the front of the block, the third top hole from the front of the block, the fourth top hole from the front of the block, and the sixth top hole from the front of the block.

When the Ardun cylinder heads are used on a 1949-53 Ford or Mercury flathead V-8 engine block, the water passage hole at the very front of the deck on each side of the

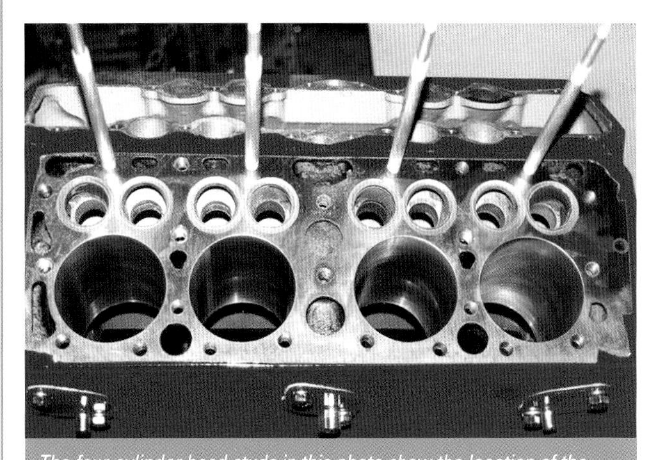

The four cylinder head studs in this photo show the location of the four head-bolt holes that must be plugged prior to installing the Ardun cylinder heads. These four holes must be plugged on both sides of the engine block. The exhaust port block-off plates with the oil drain line fittings are visible.

block must be tapped for a 1/8" N.P.T. stainless steel plug. Use Permatex aviation form-a-gasket when installing the plugs. These two water passage holes would otherwise be open and exposed due to the cylinder head not covering them.

For redi-stripping the block, and for Glyptal application, refer to Section I.

Cylinder Boring

The block described in this section will be bored and the cylinders honed and de-glazed, resulting in a final bore of 3 5/16" (3.3125"). You should purchase the pistons beforehand and deliver them to the machine shop with the block. The machine shop will then measure each piston with a micrometer and bore the block accordingly to ensure there is 0.004" piston-to-bore clearance (after cylinder honing), measured below the bottom of the wrist pin perpendicular to the wrist pin. This is the piston clearance Ross Racing Pistons recommends for these pistons. The engine block is usually bored to within 0.003" to 0.004" of the final bore and then honed and de-glazed, resulting in the final cylinder bore.

Align Hone

The engine block in this section did not require align honing.

The stock main bearing caps and bolts in a Ford flathead V-8 engine used for daily street use are of sufficient strength to withstand normal stress in the bottom end. If an Ardun engine is going to be highly modified for street use, then main bearing cap support bridges and aircraft quality 1/2"-diameter main bearing cap bolts should be installed. In most instances, the oil pan does not have to be modified to clear the main bearing cap support bridges.

Luke's used to mill the main bearing caps flat and place the support bridges on top. The Offenhauser #3408 main bearing cap support bridges (for 1949-53) have a bolt in the center of the bridge, which tightens against the center of the main bearing cap. After a recent review of both of these systems, Luke's is now producing a revised main bearing cap support bridge. This consists of milling flat the center of the main bearing cap slightly and using spacers with the bolts to level the bridge. This system will spread the stress more evenly across the main bearing cap, while only minimally reducing the thickness of the main bearing cap, and also avoiding placing undue stress on a single point in the center of the cap.

If you are going to equip an Ardun engine with a blower, then you must fabricate and fit new #1 and #2 main bearing caps and install aircraft quality 1/2"-diameter main bearing cap bolts. If you are going to use the Ardun engine for all-out racing, then you should fabricate and fit an oil pan rail and main bearing cap support girdle in order to reduce high-speed stress. The use of new main bearing caps and a girdle will require align boring and align honing as well as modification to the oil pan for main bearing cap clearance.

Luke's fabricates billet steel main bearing caps and support girdles for the Ford flathead V-8 engine. Doug King supplies billet steel main bearing caps and support girdles. This is the same Doug King who owned the Ardun-powered, record-setting 1927 Ford Model T Roadster driven by Luke Balogh in 1988.

Here is the new design of main bearing cap support bridge fabricated by Luke's Custom Machine & Design. The main bearing cap is milled slightly and spacers are used to level the support bridge. This picture was taken during the mock-up stage and prior to countersinking the main bearing cap bolts and beveling the front of the bridge for oil pan clearance.

These are the billet steel #1 and #2 main bearing caps supplied by Doug King Enterprises.

This picture shows the #2 main bearing cap support bridge fabricated by Luke's.

For parallel decking and shot peening, refer to Section I.

Valve Seat Inserts

The valve seat inserts in the engine block will not be used, so it is not necessary to be concerned with their condition. The valve seat inserts in the cylinder heads will be discussed in Chapter 25.

The valve guide bosses may require some grinding using a high-speed grinder with a carbide bit, in order to ensure sufficient pushrod-to-valve guide boss clearance. The only way to check this is to install the camshaft, the assembled cylinder heads with the rocker arm assemblies, and two camshaft lifters with an intake and exhaust pushrod. Install the lifters and pushrods in the intake and exhaust bosses for a cylinder, adjust the valve lash, rotate the camshaft through the maximum lift for the intake and exhaust valves, and check the valve guide bushing bosses for clearance as you do this. Follow this procedure for each cylinder. If there is insufficient valve guide boss clearance, the pushrods will "lay" against the valve guide bosses and start to chafe. That is a quick way to destroy a set of pushrods. The valve guide bosses for the engine being described in this section did not require any grinding.

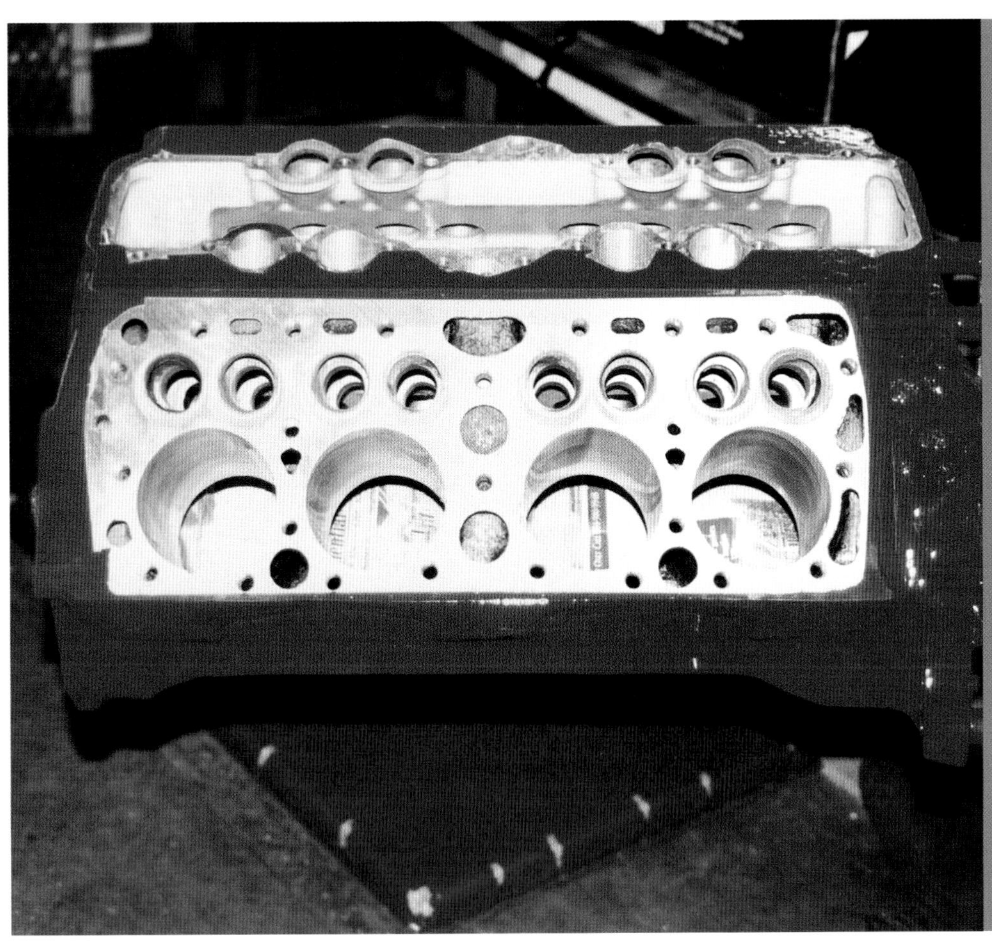

The engine block for the basis of the Ardun engine in this section has just been painted with PPG #74000 red hi-gloss polyurethane.

Valve Grind

Once again, the valve seat inserts in the engine block will not be used, so they will not be ground. The subject of valve grinding the cylinder heads will be discussed in Chapter 25.

De-Glaze

De-glaze the valve lifter bosses using a wheel cylinder hone. Do just enough honing to clean up the bosses. An absolute minimum of material should be removed in order to avoid excess valve-lifter and guide clearance, which will result in oiling problems. Do not put your drill on auto-pilot and then go for lunch!

For dealing with cracks, refer to Section I.

Cleaning and Painting

The application of polyurethane paint should be carried out in a temperature-controlled spray booth in order to obtain the maximum benefit from this type of coating. Luke Balogh and I used to paint blocks and other engine parts in the driveway of Luke's Custom Machine & Design. Aside from losing half the paint to the wind and covering ourselves and most of the neighborhood in polyurethane, there was also the thankless task of cleanup. Sanity finally prevailed. All the engine parts are now professionally painted at J & M Autobody & Paint.

Engine Block Summary

Item	Cost
1952 Canadian Mercury 255.4-ci L-head V-8 engine block; Casting Number: CIBA; 2-bolt main bearing caps; 24 stud block; Stock Bore: 3 3/16″ (3.1875"); Stock Stroke: 4.00″; Stock Compression Ratio: 6.8:1; 125 hp @ 3,700 rpm and 218 ft-lb torque @ 2,200 rpm. Engine block weight (bare): 200 lbs.	$200.00
Engine block hot tanked and redi-stripped. Engine block, main bearing caps, and main bearing cap bolts Magnafluxed.	$205.00
All threads re-tapped; main bearing caps and main bearing cap bolts shot peened; cylinder head bolt holes chamfered; valve lifter bosses de-glazed allowing for 0.0015″ valve lifter clearance. New stainless steel 7/16″ N.C. socket head set screws (8) installed in top row of cylinder head bolt holes using Permatex aviation form-a-gasket. New stainless steel 1/8″ N.P.T. plugs installed in front water passage hole, on each side of block, using Permatex aviation form-a-gasket. Exterior surface of engine block sanded and detailed. Valve lifter gallery and front of engine block painted with Glyptal #G-1228A medium grey gloss enamel. Exterior surface of engine block painted with PPG #74000 red hi-gloss polyurethane.	$360.13
Engine block converted to full-flow oil system.	$65.00
Engine block bored 0.125″ (1/8") oversize and cylinders honed and de-glazed using Sunnen 800-series 400-grit stones, final bore: 3 5/16″ (3.3125"). Piston-to-bore clearance: 0.004″ measured below bottom of wrist pin perpendicular to wrist pin.	$125.00
Engine block parallel decked to 0.010″ average, below deck.	$110.00
New 1045 steel #1 and #2 main bearing cap support bridges installed with new aircraft-quality 1/2"-diameter main bearing cap bolts, 180,000 psi.	$108.33
ENGINE BLOCK TOTAL:	**$1,173.46**

CHAPTER 22
CRANKSHAFT

Purchase

The 1949-53 Mercury #6303 cast alloy steel crankshaft is a very good-quality item and is entirely adequate for use in a street performance Ardun engine.

The 1949-53 Ford and Mercury crankshafts had two oil holes in each connecting rod journal for the lubrication of the non-floating connecting rod bearings. The pre-1949 Ford and Mercury crankshafts had one oil hole in each connecting rod journal for the lubrication of the full-floating connecting rod bearings. As a matter of interest, the 1946-48 Canadian Ford and Mercury crankshafts had two oil holes in each connecting rod journal for the lubrication of the full-floating connecting rod bearings. You cannot use non-floating connecting rods and bearings with a full-floating crankshaft (one oil hole in each connecting rod journal) but you can use a non-floating crankshaft (two oil holes in each connecting rod journal) with full-floating connecting rods and bearings.

For Magnafluxing, refer to Section I.

Shot Peen and Plug Removal

All the 1949-53 Ford and Mercury flathead V-8 crankshafts had connecting rod journal oil-passage plugs installed. There was one plug at the end of each journal, and these

The factory pressed-in connecting rod journal oil-passage plug has been removed and is now ready to be tapped for a 3/8" N.P.T. plug. The offset grind of the connecting rod journal can be seen, indicating this is a 4 1/8"-stroke Mercury crankshaft.

The 1949-53 Ford #8BA-6303 crankshaft with a 3.75" stock stroke has been Magnafluxed, aligned, shot peened, and ground smooth. The main journals have been ground 0.010" undersize, the connecting rod journals have been ground 0.020" undersize, and the factory pressed-in connecting rod journal oil plugs removed and new stainless steel 1/8" N.P.T. plugs installed. Aside from the shorter stroke, this crankshaft is every bit as good as the 1949-53 Mercury 4"-stroke model.

The 4⅛"-stroke Mercury crankshaft used in the engine built for this section has been Magnafluxed, shot peened, aligned, ground, oil holes chamfered, and the journals polished. It is being fitted in order to check the piston height-to-deck clearance.

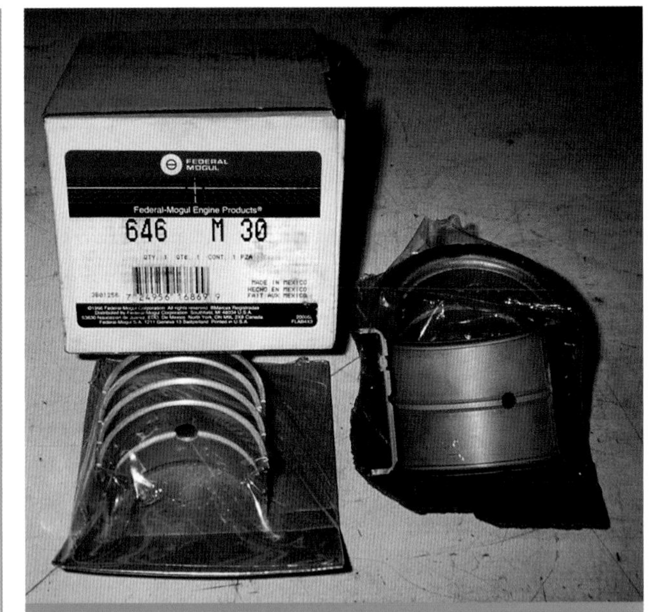

Here is a set of Federal Mogul #646-M-30 main bearings, 0.030" oversize, for the 1949-53 Ford 3½" stoke or the Mercury 4"-stroke crankshafts.

This is a good front view of the Speedway Motors #912-S12853 one-piece oil seal and Luke's Custom Machine & Design crankshaft sleeve.

plugs led to a sludge trap inside the journals. The factory plugs were pressed-in; you should remove them in order to clean out the sludge traps and tap the holes for installation of stainless steel N.P.T. plugs. The holes vary in size for ⅛″ N.P.T., or ¼″ N.P.T., or ⅜″ N.P.T. plugs.

For measuring straightness, chamfering, and polishing, refer to Section I.

Re-Grinding and Cleaning

If the connecting rod journals of the 1949-53 Mercury 4.00″-stroke crankshaft are offset ground 0.0625″ and reduced in diameter to 1.9985″, the result is a 4⅛″ (4.125″) stroke when used with the 1942 Ford #21A-6200 connecting rods and custom pistons. If the block is bored to 3⅜″ (3.375″) and the 4⅛″ (4.125″) stroke crankshaft is used, you would then have the famous "three-eights by three-eights" engine of 295-ci displacement. If the engine has a 3 5/16″ (3.3125″) bore and a 4⅛″ (4.125″) stroke, the displacement would be 284 cubic inches.

The stock 1949-53 Ford #6303 crankshaft with the 3¾″ (3.75″) stroke is often overshadowed by the Mercury 4″ stroke crankshaft. The Ford crankshaft is the same high quality as the Mercury crankshaft. If the Ford crankshaft connecting rod journals are offset ground 0.0625″ and then reduced to 1.9985″ diameter, the stroke would be 3⅞″ (3.875″). This stroke combined with a 3 5/16″ (3.3125″) bore results in another famous flathead engine, the "eighth by eighth" of 267-ci displacement. A 3⅜″ (3.375″) bore and a 3⅞″ (3.875″) stroke produces a displacement of 277 cubic inches. The 1942 Ford #21A-6200 connecting rods with the full-floating bearings and custom pistons must be used with the 3⅞″ (3.875″) stroke crankshaft.

Main Bearings

Apparently Clevite 77 (Michigan Bearings) standard-size main bearings are no longer available for the 1949-53 Ford or Mercury flathead V-8 engine. As a result, Sealed Power (Federal Mogul) #646-M standard size main bearings are used with the Ford or Mercury crankshaft standard size main bearing journals. The Federal Mogul bearings are good quality items.

For information on the crankshaft gear and pulley, refer to Section I.

Crankshaft Summary

1949-53 Mercury #6303 cast alloy steel crankshaft; Casting Number: D2613; main journal diameter: 2.498″-2.499″; connecting rod journal diameter: 2.138″-2.139″; non-floating connecting rod bearings; Stock Stroke: 4.00″. Identity Number: CS6713. Crankshaft weight: 67 lbs.	$400.00
Crankshaft Magnafluxed, aligned, and shot peened; main bearing journals ground 0.020″ undersize; connecting rod journals offset ground 0.0625″ and reduced to 1.9985″ diameter and 0.010″ undersize; oil holes chamfered; journals polished; and crankshaft balanced. Factory crankshaft connecting rod journal oil plugs removed and new stainless steel ⅜″ N.P.T. plugs installed using Loctite.	$270.00
New Federal Mogul #646-M-Std. main bearings, standard size, installed allowing for 0.002″ crankshaft clearance and 0.004″ end play. Main bearing cap bolts torqued to 105 ft-lb using Molykote.	$119.13
1949-53 Ford #6306 cast iron helical crankshaft gear, 22 teeth, and Ford #6310 oil slinger installed with Ford #357654-S crankshaft gear woodruff key. Luke's new crankshaft oil seal sleeve installed. 1949-53 Ford Truck #GAUB241815 crankshaft pulley, 7.00″ diameter, double groove, installed with Ford #74153-S crankshaft pulley woodruff key and Ford #351590-S crankshaft pulley bolt washer with Ford #20639-S crankshaft pulley bolt. Crankshaft pulley bolt installed using Loctite and torqued to 50 ft-lb. Oil slinger painted with Glyptal #G-1228A medium grey gloss enamel. Crankshaft pulley glass beaded and painted with Endura #EX-2C black 160 hi-gloss polyurethane.	$135.87
CRANKSHAFT TOTAL:	**$925.00**

CHAPTER 23
CONNECTING RODS AND PISTONS

Purchase

The connecting rods suitable for use in a street performance Ardun engine are those found in the 1949-53 Ford flathead V-8 engine. The casting number for these connecting rods is 8BA6205A or 8BA, and they use non-floating connecting rod bearings. The average weight of #8BA6205A connecting rod is 532 grams.

If you plan to equip an Ardun engine with a blower or use it for drag racing or salt flat racing, then you should box the stock flathead connecting rods. There is another alternative that is actually less expensive and stronger than boxing the stock flathead connecting rods. Luke's Custom Machine & Design has a source for custom "H" beam connecting rods. These quality 4340 forged steel connecting rods are the stock 7.00″ length (center to center). The bronze bushings are the stock flathead diameter, and the big end is 2.125″ diameter for use with the Clevite 77 #CB-610P small block Buick V-6 and V-8 connecting rod bearings. The crankshaft connecting rod journals must be turned down to 2.00″ diameter in order to use these connecting rods. The 12-point cap screw bolts are 8740 steel, ⅜″ diameter, and 190,000 psi rated. These connecting rods have been Magnafluxed, shot peened, and stress relieved. They are fitted with dowel alignment sleeves to ensure precise connecting rod cap alignment. All this for the affordable price of $500 for a set of connecting rods.

The average weight of the custom "H" beam connecting rod is 642 grams. There is a lot of material above the wrist pin bushing that could be removed in order to lighten these connecting rods to approximately the same weight as the #8BA6205A connecting rods. The addition of heavy metal (Mallory metal) to the crankshaft for balancing purposes is avoided if the connecting rods are lightened.

The top-of-the-line and most exotic connecting rods available for the Ford flathead V-8 engine are those custom manufactured by Crower Cams & Equipment or Cunningham Rods. You will have to indenture your children in order to pay for them!

The 1949-53 Mercury #6303 crankshaft connecting rod journals can be offset ground 0.0625″ and then reduced in diameter from 2.138″–2.139″ to 1.9985″, resulting in a 4⅛″ (4.125″) stroke. The 1942 Ford #21A-6200 full-floating connecting rods for the small journal diameter (1.998″ to 1.999″) can then be used. Many of the pre-1942 Ford connecting rods were designed with the small journal size; however, the model 21A connecting rod is considered the strongest of that type.

These are the "H" beam connecting rods available through Luke's. Connecting rods such as these should be used for a blown Ardun or one that is going to be used for all-out racing.

Here is a 1942 Ford #21A-6200 full-floating connecting rod. There are no tang (tab) notches in the connecting rod and cap bearing surface, indicating this assembly is for full-floating bearings.

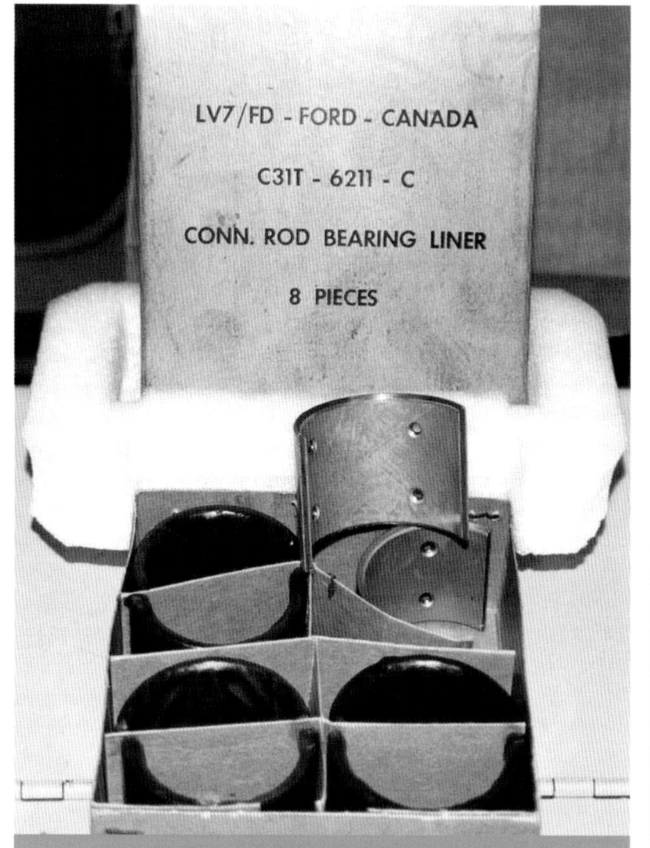

Here is a NOS (new-old-stock) set of Canadian Ford Military flathead V-8 small-journal full-floating connecting rod bearings.

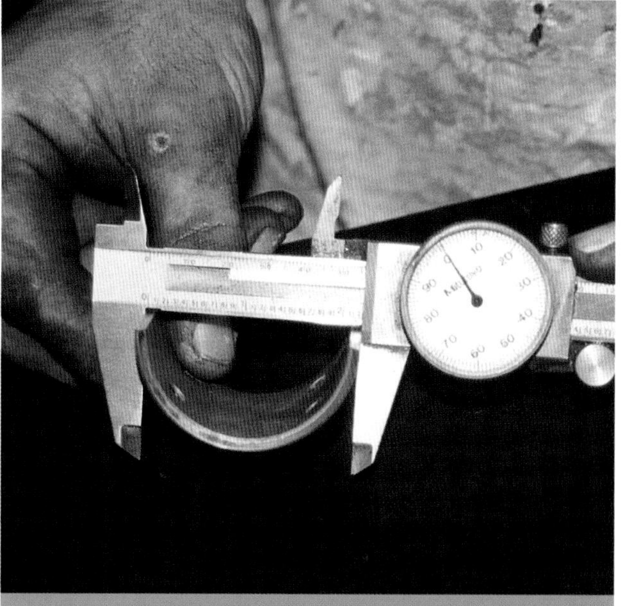

The outside diameter of a full-floating connecting rod bearing is being measured with a micrometer in order to find the spread of the bearing. The spread for a small-journal full-floating connecting rod bearing should be 2.2127" to 2.2130".

The bearing side width being checked. The width of the connecting rod journal is measured with an inside micrometer, the width of the bearing is measured (as shown), and the difference between these two measurements is the bearing side clearance. Incidentally, those are the hands of "Tony the Australian sheepherder."

This is how the "spread" (end width) is increased with full-floating bearings. The bearing is laid flat on a block of wood, and the center of the back of the bearing is tapped with a rubber mallet. Very hi-tech!

This is how the spread of the bearing is decreased. One end of the bearing is placed on a block of wood, held by one hand (not shown for clarity purposes), and the other end is tapped with a rubber mallet.

The 1942 Mercury model 19A is the next choice if the model 21A connecting rods are not available. Lots of full-floating connecting rods are around today and they should be reasonably priced. The average weight of a #21A-6200 connecting rod is 474 grams and the diameter of the "big end" (crankshaft end) is 2.2195″ to 2.220″.

For Magnafluxing and shot peening; aligning, re-sizing and re-bushing; and de-beaming, refer to Section I.

This picture shows the full-floating connecting rod bearings installed on the crankshaft with one connecting rod attached to one of the journals.

Connecting Rod Bearings

If the 1949-53 Mercury #6303 crankshaft connecting rod journals are offset ground, resulting in the 4⅛″ (4.125″) stroke, full-floating connecting rod bearings must be used with the 1942 Ford #21A-6200 connecting rods. It is my understanding that Clevite 77 (Michigan Bearings) and Federal Mogul no longer produce this type of flathead connecting rod bearing. If this is the case, then the only sources for NOS (new-old-stock) full-floating connecting rod bearings are automotive stores such as Egge Parts House, JobLot Automotive, or an ogre hoarding things. Hit the Internet and the telephone and pray a lot! The crankshaft used in the engine in this section had a 4⅛″ (4.125″) stroke and was in very good condition, although the connecting rod journals required some minor cleanup. Luke's just happened to have a set of NOS Canadian Ford Military #631T-6211-C full-floating connecting rod bearings, 0.010″ oversize, on hand.

If you are fortunate enough to obtain some NOS bearings and they are covered in the factory cloth with the protective wax coating, soak the bearings in hot water for a few minutes. The wax coating and the cloth will then be easily removed. Once again, my thanks to Tom Hood for this worldly advice, especially after I have wasted hours removing the stupid stuff with lacquer thinner, grease remover, and solvent!

The installation of full-floating connecting rod bearings in a Ford flathead V-8 is not as simple as the installation of the non-floating connecting rod bearings. Three important measurements that must be performed to ensure the proper bearing clearance. The first is the clearance between the bearing and the connecting rod journal, which should be 0.0015″

to 0.0035″. The second clearance is between the big end of the connecting rod and the bearing, which should also be 0.0015″ to 0.0035″. The final clearance to check is the bearing side width with the width of the connecting rod journal, which should be 0.005″ to 0.015″ less than the journal.

In order to find the "spread" (end width) of a full-floating connecting rod bearing, measure the outside diameter of the bearing with a micrometer. The spread for a small journal full-floating connecting rod bearing should be 2.2127″ to 2.2130″. This procedure also ensures the bearing is round and not out of shape.

There is a crude but effective method of adjusting the spread of the connecting rod bearings. If there is not enough spread, place the bearing with both ends flat on a block of wood and tap the center back of the bearing with a rubber mallet. If there is too much spread, place one end of the bearing on a block of wood and tap the other end with a rubber mallet. This is definitely "mickey mouse" engine building, but it works! If machine shop personal adjust the spread using this procedure, they should not do it when the engine's owner is present. If the owner ever saw this, he will think they have gone wacko and will probably grab his engine and run off into the sunset!

One important item that you must watch when installing bearings, whether they are the main bearings or the connecting rod bearings, is the tang (tab). It is not unusual to find bearings where the tang is too wide for the slot in the main bearing bores or the connecting rod. On some rare occasions the thickness of the tang is excessive, which pushes the bearing outward. This situation will result in the immediate destruction of the bearing when the engine is initially started.

Pistons

The Ford flathead V-8 engine with a 3³⁄₁₆″ (3.1875″) bore, 3¾″ (3.750″) stroke, and stock pistons used with the Ardun aluminum cylinder heads resulted in a 6.06:1 compression ratio. If the same engine was used and Ardun #1107 (A1) low dome racing pistons were substituted, the compression ratio was 8.85:1. If the Ardun #1101 (A2) high dome racing pistons were used, an 11.6:1 compression ratio was realized.

A used set of the Ardun #1102 (A2) high dome, 12.3:1 compression ratio, cast aluminum pistons was discovered in the bowels of Luke's shop. These pistons were for a stock 3³⁄₁₆″ (3.1875″) bore and a 4.00″ stroke, and they are the three piston ring design with ⁵⁄₆₄″ top and second compression ring width and ⁵⁄₃₂″ width oil ring. Cast on the inside of these pistons was: "J.E.," "141," and "X." The wrist pin is of the taper-wall design, 2.850″ length, and 0.750″ diameter. Each piston weighed 447 grams, and each wrist pin weighed 80 grams. The stock Ford #6140 wire-type wrist pin retainers were used.

The pistons used in the engine in this section are manufactured by Ross Racing Pistons using forged 2618 T-61 aluminum and have a slightly raised flat top. The pistons are the three-ring design and weigh 287 grams. The wrist pins are chrome moly straight-wall steel weighing 120 grams. Double Spiro Lox retainers (the ultimate) are supplied with the pistons.

The pistons for an Ardun engine, custom made by Ross Racing Pistons, will allow just about any compression ratio to be achieved. Simply supply Ross with all your engine details (bore, stroke, connecting rod length, camshaft specifications, valve sizes, cylinder head volume, carburetor cfm,

These are original Ardun #1102 (A2) high dome cast aluminum pistons with taper wall wrist pins. Compare these with the Ross Racing Pistons and you will see how far technology has come in 50 years.

These are the Ross Racing Pistons for the Ardun engine in this section. These pistons are for a 3⁵⁄₁₆" bore and 4⅛" stroke and are designed for an 8.5:1 compression ratio. The pistons rings are a Total Seal #CR7124-10 classic conventional street set with a ductile iron moly coated top ring. This complete setup is the best value for your money and is perfect for a street performance Ardun engine.

This picture shows a Ross piston installed in order to check the clearance of the lower edge of the piston from the deck. The clearance was 0.010".

etc.), and they will manufacture the pistons accordingly. The engine in this section will have an 8.5:1 compression ratio. The maximum compression ratio a street performance Ardun engine will tolerate using today's highest-octane unleaded gasoline is approximately 9.5:1. Not all areas of North America have good 94-octane unleaded gasoline; hence, the 8.5:1 compression ratio.

The piston rings Ross Racing Pistons supplies are the Total Seal #CR7124-10 classic conventional street set consisting of metric rings. The top piston rings are ductile iron moly coated, the second rings are cast iron, and the oil rings are standard tension. The top piston ring groove width is 1.5 mm, the second piston ring groove width is 1.5 mm, and the oil ring groove width is 3.0 mm. These piston rings are not considered file-fit rings and usually do not require any additional gapping. On most occasions they can be installed as they come out of the box. However, these piston rings did require gapping for the engine being described in this section of the book. Closely adhere to Total Seal's instructions for checking the piston ring gap. For the engine being described in this section of the book, that is: top ring 0.015", second ring 0.012", and oil ring 0.015".

After the engine block is parallel decked, and prior to balancing the rotating assembly, the height of the lower edge of the Ross piston just below the top must be checked to ensure it is below the height of the deck and therefore does not protrude into the combustion chamber of the cylinder head. This is an extremely critical measurement and it must be carried out accurately. The lower edge of the top of the Ross piston must be a minimum of 0.010" below the deck. If there is less than this depth, the outer edge of the pistons (approximately ⅛" width) will have to be machined to correct this.

For balancing, refer to Section I.

Gaskets

Fel-Pro produces a complete gasket set for the 1949-53 Ford or Mercury flathead V-8 engine. It is unfortunate that the cylinder head gaskets cannot be used with the Ardun cylinder heads. There is always a "normal flathead" owner around that could use a spare set of head gaskets, so a person might be able to sell them for a huge amount of money!

The well-known Ardun engine builder Cotton Werksman has the Ardun cylinder-head gaskets manufactured by Victor/Reinz, part #GX-13173-1. These superior-design nitroseal head gaskets are graphite-coated, which allows the aluminum cylinder head to slide on the gasket without experiencing leaks. The only drawback to these gaskets is that the maximum cylinder bore size they will accommodate is 3⁵⁄₁₆" (3.3125"). They are available for $100 each from Luke's. Speedway Motors sells a standard style of Ardun cylinder head gaskets, part #910-15891, at $94.95 for a pair.

This is the graphite-coated Ardun cylinder head gasket that Cotton Werksman has manufactured by Victor/Reinz, part #GX-13173-1.

Connecting Rods and Pistons Summary

1942 Ford #6200 forged steel connecting rods; Model Number: 21A; full-floating connecting rod bearings. Connecting rod length: 7.00″. Connecting rod ratio: 1.70 (with 4⅛″ stroke).	$80.00
Connecting rods Magnafluxed, shot peened, aligned, re-sized, and balanced. New Sealed Power (Federal Mogul) #9024VA wrist pin bushings, 0.8125″ o.d., installed allowing for 0.002″ clearance. New Pioneer #CRN-731 connecting rod nuts installed using Loctite and torqued to 45 ft-lb.	$286.85
New Canadian Ford Military #631T-6211-C full-floating connecting rod bearings, 0.010″ oversize, installed allowing for 0.002″ crankshaft and connecting rod clearance and 0.010″ side clearance. Connecting rod bearing spread (end width): 2.2127″.	$180.00
New Ross Racing Pistons forged 2618T-61 aluminum flat top pistons; 8.5:1 compression ratio; 0.125″ (⅛″) oversize; piston weight: 287 grams, each. Full-floating heat treated and case hardened 4340 chrome moly steel straight-wall wrist pins with new Ross Racing Pistons #4004-J double Spiro Lox retainers. Wrist pin diameter: 0.750″; wrist pin length: 2.770″; wrist pin weight: 120 grams. Piston grooves: top ring: 1.5 mm; 2nd ring: 1.5 mm; and oil ring: 3.0 mm. New Total Seal #CR7124-10 classic conventional street, ductile moly top piston ring set, installed within manufacturer's recommended arc. Top ring gap: 0.015″; 2nd ring gap: 0.012″; and oil ring gap: 0.015″.	$646.80
Complete V-8 engine balance.	$190.00
New Fel-Pro #FS7525B complete gasket set installed.	$54.95
CONNECTING RODS AND PISTONS TOTAL:	**$1,438.60**

CHAPTER 24
LUBRICATION SYSTEM

Purchase

The 1949-53 Ford flathead V-8 oil pump is considered to be the best of all the Ford flathead V-8 oil pumps. It will provide sufficient oil volume and should provide a steady 50 to 60 psi of oil pressure for an Ardun street performance engine, even with the added requirement of lubricating the Ardun overhead valve mechanism. A new Melling #M-19 standard volume replacement oil pump will be used in the engine in this section.

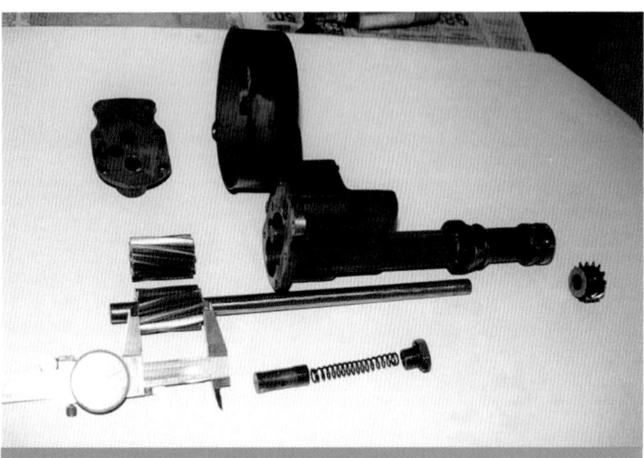

A 1949-51 Lincoln V-8 #8EL-6621-B oil pump has been disassembled, showing all the internal parts and the #8EL-6622-B oil pump cover and inlet tube attached. The gears are taller than the 1949-53 Ford flathead V-8 oil pump gears.

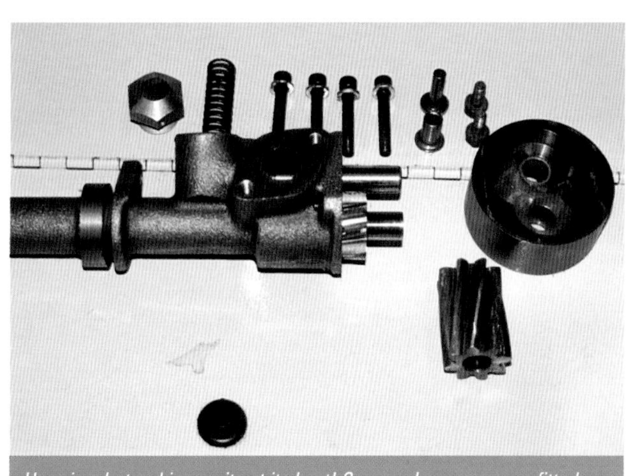

Here is a hot rod ingenuity at its best! Some unknown person fitted 1949-51 Lincoln V-8 oil pump gears in a 1949-53 Ford #6603 standard volume oil pump and then machined the extension piece, that acts as the gear cover. First class!

In years gone by, Ardun owners used the 1949-51 Lincoln V-8 #8EL-6621-B oil pump and the #8EL-6622-B oil pump cover and inlet tube, which provided sufficient oil pressure and volume at all engine speeds. The gears in the Lincoln V-8 oil pump are taller than the gears in the stock Ford flathead V-8 oil pump. The Lincoln oil pump by-pass spring was stretched to give the oil pump 60 lbs. of pressure. If you use a Lincoln V-8 oil pump, you will have to modify the stock Ford flathead V-8 oil pan in order to clear it. You could still use a Lincoln V-8 oil pump today if you could locate a new one. Dream on!

A unique oil pump was recently discovered at Luke's Custom Machine & Design. Some unknown party fitted 1949-51 Lincoln V-8 oil pump gears and shafts into a standard volume 1949-53 Ford flathead V-8 oil pump. Then an extension piece was machined for the housing that also acts as the gear cover. Very ingenious and nicely done!

Some Ardun owners may well believe a high-volume oil pump is a necessity for their engine. Such pumps are manufactured by Melling, part #M-15, or Pioneer, part #OP-15, and they are available from your local automotive parts outlet. A high-volume oil pump only provides a larger volume of oil, not an increase in the oil pressure, and it takes power away from the engine output in order to turn it. The stock 1949-53 Ford passenger car and truck oil pans usually have to be modified in order to accommodate a high-volume oil pump.

You should check the clearance between the gears and the top cover of the oil pump. This clearance should be 0.00025″ without the gasket and is accomplished by either sanding the top of the housing on a piece of thick glass if there is excessive clearance or sanding the gears on a piece of thick glass if the clearance is not adequate. After you have correctly clearanced the oil pump, thoroughly clean it, apply some motor oil to the gears, reinstall the top cover gasket using silicone sealant, and torque the bolts to 80 in-lb using Loctite.

Oil Pan and Pick-up

The best oil pans to use for a street performance Ardun engine are the 1949-53 Mercury passenger car and the 1949-53 Ford Truck models with a four-quart capacity (five quarts with the large oil filter). These oil pans have the sump at the rear. The Mercury model has a built-in oil baffle. Try to locate one of these oil pans with the matching oil pump pick-up tube and screen. The Mercury oil pump pick-up tube and screen has an attached baffle. After cleaning the pick-up tube assembly and screen filter, bolt the assembly to

This photograph shows the aluminum frame rails for an Ardun oil pan being milled at Luke's. Check the date.

The 1949-53 Mercury four-quart-capacity oil pan with the factory-installed internal baffle is a very good oil pan to use for a street performance flathead or Ardun engine. The present condition of this oil pan would make it extremely suitable as a feeding trough for livestock!

Here are the three sections that make up the custom Ardun oil pan fabricated by Luke's. This minor project represents at least 100 hours of labor!

The 1949-53 Ford Truck aluminum plate with the dust seal attached is held in place at the two rear oil pan holes with two extended bolts.

the oil pump body using silicone sealant on the gasket and torque the two bolts to 80 in-lb using Loctite. Install the oil pump with a stainless steel 5⁄16″ N.C. x 1″-length bolt and lock washer using Loctite torqued to 15 ft-lb.

Some of the 1949-53 Ford Truck #6675 oil pans had a round plate on the bottom, which could be removed for a bottom end inspection. There is one gasket inside the oil pan and one gasket outside the oil pan. These gaskets are not included in the Fel-Pro #FS7525B complete gasket set. You will have to fabricate your own using high-quality gasket material. Purchase stainless steel hardware when re-installing the plate: seven pieces of 5⁄16″ N.F. nylocks and seven pieces of AN flat washers.

This photo shows the three sections of Luke's oil pan fitted together. They have not been welded yet. This oil pan and timing gear cover are fitted with a Chevrolet big-block one-piece oil seal, another one of Luke Balogh's innovations. The engine block and water pumps have been beautifully detailed. A gorgeous start to an Ardun engine!

The 1949-53 Ford Truck oil pans came equipped with an aluminum plate that had a rubber dust seal attached. This plate was attached to the two rear oil pan holes, and the seal made contact with the starting motor plate. The 1949-53 Ford passenger cars motors came equipped with the Ford #6411 rubber dust seal that was attached to the upper edge of the starting motor plate. These two different seals are not included in the Fel-Pro #FS7525B gasket set, which is a pity, because these seals actually worked!

If an Ardun engine is to be used for drag racing or salt flat racing, then a larger capacity oil pan should be used. Luke's fabricates a beautiful seven-quart capacity (eight quarts with the large oil filter) oil pan from aluminum. This oil pan is made in sections and then welded together. The oil pan rails are welded together with 2″-square aluminum stock and then milled and drilled. The sides consist of nine pieces of sheet aluminum welded together. The bottom is a 1″-thick two-piece aluminum plate that has fins milled into it. The three sections are welded together, and then the entire unit is polished. A Chevrolet big-block front one-piece oil seal and a Chevrolet small-block rear two-piece oil seal were incorporated into this oil pan design. This is a totally spectacular oil pan and represents over 100 hours of labor!

If a Lincoln V-8 oil pump or a custom oil pan is used, the oil pump pick-up tube and screen assembly will have to be modified for clearance with the oil pan. The proper oil pan-to-pick-up tube and screen assembly clearance should be ¾″ to 1″.

Here is a 1949-53 Ford Truck oil pan with the bottom-end inspection plate installed. I guess you reached in there to pull out all the debris after the engine blew up!

The photograph shows the rear oil seal retainer installed, behind the rear main bearing, and the oil pump idler gear cover installed below it.

When the 1949-53 Ford #6754 dipstick tube and the 1949-53 Ford #6750 dipstick are installed, they protrude outward from the oil pan to the center of the exhaust tube for #7 cylinder. The Ford dipstick is not flexible, so the dipstick tube cannot be bent to clear the exhaust tube. The solution for this problem is to use a Weatherhead

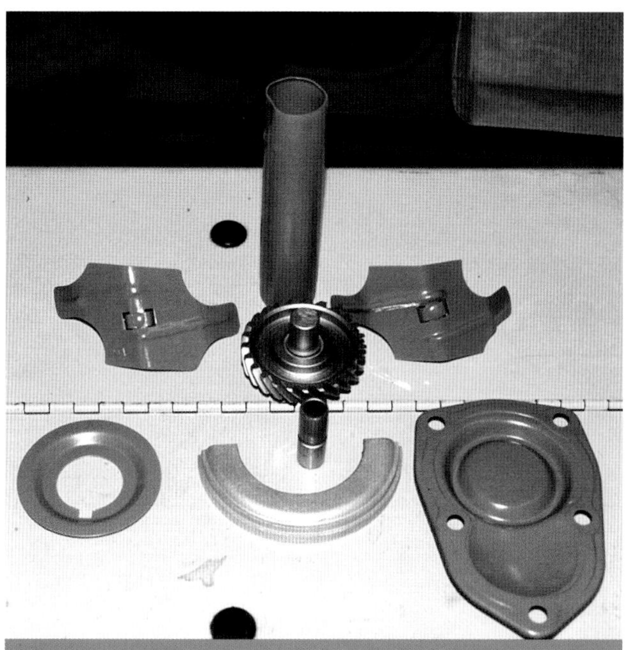

Here are the Ford #6524 valve lifter gallery oil return hole baffles (2), Ford #6756 valve lifter gallery crankcase breather tube, Ford #6310 crankshaft oil slinger, and a Ford #6658 oil pump idler gear cover all painted with Glyptal #G-1228A medium grey gloss enamel. There is also a Ford #6655 oil pump idler gear, Ford #6657 oil pump idler gear bushing, Ford #6656 oil pump idler gear shaft, Ford #6025 fuel pump pushrod bushing, and a Ford #8BA-6335 rear upper oil seal retainer. They are all ready for an Ardun engine.

#202-6 brass adapter, ⅜" tube to ½" N.P.T, and re-thread the ½" N.P.T end of the fitting using a ½" N.F. die. The fitting will now screw into the Ford #6751 dipstick tube boss. Polish the brass fitting and install it in the dipstick tube boss using silicone sealant. Use a piece of Summit Racing Equipment #220238 stainless steel tubing, ⅜" o.d. x 11½" length, for the new dipstick tube. Double flare one end of the stainless steel tubing, polish it, and bend it using a tubing bender in order to clear the #7 cylinder exhaust pipe. Install the new dipstick tube in the oil pan boss with a Weatherhead #100-6 polished brass inverted flare nut using silicone sealant. Purchase a Trans-Dapt #4958 chrome big-block Chevrolet dipstick, cut the dipstick to length, and notch the "full" level on the dipstick using a hacksaw. You now have an aristocratic means of checking the oil level!

For information on the oil pump idler gear, fuel pump pushrod bushing, and the baffles and breather tube, refer to Section I.

Oil Filter

There is no room to install an oil filter on the cylinder heads of an Ardun engine, so you will have to install a remote oil filter bracket. The Trans-Dapt #1045 remote oil filter bracket, with horizontal inlets and outlets, or the Trans-Dapt #1028 remote oil filter bracket, with vertical inlet and outlet, will be required. These units accommodate the Fram #PH8A oil filter (Ford), or you might want to use the Moroso #22400 chrome oil filter.

Here is the stainless steel rocker arm/pushrod lubrication line for the left (driver's side) cylinder head that was fabricated by Luke's. The two "collars" are attached to the two cylinder head/valve cover studs, and the forward end of the line is supported by a metal bracket. The 0.080" holes in the line spray oil on the ends of the rocker arms and pushrods.

These are polished brass oil line fittings at the rear of the Ardun engine block in this section. The single fitting on the left is the pressure-out line to the inlet side of the oil filter. The center double "T" fitting will connect the oil lines to the cylinder heads and an oil pressure gauge. The 90-degree assembly on the right is for the drain-back line from the outlet side of the oil filter. Amazingly enough, everything fits!

The Trans-Dapt #1032 and #1047 neoprene oil filter hoses are fitted with push-on brass fittings, so they can be removed and the hoses cut to the exact length required. The ability to do this allows for a tidy installation without the oil filter hoses being draped over the engine. Another ace detailing touch!

Rocker Arm and Pushrod Lubrication

Contained in the Ardun conversion kit was an oil line system used to lubricate the rocker arms and the ends of the pushrods. A "T" fitting was installed in the rear of the engine block, and lines were then plumbed to the back of the cylinder heads to feed the rocker arm shafts in each cylinder head and spray each of the ends of the pushrods. A drain-back line was installed from the bottom of each cylinder head to the upper section of the oil pan. One of the problems encountered with the original oiling system was that the spray bars that lubricated the pushrod ends were not secured properly. Copper lines of 1/8" o.d. were used for providing the oil to the pushrods.

Luke's fabricates four "collars" for each of the two cylinder head/valve cover studs. They slide over the cylinder head studs and are secured in place with socket head set screws. The 3/16" o.d. stainless steel tubing is passed through the collars and supported at the forward end by a metal

This is the pushrod/rocker arm lubrication line for the right (passenger's side) side of the Ardun engine designed by Luke's.

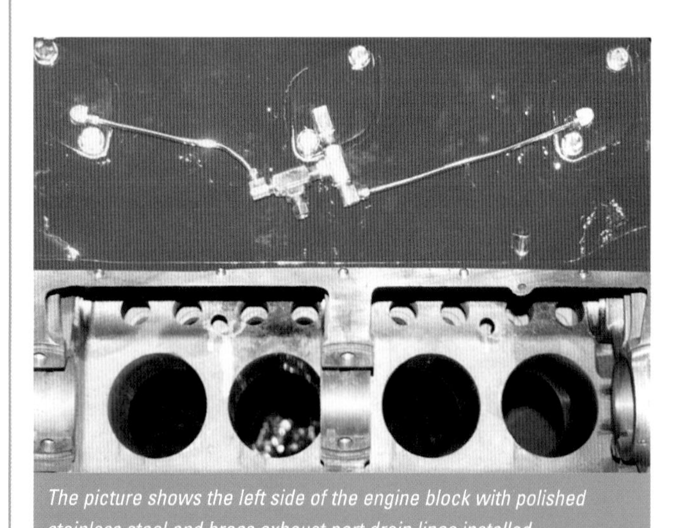

The picture shows the left side of the engine block with polished stainless steel and brass exhaust port drain lines installed.

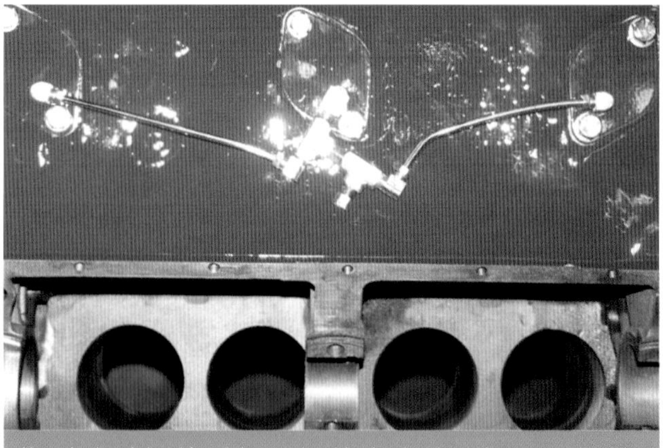

Here is the right side of the engine block with the exhaust port drain lines installed. I designed and assembled this setup for Luke's Custom Machine & Design. I am now giving serious thought to renewing all the plumbing in my house using polished stainless steel and brass!

bracket. There are 0.080″ holes drilled in the stainless steel tubing so they shoot oil at each of the eight rocker arm and pushrod ends in each cylinder head. One end of the stainless steel tubing is welded closed, and the other end attaches to the oil feed line. This is a very simple, neat, and functional oiling system.

In order to restrict the volume of oil being fed to the cylinder heads, Luke's "turns down" a pair of Holley 0.054″ carburetor jets in a lathe so they fit in the pipe thread end of the Weatherhead #202-3 adapters, 3/16″ tube to 1/8″ N.P.T These are the brass fittings that screw into the "T" fitting at the rear of the engine block.

Exhaust Port Drain Lines

The stock Ford flathead V-8 valve guides are not installed in the Ardun engine due to the use of pushrods. The absence of the valve guides permits oil to accumulate in the exhaust ports of the engine block (not the cylinder head exhaust ports) behind the Ardun #1203 exhaust port block-off plates. In order to rectify this problem, Luke's installs a drain line from the exhaust port block-off plates back to the top of the oil pan. A nifty touch!

The exhaust port block-off plates are drilled and tapped at the lowest corner of each exhaust port for 1/8″ N.P.T fittings, 3/16″ o.d. stainless steel tubing is connected to the fittings, and the lines are then plumbed to the upper center of each side of the oil pan. Summit Racing Equipment sells the 3/16″ stainless steel tubing in 20-foot lengths, part #SUM-220236. The exhaust port drain lines, the rocker arm lubrication, and the oil feed lines to the cylinder heads require the use of almost 12″ of 3/16″ o.d. stainless steel tubing.

Lubrication System Summary

New stainless steel 3/8″ N.P.T plug (Ford #6026), front oil gallery line plug, installed using Permatex aviation form-a-gasket. Ford #6025 fuel pump pushrod bushing oil hole brazed closed. Ford #6657 oil pump idler gear bushing installed with Ford #6655 oil pump idler gear and Ford #6656 oil pump idler gear shaft allowing for 0.002″ clearance. Ford #6658 oil pump idler gear cover installed with Ford #22507 oil pump idler gear cover bolts and lock washers using Loctite and torqued to 80 in-lb with stainless steel safety wire. Oil pump idler gear cover gasket installed using silicone sealant. Inside of oil pump idler gear cover, Ford #6756 valve lifter gallery crankcase breather tube, and Ford #6524 valve lifter gallery oil return hole baffles (2), painted with Glyptal #G-1228A medium grey gloss enamel.	$153.43
New Melling #M-19 standard volume oil pump (for 1949-53 Ford) installed with 1949-53 Ford Truck #6615 oil pump cover and inlet tube; Ford #6623 oil pump cover screen; and Ford #6628 oil pump cover screen spring retainer. Oil pump end clearance: 0.00025″. Oil pump cover and inlet tube gasket installed using silicone sealant and bolts torqued to 80 in-lb using Loctite. 1949-53 Ford #8BA-6335 rear upper oil seal retainer installed. Rear oil seal packings (Ford #6700) soaked in SAE 30 Wt. motor oil and installed. New Speedway Motors #912-S12853 front one-piece oil seal installed using silicone sealant.	$169.10
1949-53 Ford Truck #6675 oil pan, four quart capacity, installed with new stainless steel bolts, lock washers, and AN flat washers using Loctite and torqued to 15 ft-lb. Gaskets installed using silicone sealant. Luke's new custom dipstick tube fabricated using Summit Racing Equipment #220238 polished stainless steel tubing, 3/8″ o.d. x 11½″ length, new Weatherhead #202-6 polished brass adapter, 3/8″ tube to ½″ N.P.T, and new Weatherhead #100-6 polished brass inverted flare nut, 3/8″ tube. Fittings installed using silicone sealant. New Trans-Dapt #4958 chrome dipstick installed. Three oil return line fittings welded in the side of the oil pan. Oil pan glass beaded and painted with Endura #EX-2C black 160 hi-gloss polyurethane. Engine lubricated with six quarts Penzoil HD-30 Wt. motor oil.	$214.07

New Trans-Dapt #1028 polished remote oil filter bracket with vertical inlet/outlet; new Moroso #22400 chrome oil filter; and new Trans-Dapt #1047 neoprene rubber oil filter hoses, 3′ length ½″ N.P.T installed using pipe thread sealant. Oil filter lines and cylinder head lubrication lines installed using:

- New Weatherhead #44-8 polished brass compression fitting, ½″ tube to ⅜″ N.P.T ("pressure out" line).
- New Weatherhead #3220-8-2 polished brass reducer, ½″ N.P.T to ⅛″ N.P.T
- New Weatherhead #3325-2 polished brass male coupling, ⅜″ N.P.T
- New Weatherhead 3600-2 polished brass "T" fittings, ⅛″ N.P.T
- New Weatherhead #3300-2 polished brass female coupling, ⅛″ N.P.T
- Oil line restrictors installed using new Holley 0.054″ carburetor jets.
- New Weatherhead #202-3 polished brass adapters, 3/16″ tube to ⅛″ N.P.T
- New Weatherhead #105-3 brass inverted flare nuts, 3/16″ tube.
- New Weatherhead #41-3 polished brass compression fittings, 3/16″ tube.
- New Summit Racing Equipment #220236 polished stainless steel tubing, 3/16″ o.d. x 4′ length ("pressure out" line to cylinder heads and oil pressure gauge).
- New Weatherhead #3200-8-6 polished brass reducer, ½″ N.P.T to ⅜″ N.P.T
- New Weatherhead #3326-6 male coupling, ⅜″ N.P.T
- New Weatherhead #3300-6 polished brass female coupling, ⅜″ N.P.T
- New Weatherhead #3400-6 polished brass 90-degree elbow, ⅜″ N.P.T
- New Weatherhead #44-8 polished brass compression coupling, ½″ tube to ⅜″ N.P.T ("drain back" line). $89.76

Ardun #1203 exhaust port block-off plates painted with PPG #74000 red hi-gloss polyurethane and installed with new stainless steel bolts and lock washers using silicone sealant on gaskets and torqued to 25 ft-lb. Exhaust port block-off plate oil drain system installed using:

- New Weatherhead #402-3 polished brass 90-degree elbows, 3/16″ tube to ⅛″ N.P.T
- New Weatherhead #3400-2 polished brass 90-degree elbows, ⅛″ N.P.T
- New Weatherhead #3326-2 male connectors, ⅛″ N.P.T
- New Weatherhead #3300-2 female connectors, ⅛″ N.P.T
- New Weatherhead #3700-2 polished brass "T" fittings, ⅛″ N.P.T
- New Weatherhead #202-3 polished brass adapters, 3/16″ tube to ⅛″ N.P.T
- New Weatherhead #105-3 polished brass inverted flare nuts, 3/16″ tube.
- New Summit Racing Equipment #SUM-220236 polished stainless steel tubing, 3/16″ o.d. x 2′ length. $114.20

Cylinder head oil drain lines fabricated using new Weatherhead #66-6 polished brass compression fitting, ⅜″ tube to ½″ N.P.T; new Weatherhead #3220-4-2 polished brass reducer, ½″ N.P.T to ⅛″ N.P.T, new Weatherhead #402-6-2 polished brass 90-degree elbow, ⅛″ N.P.T to ⅜″ tube; and new Summit Racing Equipment #220238 polished stainless steel tubing, ⅜″ o.d. x 3′ length. $183.42

Luke's new pushrod/rocker arm lubrication system installed with new Summit Racing Equipment #220236 stainless steel tubing, 3/16″ o.d. x 5′ length; new Weatherhead #41-3 brass compression fittings, 3/16″ tube; and new Weatherhead #60-3 brass ferrules, 3/16″ i.d. All fittings installed using pipe thread sealant. $197.16

LUBRICATION SYSTEM TOTAL: $1,121.14

CHAPTER 25
CAMSHAFT AND CYLINDER HEADS

For information on camshaft bearings, refer to Section I.

Camshaft

The stock Ford flathead V-8 camshaft is not suitable for use in a street performance Ardun engine. An example of this camshaft would be the 1949-51 Ford #6250 passenger car model. This has an advertised duration of 229 degrees intake and 231 degrees exhaust. Lobe separation angle is 111 degrees. Valve lift is 0.293″ (0.3348″ net lift with 1.2 ratio rocker arms) intake and 0.289″ (0.3252″ net lift with 1.2 ratio rocker arms) exhaust. Valve overlap is 8 degrees, and valve lash (hot) is 0.014″ intake and 0.018″ exhaust. This camshaft is very "mild" and does not encourage the full potential of an Ardun engine. During the 1950s, racers such as Don Clark and Clem Tebow of C & T Automotive in California found that a re-ground 1932 Ford flathead V-8 steel billet camshaft was the best to use in an Ardun racing engine for added strength and endurance. The only year Ford produced a steel billet camshaft for their flatheads was 1932.

Just because an Ardun is an OHV engine does not mean you have to go bananas when choosing a camshaft! The coil binding of the valve springs, the rocker arm geometry, pushrod clearance within the cylinder heads and engine block, and rocker arm clearance with the valve spring retainers must be seriously considered. A few camshaft manufacturers produced a limited variety of camshafts for the Ardun engine in the 1950s. The technology used to choose a camshaft today far exceeds the technology that was available in the early 1950s.

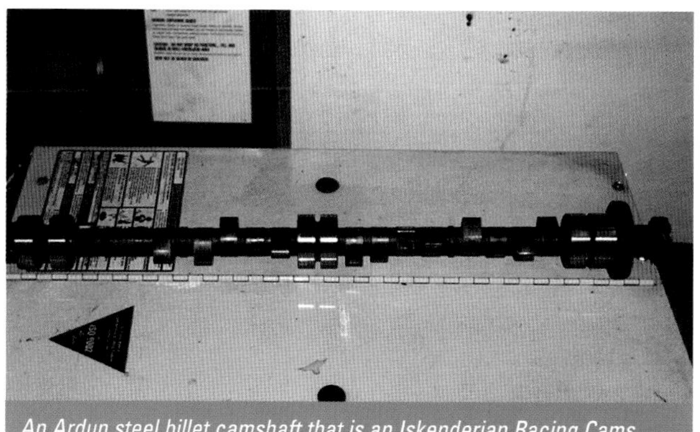

An Ardun steel billet camshaft that is an Iskenderian Racing Cams Crossflow 1 "track grind" model ("Crower X3667" is also stamped on it). This camshaft had an advertised duration of 265 degrees intake and exhaust; net valve lift of 0.318″ intake and exhaust; lobe separation angle of 114.5 degrees; overlap of 36 degrees; and valve lash (hot) of 0.018″ intake and exhaust. Definitely a rare bird!

Here is the Crower Cams & Equipment Ardun Special street-grind camshaft with an advertised duration of 268 degrees intake and exhaust; duration @ 0.050″ lift: 227 degrees intake and exhaust; lobe separation angle: 110 degrees; net valve lift: 0.398″ intake and exhaust. This is a great street camshaft for a naturally aspirated Ardun engine.

Although it is a little hard to see clearly, this photo shows the "dot" on the camshaft gear and the "dot" on the crankshaft gear vertically in line with each other. The camshaft can now be degreed in order to ensure all the specifications are correct.

The camshaft is the heart of an Ardun engine; therefore, the proper camshaft selection for this engine is an absolute must. Once again, Crower Cams & Equipment came to the rescue. The camshaft they recommended has an advertised duration of 268 degrees intake and exhaust, and duration @ 0.050″ lift: 227 degrees intake and exhaust. Net valve lift is 0.398″ intake and 0.398″ exhaust (based on 1.2 ratio rocker arms); lobe separation angle is 110 degrees. The price of this Ardun camshaft is outright with no core exchange.

Camshaft Interchange

Refer to Section I, Chapter 5, regarding camshaft interchange, before considering installing a 1932 Ford flathead V-8 camshaft in a 1946-53 Ford flathead V-8 engine.

Adapters are available for the front of a 1946-48 flathead camshaft in order to use it in a 1949-53 flathead block with the 1949-53 Ford flathead V-8 distributor. These adapters bolt to the nose of the 1946-48 flathead camshaft, and then the 1949-53 camshaft/distributor drive gear is pressed on. Luke's is one of the companies that manufactures this item at a cost of $50.

For information on degreeing the camshaft, refer to Section I.

Valve Lifters

The Ardun Engine Company originally produced two types of solid lifters (or tappets or cam followers) for their engine. The first design was similar in size to the stock Ford flathead V-8 engine solid lifters, except the upper 20% portion of the lifter was reduced to approximately half the diameter. The later model was of the taller "milk bottle" shape. Due to their shorter length, the first design lifters usually introduced pushrod-to-valve guide boss interference when used with aftermarket higher lift camshafts.

The Ardun #1024 milk bottle-shape solid lifters are non-adjustable, manufactured with high tensile nickel-chromium molybdenum steel, 3.260″ length, weigh 100 grams each, and have the same stock 1.00″ diameter as the solid lifters in the Ford flathead V-8 engine. These lifters are of good quality and will be used in the engine described in this section. Only Ardun Enterprises produces an exact replacement lifter for the stock Ardun lifter. If the Ardun lifters have been used (and they most likely have been), the bases should be re-faced by a reputable camshaft company, for a minimal fee. The milk bottle-shape lifters should be carefully checked for cracks in the pushrod seat cup.

If the Ardun solid lifters are used with a steel billet camshaft, they should have their bases hard chromed. Otherwise, they will gall and score, resulting in camshaft failure. The camshaft being provided by Crower Cams & Equipment is a standard cast iron alloy flathead camshaft that will work quite well with the stock Ardun solid lifters. Hard chroming lifters for use with today's camshafts could probably cause more problems than would be solved due to the incompatibility of different metals.

The Schubreck Racing Engine Products "diamond hard" radius lifters, for use in an Ardun engine, were previously mentioned in Section I, Chapter 5. These lifters, along with the custom Chevrolet small-block journal camshaft, are not required for a street performance Ardun engine.

The Ardun #1024 milk bottle-shape solid lifters are hollow bodied and weigh 100 grams each. These are just about the weirdest looking lifters you will ever see!

These Ardun #1024 milk bottle-shape solid lifters have just been returned from having their bases re-faced and a general tune-up. They look like new.

Valves and Valve Seat Inserts

The stock Ardun #1062 intake valves were referred to as "tulip" shaped with a head diameter of 1⅞″ (1.875″), a stem diameter of ⅜″ (0.375″), 4.875″ overall length, and a weight of 122 grams each. The Ardun intake valves should be taken to a competent machine shop in order to reduce the head size to 1¾″ (1.75″), which will result in a weight of 115 grams each. The stock Ardun #1063 exhaust valves were also referred to as "tulip" shaped with a head diameter of 1½″ (1.50″), a stem diameter of ⅜″ (0.375″), 4.695″ overall length, and a weight of 103 grams each. The exhaust valves were austenitic, defined as "a non-magnetic solid solution of ferric carbide or carbon in iron, used in making corrosion-resistant steel." This was named after Sir William Chandler Roberts-Austen (1843-1902), a British metallurgist.

The Ardun #1062 intake valves and Ardun #1063 exhaust valves were reported to be ⅛″ (0.125″) diameter too large for the stock Ardun valve seat inserts. Therefore, the valves had to be trimmed to accommodate the valve seat inserts, or the valve seat inserts had to be opened up to fit

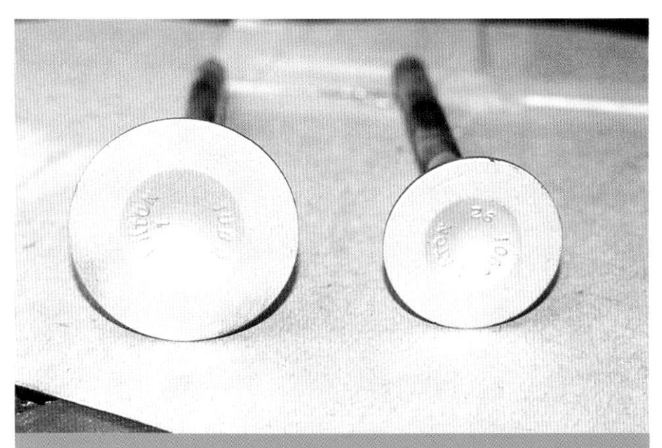

Here is a stock Ardun intake valve with a head diameter of 1⅞" left and 4.785" overall length and a stock Ardun exhaust valve right with a head diameter of 1.50" and 4.60" overall length. The intake valve had "Eaton 1" and "1062" in raised letters on the head, and the exhaust valve had "Eaton 26" and "1063" in raised letters on the head.

This photograph shows a set of Ardun #1062 intake (1¾") and #1063 exhaust (1½") valves. The valve heads and stems have just been polished and are now ready to participate in a Serdi-machined multi-angle blueprint valve grind.

the valves—or both of these options utilized. C & T Automotive recommended the optimum valve size to be 1¾" (1.750") for the intake and 1 13/32" (1.40625") for the exhaust. The stock Ardun #1063 exhaust valve was considered by some racers to be excessively heavy. C & T Automotive suggested a practical weight for the intake valves to be 122 grams and 94 grams for the exhaust valves. The entire stock valvetrain in the Ardun engine was not well matched, which curtailed any high rpm use, especially with trucks. This was probably the first production rev-limiter!

The valves in the Ardun engine described in this section appeared to have been hardly used and were in excellent condition. All the valves were closely inspected for any damage and each entire valve was polished on a lathe prior to being sent out for a Serdi-machined multi-angle blueprint valve grind.

The 1951 Chrysler V-8 hemi 331-ci intake and exhaust valves have been successfully used in the Ardun cylinder heads. The intake valves have a head diameter of 1 13/16" (1.8125"), ⅜" (0.375") diameter stems, and 5.055" overall length. The exhaust valves have a head diameter of 1½" (1.500"), ⅜" (0.375") diameter stems, and 5.055" overall length. The overall length of the Chrysler hemi valves was reduced in order to be similar in length to the stock Ardun valves. A note of caution regarding used Chrysler hemi exhaust valves: The metal in the exhaust valves would appear to crystallize after lengthy use. If a used hemi exhaust valve is placed in a vise and the valve head is hit with a hammer, the head will snap off. Save some serious grief and buy new valves!

Manley Performance Parts can custom make stainless steel valves with the ⅜" stem diameter, 1.75"/1.50" head diameter, and the same overall length as the stock Ardun valves. They have quoted an estimated price of $22 each for Ardun stainless steel Race Master or Race-Flo valves. If, for some reason, an Ardun owner wants to stay with vintage parts, the 1951 Chrysler V-8 hemi 331-ci valves are still available from Egge Parts House. The intake valves are #V1937 at $23 each, and the exhaust valves are part #S1936 at $25 each.

There were a very few reported instances of the stock Ardun #1028 intake valve seat inserts and the stock Ardun #1029 exhaust valve seat inserts coming loose as a result of the different expansion rates between the bronze metal used for the construction of the valve seat inserts and the aluminum material of the cylinder heads. A top-quality machine shop can prevent this from happening.

The stock Ardun valve seats in the cylinder heads described in this section were carefully examined, and all were found to be in apparent good order and condition. As a result, they will remain in the cylinder heads without any modification other than the Serdi-machined multi-angle blueprint valve grind.

A number of different types of replacement valve seat inserts are available. An example would be those manufactured by Snyder Industries, Inc. Their 50000 "nickel" series contains a high nickel content of approximately 41% with the remainder consisting of approximately eight different metals, with iron being the most common. Their 70000 "diamond" series is referred to as "cermat" (similar to ceramic but retains the ability to be machined like metal), and consists of approximately 12 different metals with the most common being iron. A clearance of 0.007″ to 0.008″ is required to press-fit these types of valve seat inserts in aluminum cylinder heads.

The Ardun #1001 cylinder head is fitted with the Ardun #1028 intake and #1029 bronze valve seat inserts. The Ardun #1013 intake and #1014 exhaust bronze valve guides can be seen just below the valve seat inserts.

A Serdi valve grinding machine at work on an intake valve seat in an Ardun cylinder head. This is the ultimate in valve grinding.

In order to obtain the best possible valve grind in today's world, the valves should be installed using a Serdi-machined multi-angle blueprint valve grind. The cylinder heads, valves, and associated valve gear were delivered to High Performance Engines where "T-Bone," the wizard of all cylinder heads, performed his usual magic on them. The cylinder heads used in the engine described in this section were the fourth set of Ardun cylinder heads Serdi-machined by High Performance Engines.

A Serdi valve grinding machine must be "knocked down" in order to perform a multi-angle blueprint valve grind for a Ford flathead V-8 engine block. This procedure is not necessary for OHV cylinder heads, which results in some cost savings. The estimated cost for a Serdi-machined multi-angle blueprint valve grind for 8-cylinder OHV cylinder heads is $135.

Valve Guides

The Ardun #1013 intake valve guides and the Ardun #1014 exhaust valve guides were produced using phosphor bronze material, and they are replaceable. These valve guides are of good quality and can still be used today. If there is excessive clearance between the valve stem and the valve guide, a K-Line #KL1842STA universal length ⅜″ (0.375″) "bronze bullet" valve guide liner can be inserted. These are available from your preferred automotive parts dealer or can be obtained and installed at your local machine shop.

If it is necessary to replace the Ardun valve guides, SI Industries manufactures high-quality bronze replacements, part #VG19220/00 (0.5965″ o.d.; 0.3732″ i.d.; 2.50″ L.).

The Ardun #1014 bronze exhaust valve guide is a very durable item and can be easily repaired or replaced if it is worn.

This photograph shows the Ardun #1013 bronze intake valve guides in the foreground with the Ardun #1071 valve spring seat cup (valve spring washer). The Ardun #1014 bronze exhaust valve guides can be seen in the background.

Here are the original Ardun #1072 outer and Ardun #1073 inner-valve springs with the Ardun valve stem locks. The two tightly wound coils at one end of the valve spring define these as "directional" coils. These were not very good valve springs, even for mild Arduns, but they do make wonderful nostalgic collector items.

If the owner of an Ardun engine would prefer to use 11/32″ stem diameter valves instead of the stock 3/8″ stem diameter valves, the Manley Performance Parts, Inc. #42158 bronze valve guide sleeves can be installed by a machine shop at minimal cost.

Valve Springs

The combination of the stock Ardun #1072 outer valve springs and Ardun #1073 inner valve springs is only suitable for a camshaft lift (not valve lift) of up to 0.285″, which is really pushing the margin of safety. Any lift over that results in the stock outer and inner valve springs binding, causing fatigue, which will eventually lead to the valve springs breaking. There should be a minimum of 0.060″, preferably 0.100″, clearance between the valve spring coils, with the valves in their fully open position. In order to establish the parameters for replacement valve springs, it was first necessary to determine the o.d. and i.d. of the stock Ardun inner and outer valve springs, as well as the installed height. The intensive search for this information was almost futile. Fortunately, Luke's had a stock set of Ardun valve springs, which enabled me to approach Bud Child of High Performance Engines with a request to measure the set of stock Ardun inner and outer valve springs. This resulted in the following information:

	Outer Spring	Inner Spring
Overall length	2.100″	1.645″
Outside diameter	1.460″	0.915″
Inside diameter	1.150″	0.670″
Coil Bind	1.150″	0.950″

The inner and outer valve springs were measured combined: 30 lbs. @ 1.750″, 60 lbs. @ 1.570″, 85 lbs. @ 1.475″, 90 lbs. @ 1.450″, 130 lbs. @ 1.300″, and 146 lbs. @ 1.235″. These were used valve springs; therefore, the estimated installed height for new stock Ardun inner and outer valve springs is 85 lbs. @ 1.550″ valves closed. The stock Ardun valve springs have two tightly wound coils at one end, referred to as directional coils. This end of the valve spring is installed on the cylinder head, not the valve spring retainer.

In the 1950s a number of Ardun racers used Ford F-8 Truck, Lincoln V-8, or 1952-56 Oldsmobile V-8 outer valve springs and special inner valve springs, such as those offered by Chet Herbert, in order to successfully use a camshaft with up to 0.350″ camshaft lift (not valve lift). The 1952-56 Oldsmobile V-8 outer valve springs had an installed height of 1 53/64″ (1.828125") valves closed and were rated at 156 lbs. @ 1 15/32″ (1.46875") valves open. If the 1952-56 Oldsmobile V-8 outer valve springs were combined with the Chet Herbert inner valve springs, the result was a valve-spring pressure of 125 to 130 lbs. with valves closed and 275 lbs. with valves open.

The Iskenderian Racing Cams #305-D single valve spring with damper were a popular valve spring to use in the 1970s. The characteristics of these valve springs are:

Installed height, valves closed: 130 lbs. @ 1.625″
Installed height, valves open: 218 lbs. @ 1.225″
(0.400″ valve lift)
1.430″ o.d. and 1.070″ i.d.
Coil bind: 1.125″
Color: orange/yellow

The stock Ardun inner and outer valve springs were not used in the engine described in this section as a result of the Crower Cams & Equipment camshaft having a lobe lift (not valve lift) exceeding 0.285″.

Iskenderian Racing Cams manufactures the #305-DHS aircraft-quality racing single helical coil valve

This picture shows the Iskenderian #305-DHS single-valve springs with dampers, the Iskenderian #3607-ST valve spring retainers, and the Crane Cams #99098-1 valve stem locks. These valve springs and the Iskenderian #305-D (when new) are excellent valve springs to use in a street performance Ardun engine.

springs with damper, oil tempered, shot peened, silicon chrome. These are an improved version and a replacement for the original #305-D single valve springs, and they will be used in the Ardun engine described in this section. Their characteristics are:

Installed height, valves closed: 95 lbs. @ 1.812″
Installed height, valves open: 185 lbs. @ 1.362″ (0.450″ lift)
1.430″ o.d. and 1.070″ i.d.
Coil bind: 1.120″
Maximum lift: 0.450″
Color: orange/yellow

Ardun intake valves that are 4.755″ overall length and Ardun exhaust valves that are 4.565″ overall length will require the use of Crane Cams #99480-16 single valve springs with damper and Crane Cams #99944-16 valve spring retainers:

Installed height, valves closed: 90 lbs. @ 1.578″
Installed height, valves open: 260 lbs. @ 1.20″ (0.400″ lift) or 280 lbs. @ 1.100″ (0.478″ lift)
1.460″ o.d. and 1.060″ i.d.
Coil bind: 0.935″
Maximum lift: 0.510″
Color: red/olive green

The stock rocker arm ratio in an Ardun engine is 1.2. Most OHV engines have a rocker arm ratio of 1.5 or better. In order to optimize the valve spring pressure in an Ardun street performance engine, there is a simple method to calculate the installed height of the valve springs:

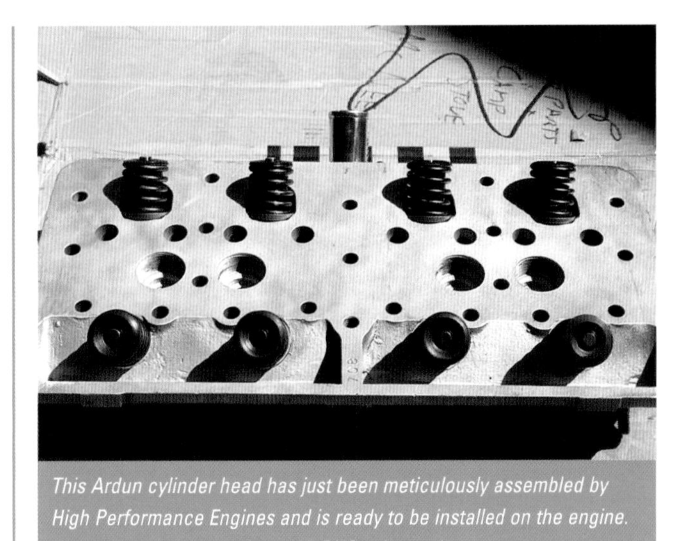

This Ardun cylinder head has just been meticulously assembled by High Performance Engines and is ready to be installed on the engine. Those are the Iskenderian #305-DHS valve springs.

Measure the coil bind of the valve spring.
Add 0.100″ for valve spring coil clearance.
Add the net valve lift (not lobe lift).
The total is the installed valve spring height.

Ardun valve springs were installed with the Ardun #1071 valve spring seat cup, or as the Ardun Engine Company referred to it, a valve spring washer. The use of spring seat cups, or spring seat discs, with aluminum cylinder heads is mandatory in order to prevent the cylinder heads from galling.

Valve Spring Retainers, Locks, and Seals

The Ardun #1060 valve spring retainers were designed to be compatible with the Ardun #1072 outer valve springs and the Ardun #1073 inner valve springs. Many early Ardun racers used the stock Ardun valve spring retainer with Lincoln V-8 and Oldsmobile V-8 outer valve springs and special inner springs. The stock Chrysler V-8 valve stem locks were used with the Chrysler V-8 valves. If other than the stock valve springs are used in an Ardun engine, the valve spring retainers must be compatible with them.

The Iskenderian Racing Cams #3607-ST heat-treated chrome moly steel 7-degree valve spring retainers are recommended for use with their #305-DHS dual-valve springs. These valve spring retainers are for ⅜″ (0.375″) valve stem diameters and they are 0.060″ higher than stock; the outer step diameter is 1.065″ and the inner step diameter is 0.730″.

The Ardun #1064 valve stem locks (keys) were designed to be compatible with the Ardun #1060 valve spring retainers and the Ardun #1062 intake valves and Ardun #1063 exhaust valves. Whether the Ardun valve spring retainers are changed or not, the valve stem locks should be upgraded to new machined 4140 chrome moly heat treated steel, 7

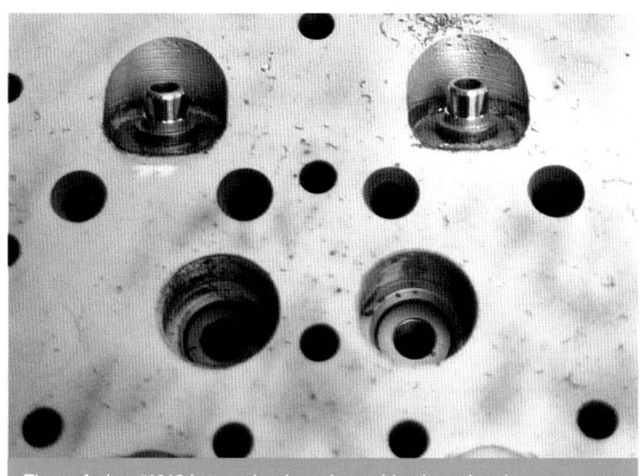
These Ardun #1013 bronze intake valve guides have just been machined in order to accept the Hastings #DT-1612 teflon/steel valve stem seals.

Here are the Enginetech #S2890 viton positive seal valve stem seals. These seals are the best type to use in a street performance engine. Valve stem seals are only required on the intake valves in an Ardun engine due to the angle of the exhaust valves in the hemi cylinder head.

degree, ⅜″ valve stem locks, such as the Crower Cams & Equipment #86111; Crane Cams #99098-1; or Iskenderian Racing Cams #VL-3/8. These are not expensive items.

A major item of importance that was missing from the Ardun cylinder heads was the valve stem seals. Valve stem seals should be used in a street performance Ardun engine for the purpose of oil control, especially with the intake valves. On a street performance Ardun engine, it is only necessary to install the valve stem seals on the intake valves due to the angle of the exhaust valves in the hemi cylinder heads. It does no harm to install the valve stem seals on the exhaust valves. There are three basic types of valve stem seals. The first is the ⅜″ polyacrylate valve stem seal, which is standard issue with the Fel-Pro #HS7908PT-4 Chrysler hemi complete gasket set. However, these will not usually work with smaller diameter or dual- and triple-valve springs. The second choice is the ⅜″ Hastings #DT-1612 "silver seal" Teflon/steel valve stem seal, which requires the valve guides to be machined for proper valve stem seal installation. These valve stem seals can be used in a street performance engine but are more commonly used for race applications. The third and best choice of valve stem seal for a street performance Ardun engine is the Enginetech #S2890 viton positive seal ⅜″ valve stem seal. You need not machine the valve guides in order to install these valve stem seals. The viton positive seal valve stem seals are available at your local performance automotive outlet for around $1 each.

Camshaft Gear and Timing Cover

The Ford flathead V-8 fiber camshaft timing gear should never be used in an Ardun engine. The added stress of the overhead valvetrain will strip the teeth off the fiber gear. A Melling #2702 aluminum camshaft timing gear is the one to use. Matched crankshaft and camshaft timing gear sets for the 1949-53 Ford flathead V-8 are available from Melling, part #2727S, and Sealed Power (Federal Mogul), part #221-2727S. The Melling and Sealed Power gears are available from your local automotive parts outlet. A chrome 1949-50 Ford #8BA-6059 cast iron camshaft timing gear cover was installed in the engine described in this section.

I have referred to the Ford #OBA-6059-A aluminum timing gear cover as the model used on the 1951-53 vehicles, and the Ford #8BA-6059 cast iron timing gear cover as the model used on the 1949-50 vehicles. In actual fact, the aluminum timing gear covers can be found on the earlier-year engines, and the cast iron timing gear covers can be found on the later-year engines. I imagine this happened during a rebuild time in the past. Unless a flathead engine is guaranteed to be 100% stock, do not assume that the type of timing gear cover is an indication of the year of the engine.

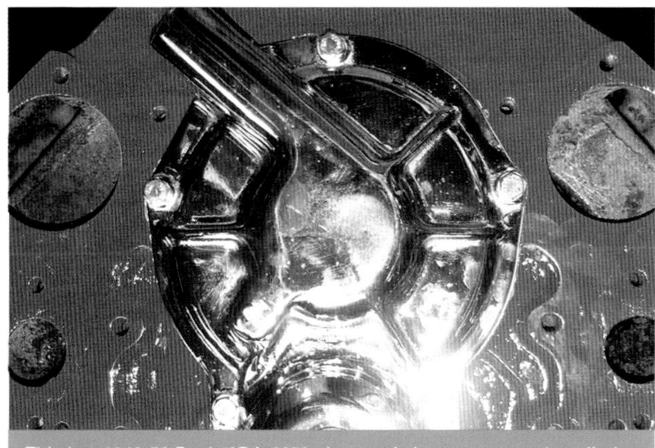
This is a 1949-50 Ford #8BA-6059 chrome timing gear cover installed with polished stainless steel bolts.

A picture is worth a thousand words! On the left is the 1951-53 Ford #OBA-6059-A aluminum timing gear cover with the distributor shaft boss. On the right is the 1949-50 Ford #8BA-6059 cast iron timing gear cover without the distributor shaft boss and painted with Glyptal #G-1228A medium grey gloss enamel.

One-Piece Oil Seal and Sleeve

There are currently a few different types of one-piece oil seals available for the front of the Ford flathead V-8 engine. However, some of those oil seals require the use of unbelievable amounts of silicone sealant in order to install them, which is totally ridiculous. I believe the Speedway Motors one-piece oil seal to be the best, and it works.

Cylinder Heads

The Ardun #1001 overhead-valve, hemispherical combustion chamber cylinder heads were cast with Alcoa 355 T-6 heat-treated aluminum alloy. These cylinder heads had a combustion chamber volume of 88 cc, and they weighed 30 lbs. (bare) each. The Ardun Engine Company advertised these heads as rating high in thermodynamic efficiency, volumetric efficiency, mechanical efficiency, mechanical reliability, and continuous output. High-handed advertising, if you ask me! These cylinder heads were the forerunners to the legendary Chrysler hemi heads.

The Speedway Motors #912-S12853 one-piece oil seal with Luke's crankshaft sleeve.

Two types of Ardun cylinder heads were produced. The first model had the water outlet elbow at the front end of the cylinder head, and the later model had the water outlet at the top center of the cylinder head, between the two middle intake ports. The Ardun #1000 OHV conversion kit for the Ford flathead V-8 (V-8-100) engine was priced at $479 by the Ardun Engine Company on March 1, 1950. This same kit was priced at $495 by the Ardun Power Products Corporation on December 1, 1950. In early 2002 I heard of a well-used Ardun complete conversion kit being offered for sale at $10,000. Now that is really and truly inflation!

The intake manifold gaskets should be used as templates to gasket-match the Ardun cylinder head intake ports. Any casting flash should be ground from inside the intake and exhaust ports. The exhaust manifold gaskets should be used as templates to gasket-match the Ardun cylinder head exhaust ports. The intake and exhaust ports can be polished, but they should not be enlarged. Use extreme caution when doing this. The material around the ports is thin in places, particularly at the pushrod bulge. The combustion chambers can be polished, but once again, only remove a minimal amount of material in order not to increase the size of the combustion chambers.

If there is any grease or oil on the Ardun cylinder heads, remove this with wax and grease remover. Glass bead the cylinder heads; this will bring them back to their original factory condition. Prior to this, make certain all the water passages are masked off with duct tape, otherwise there will be glass bead material falling out of the cylinder heads and into the engine for the next year or so. If you really want to get exotic, have someone like "Tim the polishing guy" buff the exterior surfaces of the cylinder heads; they will come up like chrome. If you do this, spray them after with Eastwood Company #10200Z diamond clear gloss finish or V.H.T. #SP-115 clear high-temperature coating to help prevent the polished cylinder heads from tarnishing.

Take the Ardun cylinder heads to your local machine shop and have them pressure tested to ensure there are no cracks. After more than 50 years, the mating surface of the Ardun cylinder heads will certainly require some attention. They have probably been improperly torqued numerous times and may well be pitted from a leaking cylinder head gasket or tiny cracks near the water jackets. Have the cylinder heads surfaced. The engine block is going to be parallel decked, so the cylinder heads should be surfaced to

Here is a photograph of a second-generation set of Ardun cylinder heads, #724 and #727. These cylinder heads were sent to Luke's by the owner in Los Angeles to have a major overhaul.

Once again, here are the Ardun #724 and #727 cylinder heads. Look closely at the bottom spark plug hole in the one on the left, notice a hole in the side.

ensure a perfect match. The estimated cost to surface the cylinder heads is $75.

The Ardun cylinder heads can be converted from 18-mm to 14-mm spark plugs using the Champion #J-202 spark plug adapter. Although 18-mm spark plugs are still available today, the heat ranges are limited. The 14-mm spark plugs, commonly known as "peanut plugs," come in a wider variety of heat ranges.

The owner of this Ardun second-generation cylinder head, #925, sent it to Luke's to have the area around one spark plug repaired.

The tip of the spark plug is recessed in the cylinder head, creating what is known as a "cartridge fire" situation. Ideally, the spark plug should be lower in the cylinder head so the spark plug tip is in the combustion chamber, thereby promoting better flame travel resulting in a cleaner and smoother running engine. The spark plugs will benefit from the cooling effect of the incoming (intake) fuel mixture and will actually run cooler at higher engine speeds. The only way to lower the spark plugs in the Ardun cylinder heads is to machine the shoulders, where the spark plugs sit, to a greater depth. The material in this area of the cylinder head is quite thin, and the chance of striking water when machining the spark plug shoulders is pretty good. Unless you have the rare ability to repair Ardun cylinder heads, leave them alone! If the spark plug adapter is removed, the spark plug is only lowered approximately ⅛" in the cylinder head. If you want to use 14-mm spark plugs, you will have to leave the spark plug adapters in place.

After all the years those spark plug adapters have been in the cylinder heads, they will certainly be a lot of fun to remove. This job should only be done by an experienced and reliable machine shop; otherwise, you will end up with some super-expensive aluminum scrap. Luke's has had to salvage Ardun cylinder heads that were damaged when inexperienced machine shops attempted to remove the spark plug adapters.

The 18 mm diameter of the spark plug hole is greater than the hole below leading into the combustion chamber of the cylinder head. When the spark plug or adapter is installed, there is a "pocket" below the spark plug or adapter and the top of the hole leading to the combustion chamber, which becomes a great dirt trap. The hole leading to the combustion chamber can be opened up using a 15/32" drill bit and then chamfering the hole on both sides, thereby minimizing the problem. This should only be done by an experienced machine shop.

Prior to the final cleaning and assembly of the cylinder heads, make certain to run an 18-mm spark plug tap through all the spark plug holes and a 14-mm spark plug tap through all the spark plug adapters, if they are being used. Use a 1½" N.F. tap to clean up the threads for the spark plug tubes. It is amazing to see the amount of strange debris that falls out of the cylinder heads when you do this!

This photograph shows how far the spark plug is recessed in the Ardun cylinder head, creating a "cartridge fire" situation. That is a 14-mm spark plug.

This is a Champion #J-202 spark plug adapter. This item was installed to convert the Ardun cylinder heads from 18-mm to 14-mm spark plugs.

This photograph shows one of the Ardun cylinder heads that will be installed on the engine described in this section. The cylinder head has been surfaced and the valves have been installed with a Serdi-machined multi-angle blueprint valve grind.

This is the aluminum plug machined by Luke's for the repair of Ardun cylinder head #925. Luke Balogh put a lot of work into this repair and probably saved the owner from a nervous breakdown!

The Ardun Engine Company provided cylinder-head studs for use with their cylinder heads. The studs have 7/16″ N.C. threads where they screw into the block and 7/16″ N.C. threads where the nuts are attached on the cylinder heads. The Ardun #1055 studs are the 4 13/16″ length "short" studs; the Ardun #1056 studs are the 5 3/8″ length "medium" studs; and the Ardun #1058 studs are the 9 13/32″ length "long" studs. The upper 2 3/32″ of the long studs are used to secure the valve covers. There are 12 short studs; 24 medium studs; and 4 long studs. In addition, the Ardun #1070 studs are 5 13/16″ length and used to secure the valve covers. There are two of those studs. The stock Ardun cylinder head studs are acceptable for use in a street performance engine. The stock pre-1949 Ford flathead V-8 cylinder-head studs had fine threads on the nut end of the studs. Why the stock Ardun cylinder head studs did not have the same fine thread is anyone's guess. This type of oversight is referred to as a "design flaw!"

Automotive Racing Products (ARP) very likely produces the best automotive engine fasteners available today. The cylinder-head studs are manufactured using 8740 chrome moly steel with a black oxide finish rated at 190,000 psi. The washers are hardened and parallel ground, and the aerospace-quality nuts are 12-point. A complete custom-made ARP head stud kit for the Ardun engine, with the valve cover acorn nuts and washers, is available from Don Ferguson at Ardun Enterprises. The ARP head stud kit is expensive at $520 but it is a necessary item for upgrading an Ardun engine that is to be used for all-out racing or equipped with a blower.

The Ardun #1036 hardened flat washers and the Ardun #1037 nuts were used on the studs. There are 40 of each of those items. Six each of the Ardun #1031 flat washers and the Ardun #1015 acorn nuts were used to secure the valve covers. The cylinder-head stud nuts are torqued to 55 ft-lb. A good cleaning and an expert glass beading will bring the Ardun cylinder-head studs, nuts, and washers back to almost-new condition. If the Ardun #1036 flat washers are pitted or missing, they should be replaced with new Manley Performance Parts #42102 heat-treated head bolt washers. None of the cylinder head stud nuts are outside the valve covers, so you will not require any chrome acorn nut covers. The cylinder head studs should be installed in the engine block using Permatex aviation form-a-gasket, the shaft of the studs should be coated with anti-seize compound, and Molykote should be used when installing the stud nuts. The Victor/Reinz cylinder head gaskets should be installed "dry" without using a cylinder-head gasket sealant.

Pushrods and Rocker Arms

The Ardun #1099 intake pushrods and Ardun #1100 exhaust pushrods are designed for use with the milk bottle-shape camshaft lifter. The Ardun #1061 intake pushrods and Ardun #1074 exhaust pushrods are designed for use with the first-generation Ardun camshaft lifter. These pushrods were manufactured using high-tensile nickel-chromium molybdenum steel and are a tapered design. The Ardun #1099 intake pushrod was 8.570″ overall length, 0.385″ diameter (at the center), and weighed 71 grams. The Ardun #1100 exhaust pushrod was 10.00″ overall length, 0.385″ diameter (at the center), and weighed 81 grams. The Ardun #1025 ball joint was attached to the camshaft lifter end of the pushrod and the Ardun #1026 ball socket was attached to the rocker arm end of the pushrod, creating a one-piece unit. The pushrod lengths for use with the first generation camshaft lifter are estimated to be 1.50″ longer. The stock Ardun pushrods were solid and heavy, and as a result of this, they will not be used in the engine described in this section.

These are the Ardun cylinder heads studs, from the top: #1058 long stud, #1056 medium stud, #1055 short stud, #1070 valve cover stud, #1036 flat washer, and #1037 nut.

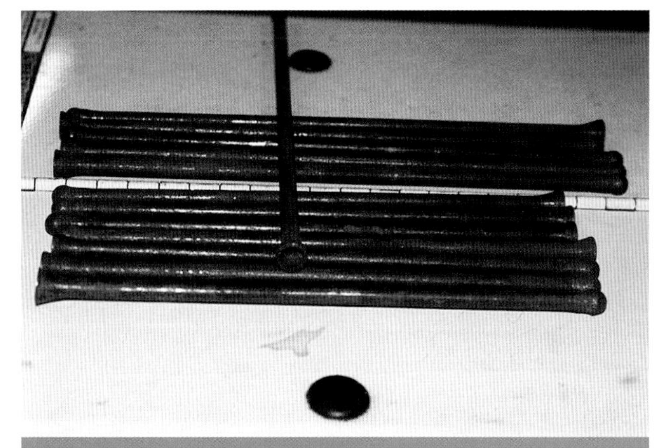

This photograph shows the stock Ardun #1099 intake and Ardun #1100 exhaust pushrods. The intake pushrods weighed 71 grams each and the exhaust pushrods weighed 81 grams each.

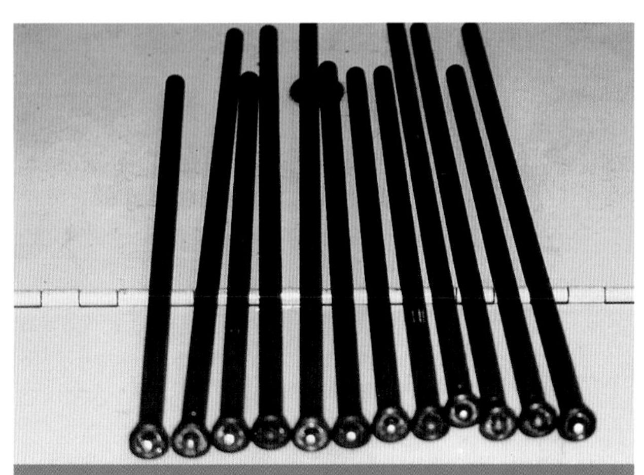

These are the Smith Brothers pushrods used in the engine described in this section. The intake pushrods weigh 58 grams each and the exhaust pushrods weigh 67 grams each. These pushrods weigh approximately 20% less than the stock Ardun pushrods.

Smith Brothers Pushrods non-adjustable 5⁄16"-diameter pushrods are manufactured from hardened, tempered, 4130 seamless chrome moly steel, with heat-treated ball and cup ends. Smith Brothers Pushrods have been in business since 1953 and produce some of the finest pushrods available today.

Smith Brothers pushrods were used in the engine build up in this section The intake pushrods are non-adjustable, 8.605″ overall length, 0.310″ diameter (at the center), and weigh 58 grams. The exhaust pushrods are non-adjustable, 10.010″ overall length, 0.310″ diameter (at the center), and weigh 67 grams.

After the Ardun cylinder heads are bolted to the engine with the rocker arm assemblies in place, the free movement of the pushrods must be checked, ensuring they do not bind in any position within the engine block or the cylinder heads. Any portion of the engine block or cylinder head that interferes with a pushrod should be carefully ground away.

The second design Ardun rocker arm assemblies will be installed in the engine described in this section. Each assembly consists of the following parts:

- 2 each: Ardun #1006 intake rocker arm shaft end supports
- 1 each: Ardun #1003 intake rocker arm shaft center support
- 1 each: Ardun #1021 intake rocker arm shaft
- 3 each: Ardun #1079 rocker arm shaft support allen head set screws
- 3 each: Ardun #1078 jam nuts
- 8 each: Ardun #1065 rocker arm bushings
- 2 each: Ardun #1008L left-hand intake rocker arms
- 2 each: Ardun #1008R right-hand intake rocker arms
- 16 each: Ardun #1053 end washers
- 4 each: Ardun #1077 washers
- 8 each: Ardun #1027 rocker adjustment screws
- 8 each: Ardun #1075 jam nuts
- 4 each: Allen head end plugs
- 2 each: Ardun #1005 exhaust rocker arm shaft supports
- 1 each: Ardun #1020 exhaust rocker arm shaft
- 2 each: Ardun #1007L left-hand exhaust rocker arms
- 2 each: Ardun #1007R right-hand exhaust rocker arms
- 2 each: Second design rocker arm "short" locating springs
- 4 each: Second design rocker arm "medium" locating springs
- 1 each: Second design rocker arm "long" locating spring
- 2 each: Second design end supports for rocker arm shafts

The first design Ardun rocker arm assemblies used the Ardun #1076 retaining rings to hold the rocker arms in position on the rocker arm shafts, while the second design used the rocker arm shaft springs for this purpose. The first design rocker arm assemblies did not have the two end supports attached to the two rocker arm shafts on each cylinder head, while the second design utilized these end supports. The lack of the two end supports for the rocker arm shafts would have permitted the rocker arm shafts to flex, creating a very undesirable situation. The second design Ardun rocker arm assemblies are the superior model.

The Ardun #1003 intake rocker arm shaft supports and the Ardun #1005 exhaust rocker arm shaft supports are bolted to their respective rocker arm shafts. The intake and exhaust rocker arms "float" on the rocker arm shafts, unlike

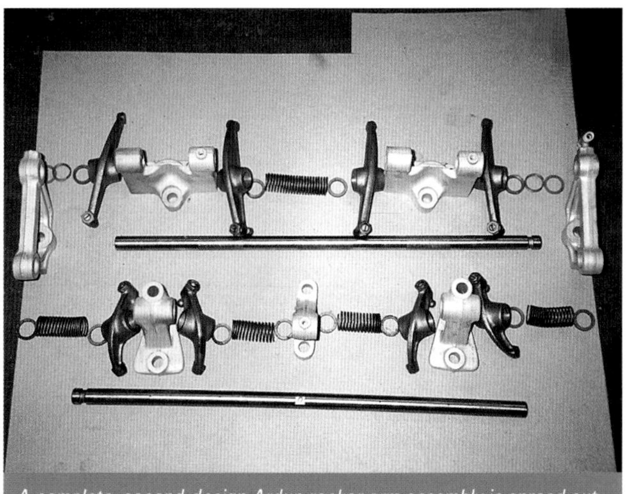

A complete, second-design Ardun rocker arm assembly is spread out prior to assembly. Memorize this!

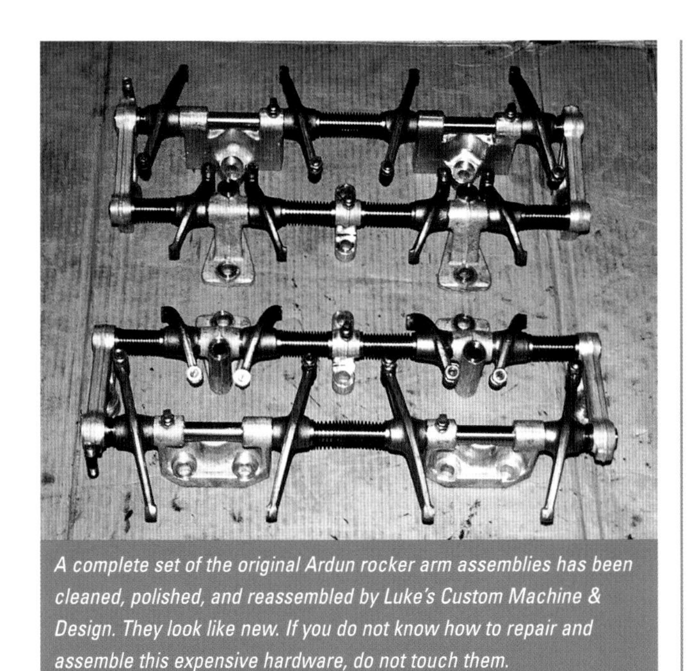

A complete set of the original Ardun rocker arm assemblies has been cleaned, polished, and reassembled by Luke's Custom Machine & Design. They look like new. If you do not know how to repair and assemble this expensive hardware, do not touch them.

the majority of OHV engines where the rocker arms are stud mounted. The rocker arm shaft springs are used to assist with maintaining the proper positioning of the rocker arms on the rocker arm shafts. There are two short springs, four medium springs, and one long spring on each rocker arm assembly. In the majority of situations, the rocker arm shaft springs are in good condition, although they might have some surface rust on them. The springs can be glass beaded and then oiled well.

If you are not experienced with the disassembly and reassembly of the Ardun rocker arm assemblies—and the majority of people are not—do not touch them! Find an experienced machine shop or a party that is known for his expertise with Ardun engines. If you insist on cleaning and reassembling your own rocker arm assemblies, take some photographs or make sketches as you disassemble them. Take your time and do the job properly. Any mistake you make with the re-assembly of these parts will result in a very expensive and heart-wrenching situation. Remember, these parts are almost impossible to replace.

The stock Ardun rocker arms were manufactured using high tensile nickel-chromium molybdenum steel, and they are lubricated using a full-pressure oiling system. The rocker arms have ratio of 1.20. This means that the camshaft lobe lift, less the valve lash, is multiplied by 1.2, resulting in the maximum net valve lift.

The rocker arm shafts should be gently polished on a lathe using 600 grit wet sandpaper. You can glass bead the rocker arms and the cast aluminum rocker arm stands, provided you use a fine-grade of glass material. Remember to plug the rocker arm bushings in the rocker arms with a plastic tube or metal shaft before glass beading them. The pallets (tips) of the rocker arms, which contact the valves, should be re-faced. This procedure should only be done by a premium quality machine shop to avoid completely destroying the rocker arms.

The socket head set screws at the end of the rocker arm shafts should be removed and the internal area of the shafts thoroughly cleaned out. Make certain all the oil supply holes in the rocker arm assemblies are clear. The rocker arm shaft to rocker arm shaft bushing clearance should be a maximum of 0.002″. Anything more than this will require the installation of new rocker arm shaft bushings. After the rocker arm assemblies are "better than hospital clean," assemble them using generous amounts of motor oil. Install the rocker arm adjustment screws and jam nuts, the rocker arm shaft set screws and jam nuts, and the rocker arm shaft socket head set screw plugs using anti-seize compound.

The rocker arm assemblies used on the engine in this section were in very good condition. Those assemblies were completely dismantled, a thorough cleaning was carried out, and the shafts were polished. The rocker arm pallets (tips) did not require any reconditioning.

If you have just managed to marry someone extremely wealthy and that person actually likes you, you could purchase a set of beautiful 17-4 stainless steel roller tip rocker arms from Ardun Enterprises. These 1.325-ratio rocker arms have an internal oil passage for lubricating the pushrod ends, which eliminates the need for rocker arm spray bars. The current price for a complete set of rocker arms is $1,600. A street performance Ardun engine does not really require this item.

Water Outlets

The Ardun #1018 water outlet elbows used on the early model of the Ardun cylinder heads were attached using the Ardun #1032 stud that screwed into the cylinder head. Ardun #1012 water outlet elbow gaskets were used, and the water outlet elbows were held in position with the Ardun #1034 washers and Ardun #1035 acorn nuts. These water outlet elbows mounted on the front of the cylinder heads and at the rear of the cylinder heads there was a plug. This plug assembly consisted of the Ardun #1019 plug (blanking cover), Ardun #1012 gasket, Ardun #1032 stud, Ardun #1034 washer, and the Ardun #1035 acorn nut.

The Ardun #3402 water outlet elbows were used on the later model Ardun cylinder head, which had the water outlet elbow attached to the top center of the cylinder head using three studs, lock washers, and nuts. The Ardun water outlet elbow gaskets for the later model Ardun cylinder heads are no longer available. You will have to fabricate your own water outlet elbow gaskets from a sheet of good-quality gasket material. A simple process! Use polished stainless steel acorn nuts to install the water outlet elbows.

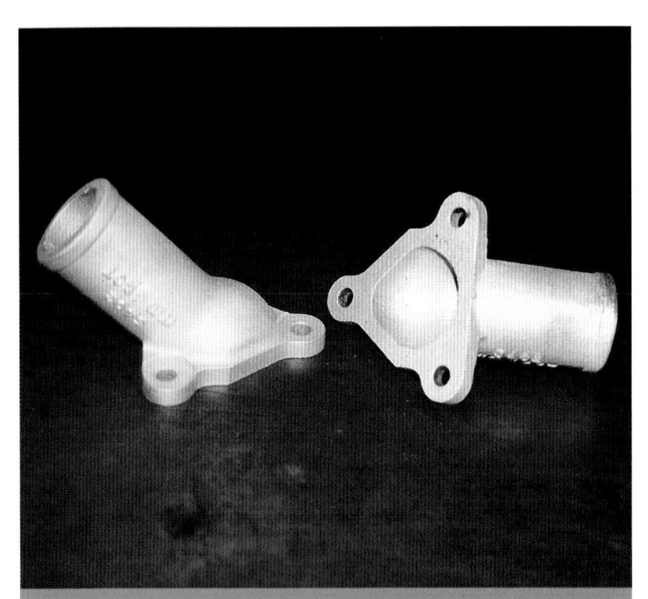

This is a pair of the Ardun #3402 cast aluminum water outlet elbows for the second generation of Ardun cylinder heads. They mount on the center top of the cylinder head.

The positioning of the water outlet elbow at the front of the first design Ardun cylinder head will interfere with a stock location 1949-53 Ford flathead V-8 distributor. The second design Ardun cylinder head is certainly more versatile for ignition systems.

Although the addition of the Ardun cylinder heads to a Ford flathead V-8 engine will result in the engine running cooler, your vehicle will be driven on the street. Therefore, it should have thermostats installed. Removing the thermostats will cause the coolant in the engine to start to move too fast for the heat to be dissipated. In years past, Ardun owners found that the thermostats for a Renault Dauphine fit the radiator hoses. In this day and age, you will have to amble down to your local automotive parts dealer to find two 180-degree F thermostats that fit inside the radiator hoses. Or, you can install a metal washer with a ½″ or 1″ opening in each of the top radiator hoses.

Valve Covers

The Ardun #1002 valve covers (rocker covers) were cast with non-sonorous aluminum, which means sound deadening. The Ardun valve covers had "ARDUN" and "NEW YORK" (in smaller letters below the "ARDUN") cast into the outside center surface. Some of the first and extremely rare models also had "MADE IN ENGLAND" in still smaller letters cast below the "NEW YORK," while other valve covers had "ARDUN" only. The Ardun #1016 valve cover gaskets were used to seal the valve covers. Each of the valve covers was secured with three Ardun #1031 washers and three Ardun #1015 acorn nuts.

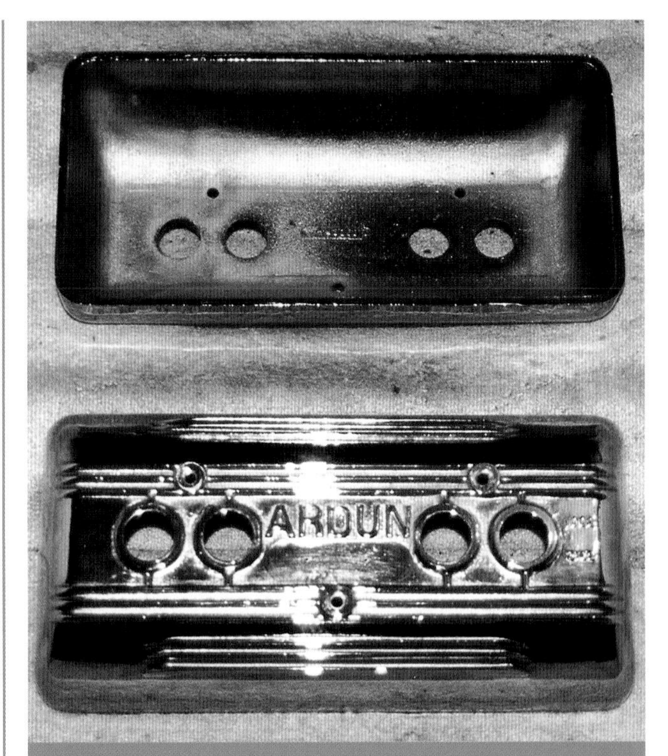

Here is a pair of Ardun #1002 non-sonorous aluminum valve covers that have been chrome plated. The old flathead almost disappears with these in place!

This photograph shows Luke's neoprene rubber valve cover gasket installed around the lip of the valve cover. These are great gaskets, and they are re-useable.

It is not uncommon to find a broken fin on an Ardun valve cover, possibly as a result of some oaf dropping the valve cover after removing it in order to see what was underneath! The broken fins can be repaired by a reliable machine shop. The Ardun valve covers buff up superbly, and it should be mandatory for Ardun engine owners to do this. Contact "Tim the polishing guy" or one of his clones!

Luke's has the Ardun neoprene rubber valve-cover gaskets specifically manufactured by a gasket company. The gaskets are channel shaped, reuseable, and slip onto the lip of the valve cover. The ends are placed at the top of the valve cover and glued together. This is the only source of Ardun valve-cover gaskets that I am aware of. The price is $45 for a pair of the gaskets.

Estimated Costs

It would appear to be almost impossible to establish a price for a used Ardun conversion kit in good condition; only market forces would determine what that value would be. In order to arrive at an estimated cost for the Ardun cylinder heads and associated parts, I have based the total cost at $10,000. This price was mentioned earlier in this section, and it may or may not seem realistic. However, based on the fact a new high-tech Ardun conversion kit from Ardun Enterprises costs $13,000, it would then follow that $10,000 for a used original Ardun kit is not out of line.

If the total cost of the pushrods, valves, valve springs, valve spring seat cups, valve spring retainers, valve stem locks, cylinder head stud kit, and intake manifold are estimated to be $2,500, this would leave $7,500. The pair of cylinder heads, with the valve guides, valve seat inserts, and water outlet elbows are then estimated to be worth $5,000. The pair of complete rocker arm assemblies are estimated to be worth $1,000. The pair of valve covers, with spark plug tubes, are estimated to be worth $800. The camshaft lifters are estimated to be worth $350, and the valley cover is estimated to be worth $350. These are the numbers I use in the summary below.

Camshaft and Cylinder Heads Summary

Item	Cost
New Clevite 77 #SH-21S camshaft bearings installed allowing for 0.002″ camshaft clearance and 0.007″ camshaft end play.	$26.12
New Crower Cams & Equipment Ardun Special "street grind" cast iron alloy solid lifter camshaft with advertised duration: 268 degrees intake and exhaust; duration @ 0.050″ lift: 227 degrees intake and exhaust; net valve lift: 0.398″ intake and exhaust; lobe separation angle: 110 degrees; valve lash (hot): 0.012″ intake and exhaust. Camshaft degreed. Camshaft journal diameter: 1.7965"-1.7970″. Ford #6254 rear camshaft gear (camshaft to oil pump idler gear) and 1949-50 Ford #7RA-6254-B camshaft gear (camshaft to distributor) installed.	$284.96
Ardun #1024 high tensile nickel-chromium molybdenum steel milk-bottle shape solid lifters, bases re-faced, stock 1.00″ diameter, 3.260″ length, installed. Weight: 100 grams, each.	$439.03 (estimated)
New Smith Brothers Pushrods 0.310"-diameter non-adjustable intake pushrods, 8.605″ overall length, 4130 seamless chrome moly steel. Weight: 58 grams each. New Smith Brothers Pushrods 0.310"-diameter non-adjustable exhaust pushrods, 10.010″ overall length, 4130 seamless chrome moly steel. Weight: 67 grams, each.	$139.84
Iskenderian Racing Cams #305-DHS aircraft quality racing single helical coil valve springs with damper, oil tempered, shot peened, silicon chrome. Installed height: 95 lbs. @ 1.812″ valves closed and 185 lbs. @ 1.362″ (0.450″ lift) valves open; 1.430″ o.d. and 1.070″ i.d.; coil bind: 1.120″; maximum lift: 0.450″; color: orange/yellow. New Iskenderian Racing Cams #3607-ST heat-treated chrome moly steel 7 degree valve spring retainers, 3/8″ stem diameter, 0.060″ higher than stock, installed with new Crane Cams #99098-1 machined 4140 chrome moly heat-treated steel, 7 degree valve stem locks, standard height, black oxide finish. Ardun #1071 spring seat cups installed.	$193.66

Ardun #1062 intake valves, 1¾″ (1.750") diameter, ⅜″ (0.375") diameter stems, 4.875″ overall length, weight: 115 grams, each; (marking: "Eaton 1"); and Ardun #1063 "austenitic" exhaust valves, 1½″ (1.50") diameter, ⅜″ (0.375") diameter stems, 4.695″ overall length, weight: 103 grams, each; (marking: "Eaton 25"). Valves installed with Serdi-machined multi-angle blueprint valve grind. New Enginetech #S2890 viton positive seal valve-stem seals installed on intake and exhaust valve guides.	$524.67
New Melling #2702 helical camshaft timing gear, 44 teeth, installed with Ford #6258 lock washer plate and Ford #350400 camshaft gear bolts using Loctite and torqued to 20 ft-lb. 1949-50 Ford #8BA-6059 chrome cast iron timing gear cover installed with new polished stainless steel bolts and lock washers using Loctite and torqued to 15 ft-lb. Gasket installed using silicone sealant. Inside of timing cover painted with Glyptal #G-1228A medium grey gloss enamel.	$169.12
Ardun #1001 (second design) OHV 355T-6 cast aluminum hemispherical combustion chamber cylinder heads, 88-cc combustion chamber volume, with Ardun #1028 phosphor bronze intake valve seat inserts and Ardun #1029 phosphor bronze exhaust valve seat inserts, and Ardun #1013 phosphor bronze intake valve guides and Ardun #1014 phosphor bronze exhaust valve guides installed. Ardun #3402 polished aluminum water outlet elbows installed with new polished stainless steel acorn nuts, lock washers, and AN flat washers using silicone sealant on the water outlet elbow gaskets. Cylinder head identity numbers: 708 and 729. Cylinder head weight: 30 lbs, each (bare).	$5,013.95 (estimated)
Cylinder heads glass beaded and re-surfaced. Champion #J-202 spark plug adapters removed. New Victor/Reinz #GX-13173-1 "nitroseal" cylinder head gaskets installed. Ardun #1055, #1056, and #1058 cylinder head studs installed using Permatex aviation form-a-gasket. Ardun #1037 cylinder head stud nuts and Ardun #1036 flat washers installed using Molykote and torqued to 50 ft-lb.	$686.67
Ardun second design complete rocker arm assemblies with Ardun #1021 and #1020 rocker arm shafts; Ardun #1008L and #1008R high tensile nickel-chromium molybdenum steel intake rocker arms; and Ardun #1007L and #1007R high tensile nickel-chromium molybdenum steel exhaust rocker arms installed.	$1,000.00 (estimated)
Ardun rocker arm assemblies rebuilt by Luke's.	$130.00
Ardun #1002 chrome-plated non-sonorous aluminum valve covers installed with Ardun #1070 valve cover studs, Ardun #1031 washers, and Ardun #1015 acorn nuts. Luke's new neoprene rubber valve cover gaskets installed with valve covers torqued to 15 ft-lb.	$890.00 (estimated)
CAMSHAFT AND CYLINDERS HEAD TOTAL:	**$9,498.02**

CHAPTER 26

INTAKE SYSTEM

For information on carburetors and detailing, refer to Section I.

Intake Manifold

The stock Ardun intake manifold consisted of two Ardun #1009 cast aluminum logs, one bolted to each cylinder head, along with an Ardun #1069 connector joining the two logs. A single Holley 94 (or Stromberg 97) carburetor was mounted on top of the connector or, as it was described by the Ardun Engine Company, the carburetor adapter. This intake manifold was not the greatest design and efficiency, to put it mildly. In the early part of 2002, a complete single carburetor Ardun intake manifold was listed for sale on the eBay website. The resulting bids reached $960, but even that amount did not achieve the reserve price. That is double what the entire Ardun conversion kit cost in 1950!

The Ardun #1009 cast aluminum intake manifold consists of two logs. A single two-barrel carburetor adapter bolts to the flanges and connects the two logs. This intake manifold was definitely not the greatest of designs.

This is the Austin Model TD, 3 deuce, dual plane, cast aluminum intake manifold for the Ardun engine. It is a beautiful piece of work and well designed to boot. The flanges fit on the intake runners, the O-rings slide onto the intake runners, and the complete unit is installed.

The Ardun Engine Company also offered the "special racing intake manifold," which had two Ardun #1069 carburetor adapters (connectors), one at each end of the intake manifold, in order to mount two Holley 94 (or Stromberg 97) carburetors. There was a block-off plate in the center of each log which, if removed, would have permitted the installation of another carburetor adapter (connector), and three Holley 94 (or Stromberg 97) carburetors could have been used. Due to the poor runner design, there was no way in the world one of these marvels was going to be installed on the street performance Ardun used in this section!

Ken Austin of Newburg, Oregon, has been custom casting intake manifolds since 1950 and Ardun intake manifolds since 1997. These intake manifolds are made of high-grade aluminum, and they are not only well designed but beautiful pieces of work. They have a unique floating flange sealed by a 3/16" cross-section O-ring, no welding required, and they are guaranteed to fit regardless of age or modification to the cylinder heads. The O-rings eliminate the need for conventional gaskets. These unpolished Ardun intake manifolds range in price from $850 to $1,250. The Ardun intake manifolds available are:

Model DD: 2 deuces, dual plane. $1,250
Model DS: 2 deuces, single plane. $850
Model TD: 3 deuces, dual plane. $1,150
Model TS: 3 deuces, single plane. $900
Model FS: 4 deuces, single plane. $950
Model QD: 4 barrel, dual plane. $1,250
Model QS: 4 barrel, single plane. $850
Model BB: blower base. $750
Model UB: universal base. $750;
available with different top plates: $150

An Austin intake manifold, Model TD (3 deuce, dual plane) will be installed on the engine described in this section. The intake manifold gaskets used as templates to scribe around the intake ports in the cylinder heads should be used as templates for the intake manifold to gasket-match the ports. Although it is unlikely that there will be any casting flash in the ports of the intake manifold, any such flash should be ground off.

This is the underside of the Austin Model TD intake manifold. "Tim the polishing guy" noted the quality of this intake manifold and on his own initiative decided to polish the underside as well. Put that guy in front of a buffing wheel and there is just no stopping him!

In order to install the Austin intake manifold, the intake manifold studs should be installed in one cylinder head only. The intake manifold is then placed in position and the intake manifold studs for the other cylinder head are installed. The intake manifold stud holes in the Austin flanges are not oval. This prevents both sets of intake manifold studs from being installed prior to placing the intake manifold in position.

The ideal intake system for a street performance Ardun engine would consist of an Austin Model QD, single quad carburetor dual plane intake manifold and an Edelbrock #1404 "performer" 4-barrel, 500-cfm carburetor. That setup would provide fuel economy, good throttle response, and reliability.

There is no complete gasket kit available for the Ardun engine. Thus, you will have to improvise in order to provide suitable intake manifold gaskets for conventional-style Ardun intake manifolds. The intake manifold on an Ardun engine is secured in place with ⅜" N.C. studs and nuts. The spacing between the studs for each intake runner is 3.00" and the diameter of the intake port is 2.00". Now go find eight gaskets that fit these dimensions! Your local automotive parts dealer should be able to help out, or you can use

This masterpiece is the three-carb setup I assembled for the Ardun engine described in this section.

This is the underside of the Austin Model TD aluminum intake manifold showing the intake runner flanges and the O-rings in place. A very nifty idea!

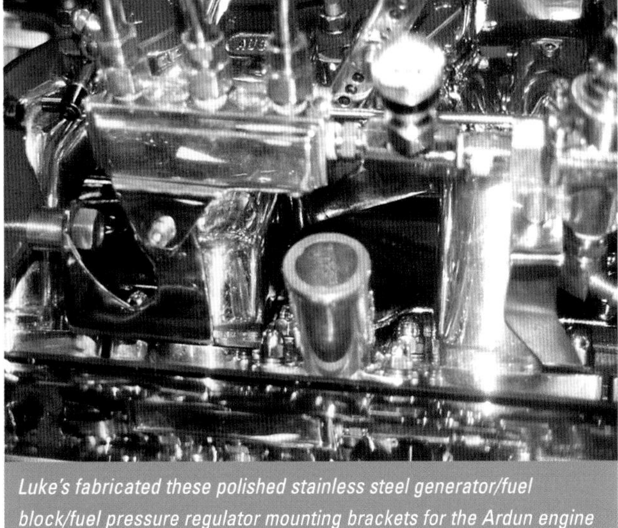

Luke's fabricated these polished stainless steel generator/fuel block/fuel pressure regulator mounting brackets for the Ardun engine described in this section.

The scouts will have to be sent out to locate eight gaskets like these for the stock Ardun intake manifold! The spacing between the intake manifold studs for each intake runner is 3.00" and the intake port diameter is 2.00."

This stock Ardun valley cover has been chrome plated, which explains why it is difficult to get a halfway decent photograph of it.

the larger exhaust manifold gaskets (tan colored) that are part of the Fel-Pro #FS7525B complete gasket set for the 1949-53 Ford flathead V-8 engine. While you are out finding the gaskets, purchase 16 stainless steel ⅜" N.C. acorn nuts and 16 stainless steel ⅜" AN flat washers for the intake manifold. This is a nice detailing touch when the acorn nuts are buffed. The intake manifold studs should be installed in the aluminum cylinder heads using anti-seize compound in order to prevent the threads from galling. Torque the intake manifold acorn nuts to 25 ft-lb.

A 1939-48 Ford #9415 fuel pump stand/crankcase breather housing will have to be used with the Ardun engine. There is no provision for a road draft/crankcase breather and crankcase breather/oil filler tube at the front of the Ardun #3261 valley cover.

For information on fuel lines and the progressive linkage, the fuel pressure regulator, and air cleaners, refer to Section I.

Valley Cover and Bolts

An Ardun #3261 cast aluminum valley cover is used to cover the intake ports and valve lifter gallery in place of the stock 1949-53 Ford flathead V-8 intake manifold. This valley cover uses the stock intake manifold gasket and is secured in place using eight of the stock intake manifold bolts and chrome acorn nut covers. Trace the outline of the valley cover on the intake manifold gasket and trim the gasket accordingly. This valley cover is fitted with a stock position generator/fan mount on the front and a flange to install the fuel pump stand/crankcase breather housing at the rear. This is another item that will look exceptional when buffed.

In the event you do not have an Ardun valley cover, Luke's fabricates these. A note about valley covers: Some aftermarket manufacturers sell them with fins on the top for other OHV engines. These fins look great until you have to clean and polish them, then you will curse the day you bought them! The valley cover is located under the intake manifold and, as a result, it is next to impossible to properly clean and polish.

Intake System Summary

New Austin Model TD polished aluminum 3 deuces, dual plane intake manifold installed with new stainless steel acorn nuts and AN flat washers using anti-seize compound and torqued to 25 ft lb. 1939-48 Ford #9415 polished fuel pump stand/crankcase breather housing installed with new polished stainless steel acorn nuts and lock washers using silicone sealant on gasket. New Speedway Motors #910-15195 crankcase breather/oil filler cap (for 1939-48 Ford) painted with Endura #EX-2C black 160 hi-gloss polyurethane. Luke's new polished aluminum fuel pump block-off plate installed. $1,374.76

3 x 2-barrel Holley 94 polished carburetors, 94/100″ (15/16″) venturi, 160 cfm (approximate), installed with new Papco #264-016 carburetor studs, 1½″ length, and new stainless steel nuts and lock washers using anti-seize compound. $682.49

New Offenhauser #6271 polished 3-carb progressive linkage installed with new polished stainless steel linkage rods using anti-seize compound. $126.23

New Holley #12-804 polished fuel pressure regulator, adjustable from 1-4 psi, installed with new Fairview #KA06-02MB90 polished brass 90-degree elbow, ⅜″ i.d. hose to ½″ N.P.T., and new Weatherhead #3220-6-4 polished brass reducer, ⅜″ N.P.T. to ?″ N.P.T. (inlet line). New Weatherhead #3320-6-4 polished brass reducer, ⅜″ N.P.T. to ½″ N.P.T. (outlet line). New polished aluminum custom 3-carburetor fuel block installed with new Weatherhead #3600-4 polished brass "T" fitting, ½″ N.P.T.; new Weatherhead #3325-4 polished brass connector, ½″ N.P.T.; new Weatherhead #3300-4-2 polished brass reducer, ½″ N.P.T. to ⅛″ N.P.T.; and new Weatherhead #3325-6-4 polished brass connector, ⅛″ N.P.T. (inlet to fuel pressure gauge). New Weatherhead #202-6 polished brass reducers, ⅜″ tube to ½″ N.P.T., and new Weatherhead #100-6 polished inverted flare nuts, ⅜″ tube (fuel block to fuel lines), installed using pipe thread sealant. New Summit Racing Equipment #220238 polished stainless steel fuel line, ⅜″ x 0.028″ wall, double annealed, 5′ length, installed. New Weatherhead #7915 polished brass carburetor fuel inlet fittings, ⅜″ tube, installed. Luke's new polished stainless steel generator/fuel block/fuel pressure regulator mounting brackets installed with new polished stainless steel screws and lock washers using anti-seize compound. New V.D.O. #153-002 fuel pressure gauge, 0-15 psi, 1½″-diameter face, installed using pipe thread sealant. $195.78

Ardun #3261 chromed aluminum valley cover installed using silicone sealant on gasket and torqued to 25 ft-lb. 1949-53 Ford #20448-S intake manifold bolts and new stainless steel AN flat washers installed with new Speedway Motors #910-10125 chrome acorn nut covers, for 9/16″ head. $463.95 (estimated)

INTAKE SYSTEM TOTAL: $2,843.21

CHAPTER 27
IGNITION SYSTEM

Distributor

The amount of money it takes to build a street performance Ardun engine dictates that an electronic ignition be used in order to protect that investment. The distributor will be mounted in the stock 1949-53 Ford flathead V-8 position. A Mallory #3727501 Unilite electronic, full centrifugal (mechanical) advance distributor will be used. This is an excellent, trouble-free distributor.

The 1949-53 Ford flathead V-8 distributor was secured in position using the Ford #12270 distributor hold-down clamp that was bolted to the right (passenger's side) cylinder head. There is no allowance on the Ardun #1001 aluminum cylinder heads for securing the distributor in the 1949-53 stock position. Luke's fabricates a polished stainless steel bracket used in conjunction with the 1949-53 Ford #12270 distributor hold-down clamp to secure the distributor in place.

Some words regarding ignition advance would appear to be in order. The fuel mixture in a cylinder must be ignited before the piston reaches the top of the compression stroke. This will then place the maximum pressure on the piston top for the power stroke. In order to do this, the timing must be controlled so there is more ignition advance at higher engine speeds than there is at lower engine speeds. The ignition advance is increased as the engine accelerates. Any vacuum advance is only a consideration at idle or at lower cruising speeds where the engine is not laboring.

The Ford flathead V-8 crankshaft makes two full revolutions for every single camshaft revolution, since the crankshaft gear has 22 teeth and the camshaft gear has 44 teeth. If the mechanical advance in a distributor is 13 degrees, the actual advance is 26 degrees. If the crankshaft has 10 degrees of advance and the distributor has 26 degrees actual advance, the result would be 36 degrees of total advance. A street performance Ardun engine should have approximately 42 degrees of total advance for the best all-around results. The Ardun engine requires a little more ignition advance than most OHV engines as a result of the "cartridge fire" situation of the spark plugs.

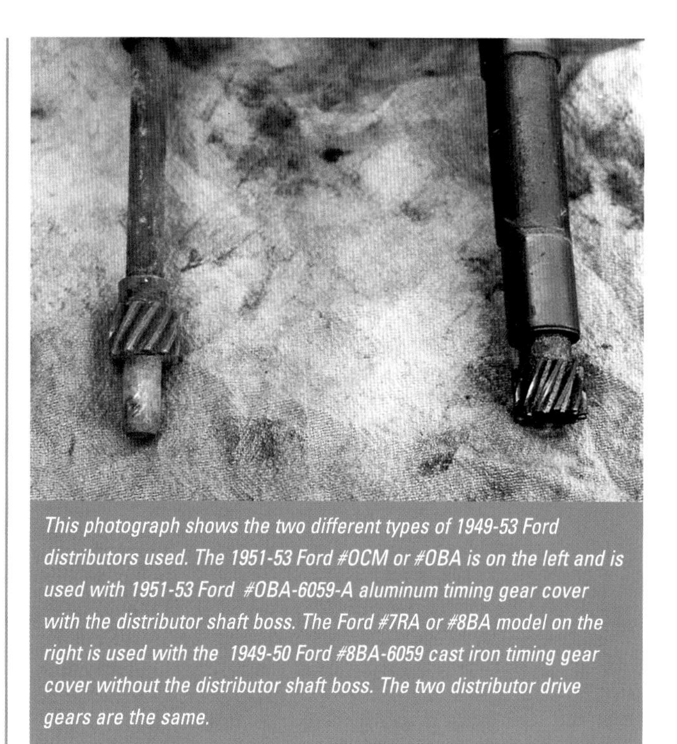

This photograph shows the two different types of 1949-53 Ford distributors used. The 1951-53 Ford #OCM or #OBA is on the left and is used with 1951-53 Ford #OBA-6059-A aluminum timing gear cover with the distributor shaft boss. The Ford #7RA or #8BA model on the right is used with the 1949-50 Ford #8BA-6059 cast iron timing gear cover without the distributor shaft boss. The two distributor drive gears are the same.

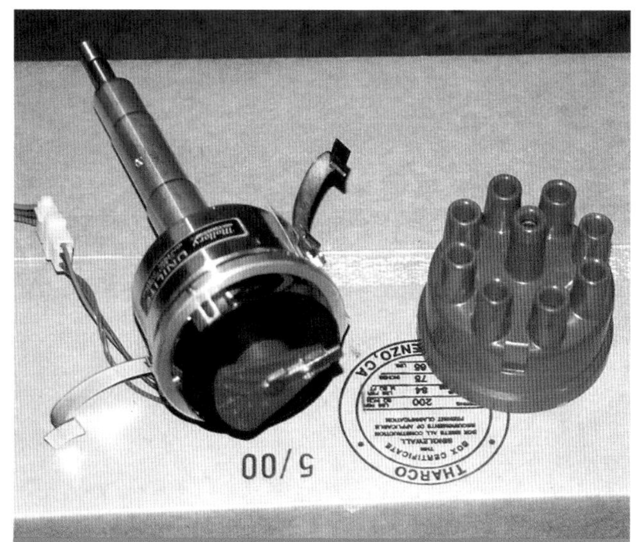

The Mallory #3727501 Unilite electronic distributor used in the Ardun engine described in this section is an excellent, compact unit.

For discussions of coil and ignition control, refer to Section I.

Spark Plug Wires and Plugs

Mallory (Mr. Gasket Company) advises that copper wire core or stainless steel wire core spark plug wires should not be used with electronic ignitions. Aside from this advisory, the engines described in this book are for street use, where there is no valid reason to use copper or stainless steel wire core spark plug wires.

The Mopar Performance (Chrysler Corporation) #4120808 hemi spark plug tube and insulator kit is a very nice and practical addition to an Ardun engine. This will assist in keeping unwanted alien critters out of the spark plug tubes! These kits are affordable and available at your local Chrysler dealer.

In the 1970s, the 18-mm spark plugs recommended for an Ardun street engine were the Autolite #BT4 (colder

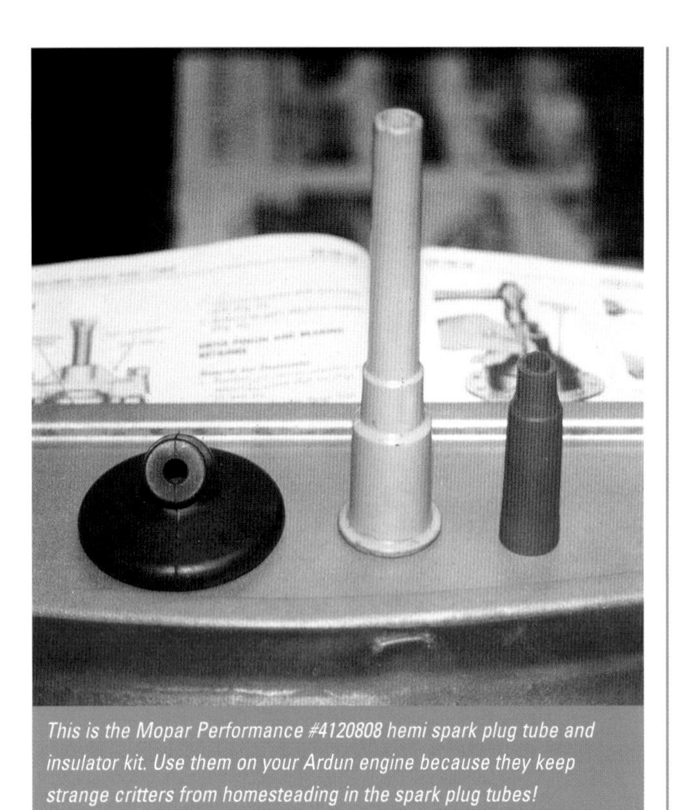

This is the Mopar Performance #4120808 hemi spark plug tube and insulator kit. Use them on your Ardun engine because they keep strange critters from homesteading in the spark plug tubes!

Here are three very different spark plugs. The one on the far left is an Autolite #377 regular gap 18 mm with a washer. The one in the middle is an NGK #WR4-1 projected nose 18 mm with a tapered seat. The one on the far right is a Champion #S59C regular gap 14 mm for use in a blown race Ardun engine. The projected nose on the NGK #WR4-1 is ⅜″ longer than the "regular gap" Autolite #377.

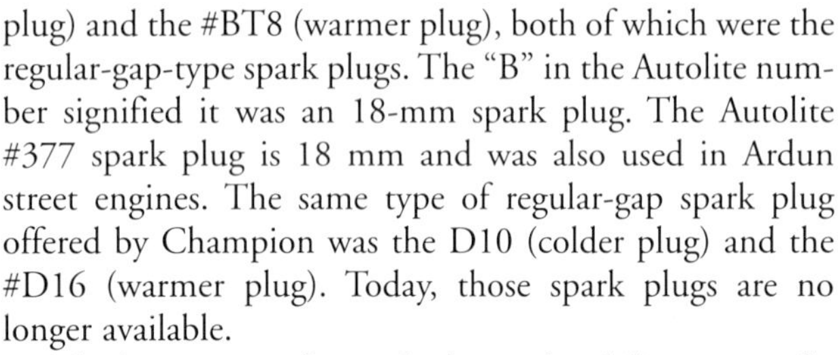

plug) and the #BT8 (warmer plug), both of which were the regular-gap-type spark plugs. The "B" in the Autolite number signified it was an 18-mm spark plug. The Autolite #377 spark plug is 18 mm and was also used in Ardun street engines. The same type of regular-gap spark plug offered by Champion was the D10 (colder plug) and the #D16 (warmer plug). Today, those spark plugs are no longer available.

The heat range of a spark plug is the ability to transfer heat from the insulator tip into the cylinder head. Each street performance engine is different, and as a result, the only certain method of finding the exact heat range for spark plugs in an engine is through trying different heat ranges. A spark plug that is too "cold" will tend to foul easily and misfire, and a spark plug that is too "hot" could cause pre-ignition.

The catalogs supplied by the major spark plug companies have a cross-reference section for the purpose of interchanging spark plugs between different manufacturers. The catalogs available today do not show the Autolite #BT4 or #BT8. The Autolite #377 cross-references to an NGK #A6, then cross-references back to an Autolite #386. The Champion #D10 does not appear anywhere; however, the Champion #D16 cross-references to an NGK #WR5. The NGK #WR5 is a projected-nose spark plug. The "W" indicates the spark plug is 18 mm, the "R" indicates it is a resistor type spark plug, and the "5" is the heat range. The NGK #WR5 cross-references to a Champion #RF11YC and an Autolite #45. The NGK #WR4-1 is one heat range hotter than the #WR5 and has a very long projected nose that is ideal for locating the spark plug tip as far down the spark plug opening in the Ardun cylinder head as possible. Even with this projected nose, the tip of the spark plug is still 0.400″ recessed in the spark plug hole.

The only drawback to the NGK #WR5 and #WR4-1 spark plugs is they have a tapered seat and therefore do not have the usual spark plug washer. This means the spark plug seats in the cylinder heads will have to be beveled in order to seat those spark plugs properly. This is a very simple task for a competent machine shop. The NGK #WR4-1 cross-references to a Champion #RF14LC and an Autolite #5125. The NGK #WR4-1 spark plugs will be used in the engine described in this section.

If the spark plug adapter is going to be used to accommodate the 14-mm spark plugs, the NGK #UR5 is a 14-mm spark plug with the same heat range as the NGK #WR5. The "U" indicates the spark plug is 14 mm, the "R" indicates it is a resistor type spark plug, and the "5" is the heat range. The NGK #UR5 cross-references with a Champion #RV12YC and an Autolite #23. The NGK #TR55-1 has a very long projected nose and is equivalent to the NGK #WR4-1. The NGK #TR55-1 cross-references to a Champion #RS12YC and an Autolite #605. This information should keep the 14-mm fans happy!

The 1949-53 Ford spring-type six-volt starting motor is the most common type and was used in vehicles equipped with a standard transmission.

The spark plug gap should be 0.050″ when using an electronic ignition system, such as the MSD or Mallory units. Always coat the threads on the spark plugs with anti-seize compound when they are being installed in aluminum cylinder heads; this will help to prevent the threads from galling.

Generator

The owner of the Ardun engine described in this section did not want the "new" look of an alternator on his engine. A 1956 Ford V-8 12-volt generator was chromed, rebuilt, and installed on the Ardun engine. A polished aluminum bracket and brace were fabricated by Luke's to mount the generator.

Starting Motor

The owner also decided to use a 1949-53 Ford flathead V-8 starting motor in order to give his engine the "classic" look. Even though this starting motor was designed for a 6-volt

The spark plug tube holes are being machined into this cast aluminum reproduction Ardun valve cover at Luke's Custom Machine & Design.

electrical system, a 12-volt system will not harm the starting motor, providing the engine is not being constantly started.

There were two types of 1949-53 Ford flathead V-8 starting motors. The most common model was the "spring type" for use with manual transmissions, and the other model was the "barrel type" for use with automatic transmissions.

Spark Plug Tubes and Retainers

The Ardun #1051 spark plug tubes (funnels) are screwed into the cylinder heads, the Ardun #1011 spark plug tube seals are positioned on the end of the spark plug tubes, and the Ardun #1052 spark plug tube retainers are screwed onto the spark plug tubes against the valve covers. The spark plug are then inserted into the spark plug tubes and torqued to 15 ft-lb using anti-seize compound. The Ardun spark plug tubes were manufactured using thin metal, which resulted in a flimsy design, and they usually rusted, causing corrosion in the cylinder-head area around them. This situation made it almost impossible to remove the spark plug tubes, and they often collapsed when a wrench was used in an attempt to remove them. The large 1½" diameter of the spark plug tubes usually meant they had to be dented with a hammer in order to clear the rocker arms. A minor detail!

In the early 1980s, Luke Balogh designed and machined stainless steel spark plug tubes with serrated brass or black anodized nuts. These were a very upscale replacement for the stock Ardun assembly. The center section of the spark plug tube is 1¼" diameter, which ensures rocker arm clearance. These serrated nuts and tubes accommodate the Mopar Performance #4120808 hemi spark plug insulator and boot assembly. This is a great-looking and practical addition to any Ardun engine. Dozens of Ardun owners throughout North America have these special nuts and spark plug tubes installed in their valve covers. Luke's is no longer producing the serrated nut and tube assembly. New gold irridited finish spark plug tubes and serrated nuts are available from Ardun Enterprises.

Here are Luke's brass serrated nuts and stainless steel spark plug tubes, the black anodized serrated nuts, and the Mopar Performance #4120808 hemi spark plug insulator and boot assembly for the Ardun engine. I am certain even Zora Arkus-Duntov would have been impressed with this assembly.

The price for a set of these spark plug tubes, seals, and serrated nuts is $350.

The installation of the Luke's spark plug tubes is very easy. The spark plug tube is installed in the cylinder head, the valve cover is secured in position, an O-ring is installed on the serrated nut, and the serrated nut is screwed onto the spark plug tube, against the valve cover. The hemi spark plug wire/tube cover is then slid over the serrated nut, resulting in a waterproof spark plug tube. Use anti-seize compound on all the spark plug tube threads when installing the spark plug tubes in the cylinder heads and the serrated nuts on the tubes.

One item that should be noted regarding Luke's spark plug tubes is that when using the Autolite #BT4, #BT8, or #377 or the Champion #D10 or #D16 conventional 18 mm spark plugs, the spark plugs must be installed before the spark plug tubes are installed. The NGK #WR5 and #WR4-one spark plugs have a smaller diameter body, thereby avoiding this situation. The 14-mm spark plugs can be installed with the spark plug tubes in place in the cylinder heads.

Ignition System Summary

Item	Price
New Mallory #3727501 Unilite electronic distributor (for 1949-53 Ford) with full centrifugal (mechanical) advance, 6061 T-6 billet aluminum, installed with Luke's new polished stainless distributor bracket and 1949-53 Ford #12270 distributor hold-down clamp using new polished stainless steel bolt and lock washer. Distributor total advance: 17 degrees @ 800 rpm; 28 degrees @ 1,800 rpm; and 41 degrees @ 3,000 rpm. New MSD #6200, Model 6A, multiple spark discharge ignition control, and new MSD #8200 Blaster 2 chrome ignition coil, 45,000 volts, installed with Luke's new polished stainless steel coil bracket.	$545.52
New Pertronix Performance Products #808290 FlameThrower high performance 8 mm spark plug wires, black 90 degree boots (removed), installed with Mopar Performance #4120808 hemi spark plug tube and insulator kit. Spectre #4245 chrome professional wire separators installed. New NGK #WR4-1 spark plugs, 18 mm, "projected nose," installed with 0.050" gap and torqued to 15 ft-lb using anti-seize compound.	$106.30
Luke's new stainless steel spark plug tubes, O-ring seals, and black anodized serrated nuts installed using anti-seize compound.	$350.00
1956 Ford V-8 12-volt generator chromed, rebuilt, and installed with Luke's new polished aluminum generator bracket and brace. Generator bracket installed with new stainless steel bolts, flat washers, and lock washers using anti-seize compound. New Super Sunny #8867C polished aluminum alternator fan and Luke's new polished aluminum generator pulley installed.	$385.46
1949-53 Ford flathead V-8 rebuilt spring-type starting motor, 6 volts, installed. Starting motor painted with Endura #EX-2C black 160 hi-gloss polyurethane.	$189.95
IGNITION SYSTEM TOTAL:	**$1,577.23**

CHAPTER 28
COOLING SYSTEM AND MISCELLANEOUS

Water Pumps

The 1949 Ford passenger car and truck water pumps used an impeller shaft with a separate bushing and a bearing. The 1950-53 Ford passenger car and truck water pumps used a combined shaft and bearing assembly. The later model shaft and bearing assembly is available as a replacement part from Fag Bearings Limited, part #W2503. The cost for this item is $12.25.

A hydraulic press is required in order to disassemble a water pump. The disassembly and the reassembly of a water pump should only be done by someone with expert knowledge of the Ford flathead V-8 water pump. Otherwise, the destruction of the water pump pulley and/or the water pump housing is almost a certainty.

Labor

The cost of the labor for checking clearances, gapping piston rings, degree camshaft, painting and detailing, cylinder head assembly, trial assembly of motor, final assembly of motor, and the initial start-up of the engine are include below.

Cooling System and Miscellaneous Summary

1949-53 Ford Truck #8RT-8503-B and #8RT-8504-B water pumps rebuilt by Luke's with new Fag Bearings Limited #W2503 shaft and bearing assembly. Water pumps installed with new stainless steel bolts and lock washers using silicone sealant on gaskets and torqued to 25 ft-lb. New Gates #15A1465 Green Stripe water pump/generator/crankshaft V-belt (11/16" x 57½" length) installed. Water pumps ground smooth and painted with PPG #74000 red hi-gloss polyurethane.	$154.59
Labor for checking bearing clearances, gapping piston rings, degreeing camshaft, fabricating oil lines, cylinder head assembly, painting and detailing, trial engine assembly, final engine assembly, and initial engine start-up.	$1,040.00
COOLING SYSTEM AND MISCELLANEOUS TOTAL:	**$1,194.59**

NOTE: The estimated output of this engine is: 300 hp @ 5,500 rpm and 323 ft-lb torque @ 4,000 rpm (See the Dyno Printouts section).

Ardun Performance Street Engine Total

Engine block	$1,173.46
Crankshaf	$925.00
Connecting rods and piston	$1,438.60
	$1,121.14
Lubrication system	
Camshaft and cylinder heads	$9,498.02
	$2,843.21
Intake system	
Ignition system	$1,577.23
Cooling system and miscellaneous	$1,194.59
TOTAL	**$19,771.25 (U.S.)**

CHAPTER 29

MISSING PARTS

Exhaust Manifolds

The exhaust manifolds are secured in place on the Ardun cylinder heads using ⅜" N.C. studs and nuts. The spacing between the studs for each exhaust port is 3.00" and the exhaust port diameter is 1⅝" (1.625"). The stock exhaust manifold gaskets supplied with the Fel-Pro #FS7525B gasket set are suitable; however, they have already been used for the exhaust port block-off plates. Your local automotive

These are the stock flathead exhaust manifold gaskets. The spacing between the exhaust port studs for each exhaust runner is 3" and the exhaust port diameter is 1⅝".

This is an Offenhauser #5272-A aluminum transmission adapter. This unit permits a Chevrolet manual transmission to be bolted to the flathead engine and also incorporates the cross-shaft throwout bearing used in the pre-1949 Fords and the 1949-51 Mercury. .

Another rare find is this Weber Tool Company 14.2"-diameter all-aluminum flywheel for the Ford flathead V-8 engine. It weighs 12.5 lbs.

Here are the two different types of 1949-53 Ford bellhousing adapters. The top one is the 1949-53 Ford Truck #8RT-6392, manufactured using cast steel. Other than that, they are the same.

This stock Ford #8602 flathead six-blade fan has been painted with Endura #EX-2C black 160 hi-gloss polyurethane.

parts dealer should be able to help out. The exhaust manifold studs should be installed in the aluminum cylinder heads using anti-seize compound in order to prevent the threads from galling, and the nuts should be torqued to 25 ft-lb.

I have not included the exhaust manifolds in the description of the engine in this section because the type of header will depend on the construction of the frame the engine will be installed in. The headers for an Ardun engine will have to be custom-made.

An interesting and unique point about the Ardun cylinder heads is that the exhaust flanges are parallel to the ground. This situation simplifies the fabrication of exhaust headers and will also guarantee an instant prairie fire if you do not use headers!

Flywheel and Flexplate

If you are going to use a Ford flathead standard transmission, you will require the stock Ford #7600 bronze pilot bushing. You can upgrade this part by using a roller pilot bearing, available from most high-performance parts outlets. An example would be the Federal #1203-FO with 1.75″ o.d. and 0.665″ i.d. for use with early Ford Transmissions.

For information on the fan, refer to Section I.

The stages of assembly that I am about to list below can be followed, or some of the later steps can be combined with some of the earlier steps. It is up to you as the owner of an Ardun engine to decide the sequence of assembly. It is only important to assemble the engine correctly without any parts leftover!

A Cam-A-Go camshaft bearing installation tool is used to install the center camshaft bearing. Do not even mildly contemplate installing camshaft bearings without this type of tool!

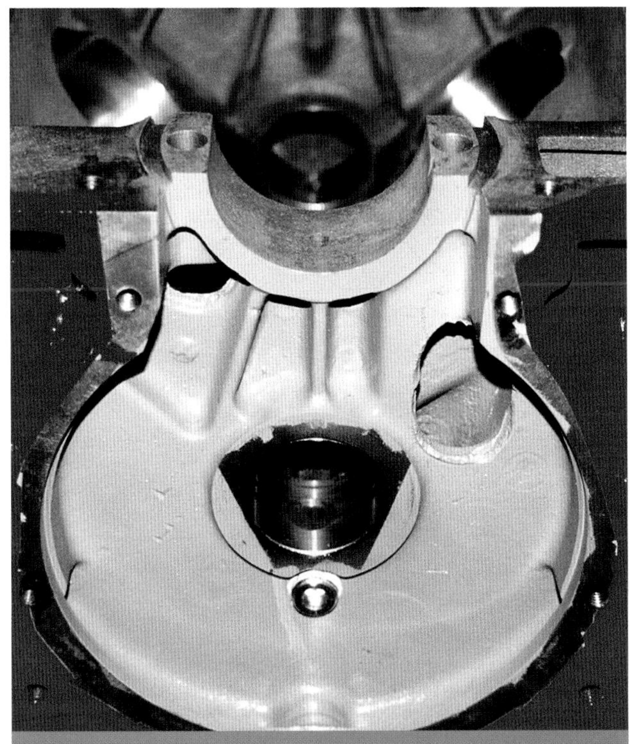

The Clevite 77 #SH-21S camshaft bearings are installed.

For information on assembling the engine block, refer to Section I. In addition, install the eight stainless steel cylinder socket head set screws for the cylinder head bolt holes, and the two stainless steel ⅛″ N.P.T. plugs for the water passages, in the engine block using Permatex aviation form-a-gasket.

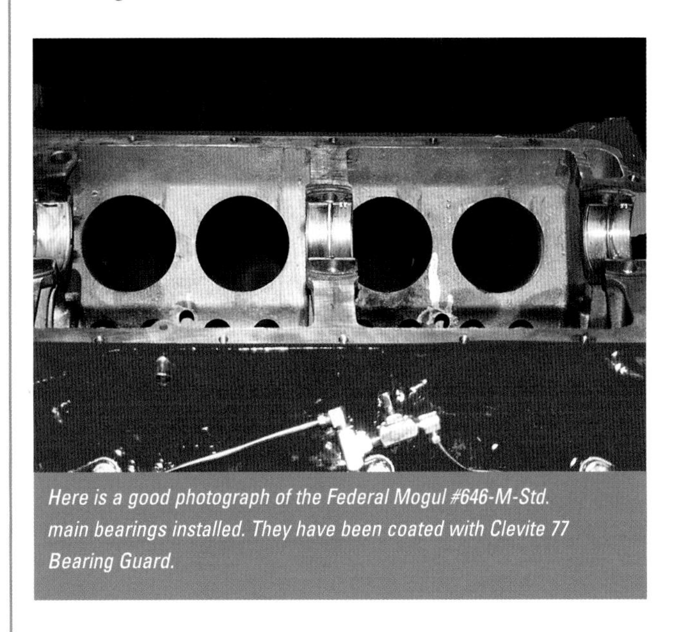

Here is a good photograph of the Federal Mogul #646-M-Std. main bearings installed. They have been coated with Clevite 77 Bearing Guard.

For crankshaft information, refer to Section I.

Connecting Rods and Pistons

Refer to Section I for information. In addition, the Ross Racing Pistons have two notches on the dome of their Ardun pistons for valve clearance. The larger notch should be at the top of each cylinder and is for the intake valve clearance. The smaller notch should be at the bottom of each cylinder and is for the exhaust valve clearance. Remember this when assembling the connecting rod and piston assemblies!

For lubrication system information, refer to Section I.

Camshaft and Cylinder Heads

Install the intake and exhaust valve camshaft lifters (tappets) for the #1 cylinder and degree the camshaft. If all the results of this exercise are in accordance with the manufacturer's specification card (timing tag), then continue with the engine assembly. If they are not, you had better find out why before proceeding any further.

Install all the valves in the cylinder heads with the valve spring seat cups, the valve stem seals, the valve springs, the valve spring retainers, and the valve stem locks. Coat everything with motor oil as you assemble it. The valve springs must be at the recommended installed height; shim as necessary.

The Ross Racing Pistons, 1942 Ford #21A connecting rods, Canadian Ford Military #631T-6211-C full-floating connecting rod bearings, and the Total Seal moly piston rings are spread out prior to installation in the engine block.

The larger notch on the dome of these Ross Racing Pistons faces the top of the engine and is for the intake valve clearance. The smaller notch faces the bottom of the engine and is for the exhaust valve clearance. Note the stainless steel ½" N.P.T. plug in the water passage opening at the very front of the deck surface.

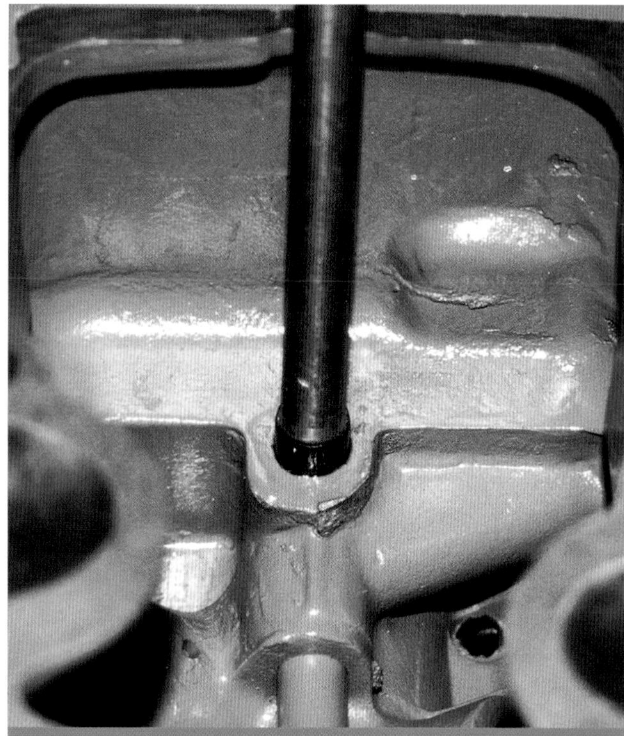
The fuel pump pushrod bushing is installed with a brass drift. Notice the great finish Glyptal paint gives to the valve lifter gallery .

Install the one-piece oil seal and the crankshaft oil seal sleeve on the crankshaft by gently tapping it into position with a piece of pipe and a hammer. Install the timing gear cover using silicone sealant on the gasket and around the oil seal. Install the timing gear cover bolts using Loctite and torque to 15 ft-lb.

Install the cord material rear oil seal in the oil pan by rolling it in place with a large socket or using the head of a large ball peen hammer and tapping the head of the hammer with another hammer. Place some putty on the oil pump pick-up screen and position the oil pan on the engine block without the oil pan gaskets. Push down firmly on the oil pan and then remove it from the engine. Measure the putty for compressed thickness. The proper oil pan-to-oil pump pick-up clearance should be ¾" to 1". If the compressed thickness is correct, carry on. If it is not, adjust the oil pump pick-up arm until the correct clearance is obtained. Install the oil pan on the engine block using silicone sealant on the gaskets. Install the oil pan bolts using Loctite and torque them to 165 in-lb. Screw the dipstick tube into the oil pan using silicone sealant and install the dipstick.

Install the engine block exhaust port block-off plates using silicone sealant on the gaskets, and torque the bolts to 20 ft-lb using Loctite. Install the exhaust port oil drain lines using pipe thread sealant on the fittings.

Install the camshaft lifters using motor oil on the camshaft lifter bosses, and coat the face (bottom) of the camshaft lifters liberally with the camshaft assembly lube provided by the camshaft manufacturer.

Install the cylinder head studs snugly in the engine block using Permatex aviation form-a-gasket, and coat the shaft of the studs with anti-seize compound. Do not over-tighten the studs. Place some putty on the piston top in any cylinder. Slide the cylinder head over the cylinder head studs. Do not install the cylinder head gasket. Slide the rocker arm assembly over the cylinder head studs, install two cylinder head stud nuts and flat washers and tighten them down lightly. Install the intake and exhaust pushrods for that cylinder. Adjust the valves for that cylinder according to the camshaft manufacturer's specifications. Rotate the crankshaft until the exhaust valve for that cylinder starts to open, and adjust the intake valve for that cylinder. Rotate the crankshaft until the intake valve for that cylinder starts to close, then adjust the exhaust valve for that cylinder. Rotate the crankshaft at least two full turns in the normal direction of rotation. Remove the rocker arm assembly and the cylinder head and measure the compressed thickness of the valve imprints in the putty on the piston top. This measurement will indicate the valve-to-piston clearance. The minimum intake valve-to-piston clearance should be 0.060″ and the minimum exhaust valve-to-piston clearance should be 0.065″ without the cylinder head gasket. The clearances for this engine were: 0.113″ intake and exhaust valve-to-piston clearance without the cylinder head gasket.

This picture shows the rear cord material oil seal installed in the upper oil seal retainer.

The bottom end is now complete and a new Melling #M-19 standard volume oil pump has been installed. The center main bearing cap support bridge was fabricated by Luke's. Notice the stainless steel safety wire through the oil pump mounting bolt.

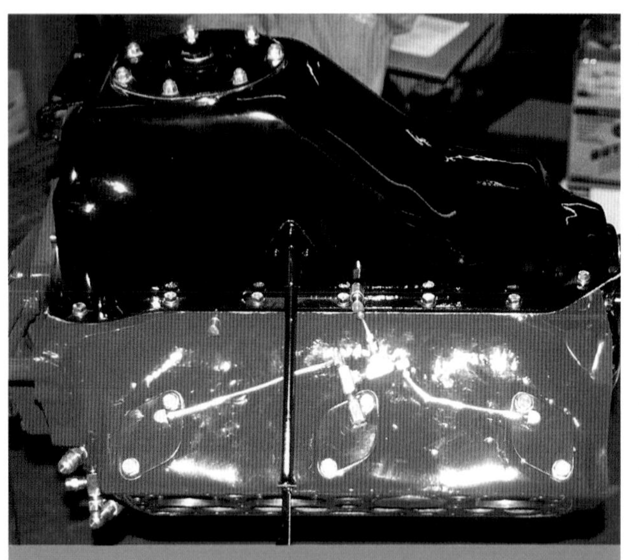

The 1949-53 Ford Truck oil pan and crankshaft pulley have been installed, and the stock exhaust port oil drain lines have all been connected. It is time to flip this baby over!

Those are the second-generation milk bottle-shape solid lifters installed. They definitely look odd sitting inside a flathead engine.

The numbers on the cylinder head studs indicate where the different length studs are located. The short studs are 6, 10, 11, 15, 18, and 20. The medium studs are 1, 3, 5, 7, 8, 9, 12, 13, 14, 16, 17, and 19 The long studs are 2 and 4. The studs are located in the same position on each side of the engine block.

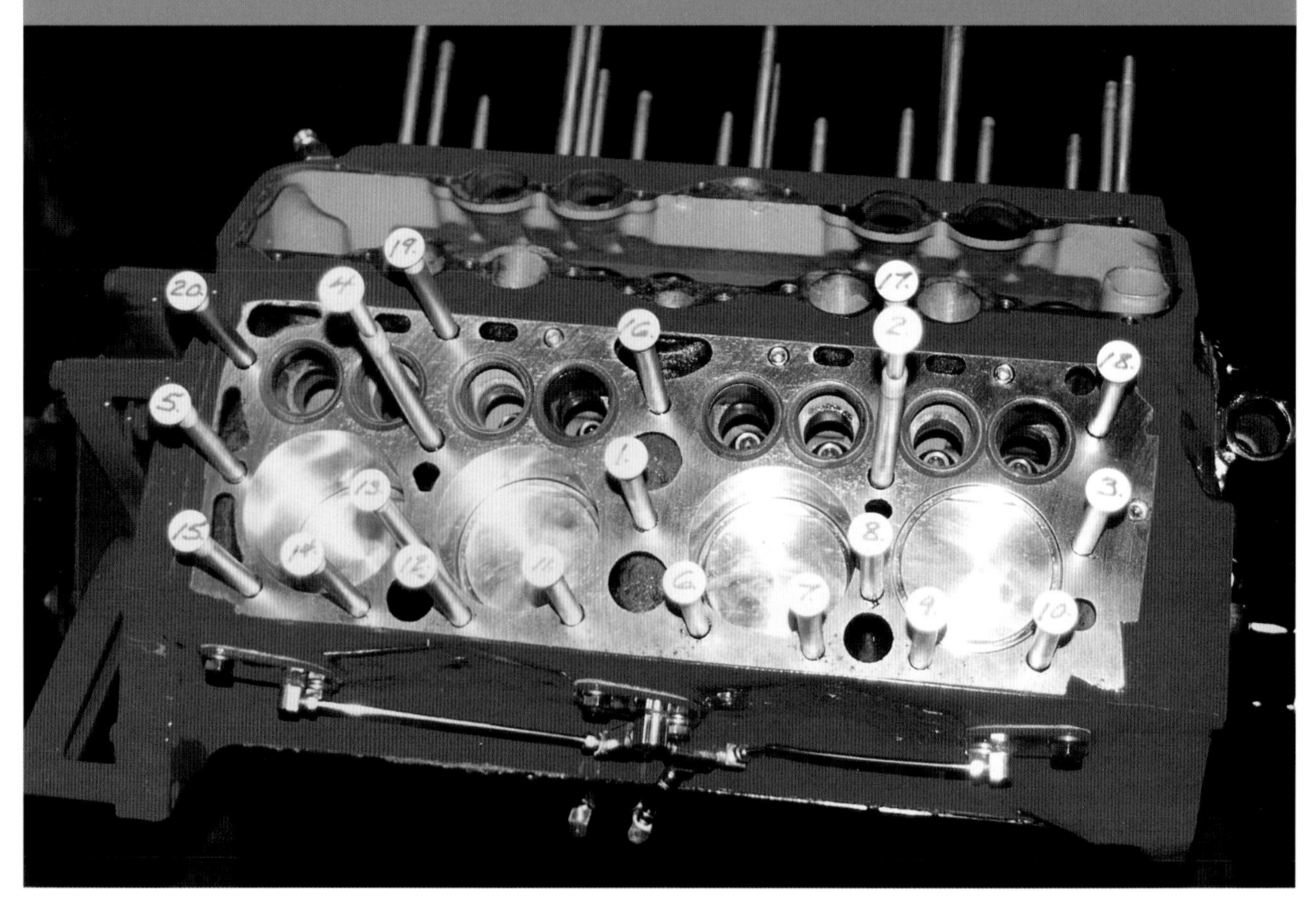

The Ardun cylinder head studs and the Victor/Reinz #GX-13173-1 cylinder head gasket have all been installed. The cylinder head studs have been coated with anti-seize compound.

Install the cylinder head gaskets dry; do not use any sealant. The cylinder head stud holes in the Victor/Reinz #GX-13173-1 cylinder head gaskets are perfectly positioned. This is a great aid in determining if the cylinder head studs are correctly aligned. If they are not, gently tweak the studs with a metal tube in order to align them. Slide the cylinder heads and rocker arm assemblies over the cylinder head studs and install the cylinder head stud nuts and flat washers using

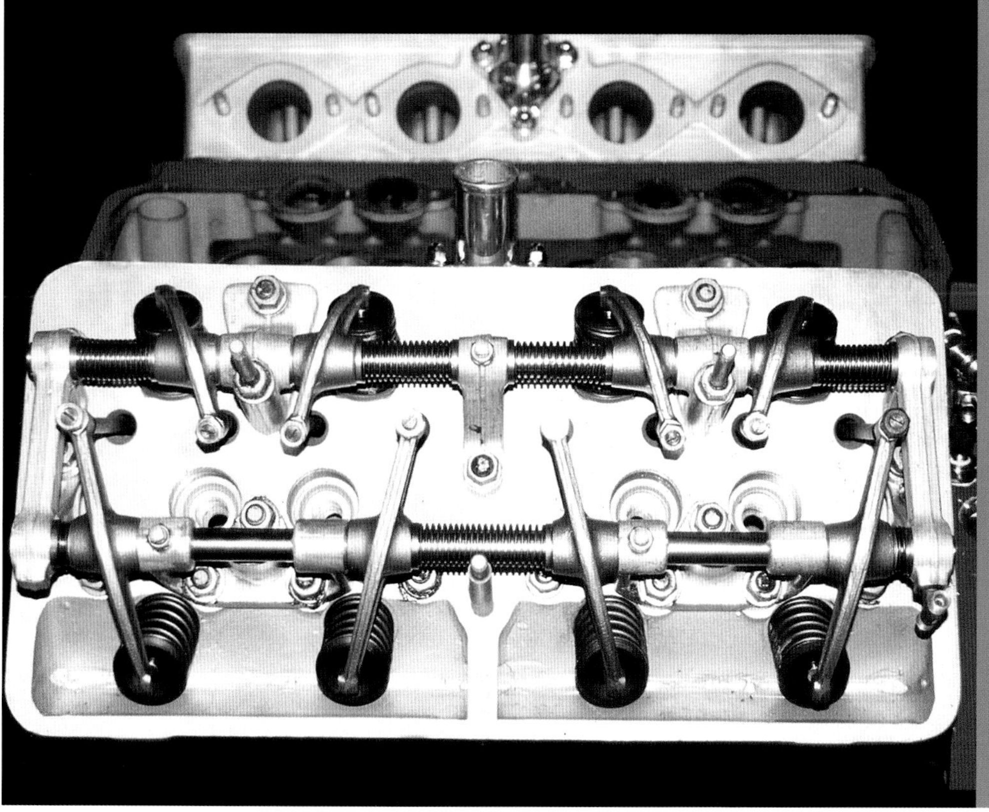

The Ardun cylinder head, rocker arm assembly, and the pushrods have all been installed. This engine is starting to look like it means business.

These are the polished stainless steel oil feed lines for the cylinder heads. Holley 0.054″ carburetor jets have been machined to fit inside the pipe thread end of the Weatherhead #202-3 brass adapters, which are the fittings in the "T" fitting that the stainless steel lines are screwed into.

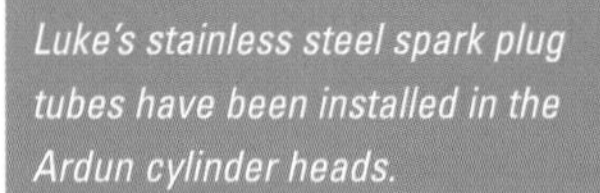

Luke's stainless steel spark plug tubes have been installed in the Ardun cylinder heads.

Molykote on the threads. Install the pushrods before tightening the cylinder head stud nuts. Torque the cylinder heads to 55 ft-lb using the manufacturer's recommended torque sequence.

Install the water outlet elbows and water outlet elbow acorn nuts using silicone sealant on the gaskets. Torque the water outlet elbow acorn nuts to 15 ft-lb.

Install the rocker arm lubrication lines.

Install the cylinder head oil feed lines and the cylinder head oil drain lines using pipe thread sealant on the fittings.

Adjust all the valves according to the procedure explained above. Gap the spark plugs to 0.050″, coat the threads with anti-seize compound, install the spark plugs, and torque them to 15 ft-lb. Install the spark plug tubes in the cylinder heads using anti-seize compound on the threads. Install the neoprene rubber valve-cover gaskets dry—do not

The right side Ardun valve cover has been installed on the engine, and the valve cover gasket is visible around the lip of the valve cover.

The Ardun #3261 chrome valley cover has been installed.

use any sealant—and install the valve covers. Install the three acorn nuts and flat washers on the valve cover studs for each valve cover and torque them to 15 ft-lb. Slide the spark plug tube gaskets over the serrated nuts and install them in the end of the spark plug tubes against the valve covers. Tighten the serrated nuts snugly; do not overtighten.

Install the stock Ford flathead V-8 intake manifold gasket using silicone sealant and then install the valley cover. Apply silicone sealant on the valley cover bolts and torque them to 25 ft-lb. Install the chrome acorn nut covers on the valley cover bolts.

Intake System

Install the carburetor studs in the intake manifold using anti-seize compound. Place the carburetor gaskets on the

Continued on page 174

The Austin Model TD intake manifold, complete with the three Holley 94 carburetors, has been installed.

The polished ⅜"-o.d. stainless steel fuel lines make a great finishing touch to a terrific intake system.

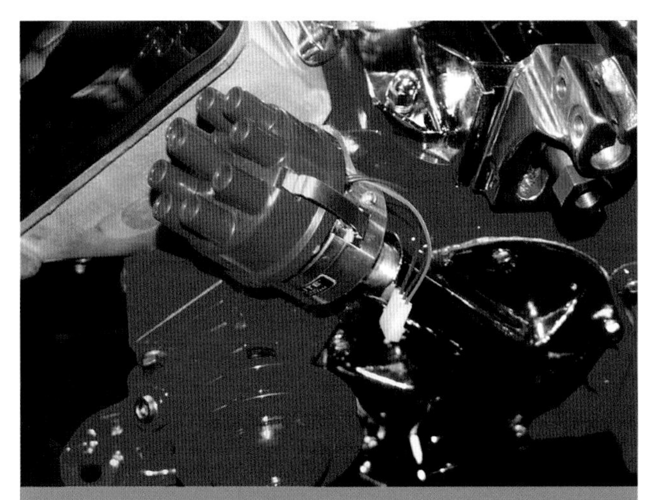

Here is the Mallory #3727501 Unilite electronic distributor installed. An Offenhauser #3499 polished aluminum fan carrier bracket is pictured above the chrome timing gear cover.

The polished stainless steel distributor bracket fabricated by Luke's Custom Machine & Design.

All the spark plug wires are neatly in position and just waiting for some juice to light up this beast!

Continued from page 171
intake manifold, and install the carburetors using anti-seize compound on the studs. Tighten the carburetor nuts snugly, but do not overtighten them. Install the carburetor linkage on the extended throttle shafts and adjust the linkage. Install the air cleaners on the carburetors.

Slide the intake manifold runner flanges onto the intake manifold runners followed by the O-rings. NOTE: Four of the flanges have notches on the face in order to provide clearance for the upper edge of the left (driver's) side of the engine block. The left cylinder head sits slightly lower on the engine block than the right cylinder head. Install the intake manifold studs in one cylinder head only, place the intake manifold on the engine, and then install the intake manifold studs in the other cylinder head. Use anti-seize compound on the intake manifold studs, and torque the intake manifold acorn nuts to 25 ft-lb. Each intake runner flange is independent of the other; however, it is best to torque the acorn nuts from the center outward. Install the fuel pump stand/crankcase breather housing using silicone sealant on the gasket and anti-seize compound on the studs. Torque the acorn nuts to 15 ft-lb.

Install the generator/fuel block/fuel pressure regulator mounting brackets and the fuel block, with the fuel pressure regulator attached, to the intake manifold. Fabricate the fuel lines from the fuel block to the carburetors using a tubing bender and a double flaring tool, then install the fuel lines.

Attach the oil line from the outboard pressure-out hole in the engine block to the inlet side of the remote oil filter, and attach the oil line from the inboard drain-in hole in the engine block to the outlet side of the remote oil filter. Use Teflon tape or pipe thread sealant on the oil line fittings.

Fill the oil filter with oil and install it on the remote oil filter bracket. Pour the required amount of motor oil in the engine. Install a temporary oil pressure gauge.

Ignition System

Install the crankshaft pulley woodruff key in the crankshaft slot using anti-seize compound and gently tap the key into position with a hammer. Apply some anti-seize compound to the snout of the crankshaft and install the crankshaft pulley. The pulley should have a snug fit, but it should not require the use of a harmonic balancer installation tool. Gently tap the crankshaft pulley onto the crankshaft using a piece of wood and a hammer. Install the crankshaft pulley bolt and washer using Loctite, and torque the bolt to 50 ft-lb.

Rotate the crankshaft until the engine is set with the #1 piston at 10 degrees before TDC (top dead center), and insert the distributor in the timing gear cover with the distributor rotor at the #1 spark plug lead position. Clamp down the distributor.

Lay out the spark plug wires and cut them to length for each cylinder. The cylinders on the right (passenger's) side of the engine are numbered 1, 2, 3, and 4 from the front, and the cylinders on the left (driver's) side of the engine are numbered 5, 6, 7, and 8 from the front. The firing order is: 1, 5, 4, 8, 6, 3, 7, 2. Slip the hemi spark plug wire/tube cover on the spark plug wire first, then the bakelite insulator tube, and then the rubber spark plug boot. Install the wires on the spark plugs and in the distributor cap. Install the ignition coil and coil bracket using anti-seize compound on the bolts. Connect the coil wire to the distributor.

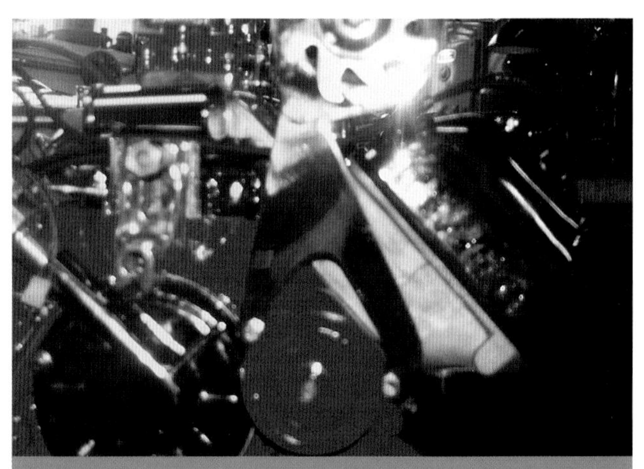

This is the polished aluminum generator mounting bracket fabricated by Luke's.

Bolt the generator to the generator mounting bracket, and install the complete unit using anti-seize compound on the bolts.

You will have to install a flywheel or flexplate in order to start the engine. Install the flywheel or flexplate bolts with Loctite and torque them to 80 ft-lb. A bellhousing and starting motor plate will have to be installed to mount the starting motor.

The 1949-53 Ford Truck #8RT-8503-B and #8RT-8504-B water pumps have been installed.

Here is the finished product, and what a great looking piece of automotive history this is! The headers are being used for the engine start-up only.

Install the starting motor using anti-seize compound on the bolts.

Cooling System and Miscellaneous

Apply silicone sealant to the water pump gaskets and bolts. Install the water pumps and torque the bolts to 25 ft-lb.

Install the water pump/alternator/crankshaft pulley V-belt, allowing for approximately ½″ to 1″ slack.

Hook up some headers (the cylinder head oil drain lines will have to be removed to do this) and mufflers, a radiator with some water in it, and the ignition system with a battery and starter switch. Start the engine, and adjust the timing and the carburetor. Allow the engine to run at approximately 2,000 rpm for 30 minutes in order to break-in the camshaft. After the engine is at full operating temperature, shut it off, allow the engine to cool, remove the valve covers, and re-torque the cylinder heads using the manufacturer's approved torque pattern. Install the valve covers with the valve cover gaskets dry and torque the valve cover acorn nuts to 15 ft-lb. Now you can sit back and truly admire "the old days elephant motor," as Tom Senter would say!

This photograph is not of two thugs you would see on "America's Most Wanted" or on posters in your local post office! That is Luke Balogh on the left and me on the right. The best part of this picture is the Ardun engine!

CHAPTER 31
DYNO PRINTOUTS

Ford Flathead V-8 259-ci Performance Street Engine

This engine consisted of the following:

- 1950 Canadian Ford engine block with full-flow oil system; block bored 0.125″ over to 3.3125″; engine block parallel decked. Ford 3½″-stroke cast alloy steel crankshaft.
- 1949-53 Ford connecting rods, casting #8BA-6205A. Ross forged aluminum pistons with Grant cast iron piston ring set.
- Melling #M-19 oil pump and 1949-53 Ford Truck oil pan.
- Iskenderian Racing Cams #811100 (8BA) Max #1 grind camshaft; Johnson adjustable lifters; 1.60″ stainless steel intake and exhaust valves; Iskenderian Racing Cams #185-G single valve springs.
- 1949-53 Ford cast iron cylinder heads.
- Offenhauser #1078 polished aluminum single quad intake manifold with Edelbrock #1404 "performer" 500-cfm carburetor.
- Chevrolet distributor with Pertronix electronic conversion kit, MSD chrome coil, and MSD control box. Pertronix 8 mm spark plug wires. GM chrome alternator.
- 1949-53 Ford Truck water pumps.

NOTE: The estimated output of this engine is 206 hp @ 5,000 rpm and 242 ft-lb torque @ 3,500 rpm.

SHORT BLOCK

Block:	FORD "FLATHEAD".	Bore:	3.313 in	Stroke:	3.750 in
Cylinders:	8	Cyl Vol:	529.7 cc	Total Vol:	258.6 ci

CYLINDER HEADS

Cylinder Heads:	Low Performance/Stock Ports And Valves		
Air Flow File:	***		
Intake Valves:	1	Exhaust Valves:	1
Intake Valve:	1.600 in	Exhaust Valve:	1.600 in

COMPRESSION

Compression Ratio:	7.50	Combustion Space:	81.5 cc

INDUCTION

Induction Flow:	500.0 cfm @ 1.5 inHg	Fuel:	Gasoline
Manifold Type:	Dual-Plane Manifold	N20:	0.0 lbs/min

Blower:	None			Intercooler:	*** %
Flow:	*** cfm	Pressure Ratio:	***	Boost Limit:	*** psi
Speed:	*** rpm	Belt Gear Ratio:	***	Surge Flow:	*** cfm
Eff:	*** %	Internal Gear Ratio:	***		

EXHAUST

Exhaust System:	H.P. Manifolds And Mufflers

CAMSHAFT

Camshaft Type:	ISKY "MAX #1".	Cam File:	***
Lifter:	Solid	Lobe Center:	110.0
Cam Specs @:	0.050-Lift	Valve Overlap:	6.0
Int Lift@Valve:	0.350 in	Int Duration:	226.0
Exh Lift@Valve:	0.350 in	Exh Duration:	226.0
Nominal Timing		Timing@ Adv(+)/Ret(-):	0.0

IVO (BTDC):	3.0	IVC (ABDC):	43.0	IVO:	3.0	IVC:	43.0
EVO (BBDC):	43.0	EVC (ATDC):	3.0	EVO:	43.0	EVC:	3.0
ICA (ATDC):	110.0	ECA (BTDC):	110.0	ICA:	110.0	ECA:	110.0

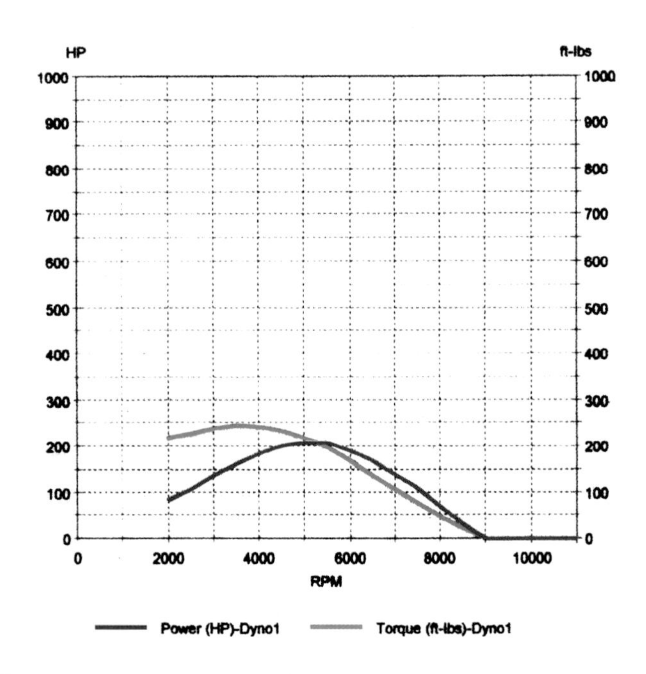

CALCULATED POWER AND ENGINE PRESSURES

Engine RPM	Power (Fly)	Torque (Fly)	Int Man Pressure	Vol Eff %	IMEP Pressure	FMEP Pressure	BMEP Pressure
2000	84	220	14.67	64.9	171.0	17.8	129.8
2500	107	225	14.66	66.9	168.3	19.3	133.0
3000	136	238	14.63	71.3	175.0	21.0	140.7
3500	161	242	14.59	74.6	175.8	22.8	143.0
4000	182	239	14.55	76.5	174.6	24.7	141.4
4500	199	232	14.50	77.1	172.0	26.7	137.0
5000	206	217	14.45	76.5	164.7	28.9	128.1
5500	206	196	14.40	74.7	154.2	31.2	116.1
6000	191	167	14.36	70.6	138.2	33.6	98.7
6500	169	136	14.34	66.2	121.5	36.2	80.6
7000	139	104	14.34	61.4	104.2	38.8	61.7
7500	110	77	14.34	57.1	89.8	41.6	45.4
8000	70	46	14.35	52.5	73.5	44.6	27.3
8500	33	20	14.36	48.6	60.5	47.6	12.1
9000	0	0	14.38	44.7	47.1	50.8	-3.5
9500	0	0	14.39	41.0	34.7	54.1	-18.4
10000	0	0	14.41	37.8	24.2	57.6	-31.5
10500	0	0	14.43	34.6	13.4	61.2	-45.0
11000	0	0	14.45	31.8	5.0	64.9	-56.4

Luke's Custom Machine & Design completed this Ford flathead V-8 engine in August 2002. The owner installed it in a daily-driven 1948 Ford pickup.

Ford Flathead V-8 286-ci Performance Street Engine

This engine consisted of the following:

- 1950 Canadian Ford engine block with full-flow oil system; main bearing cap support bridges; block bored to 3⅜″; block align honed and parallel decked; intake and exhaust ports fully ported and polished; block relieved; Mercury 4″-stroke cast alloy steel crankshaft.
- 1950-53 Ford connecting rods, casting #8BA-6205A; Jahns cast aluminum pistons with Grant cast iron piston rings.
- Melling #M-19 oil pump and 1949-53 Ford passenger car chrome oil pan.
- Iskenderian Racing Cams #818800 (8BA) 88 grind camshaft; Johnson adjustable lifters; 1.60″ intake valves and 1.50″ exhaust valves; Iskenderian #185-G single valve springs; Speedway Motors new valve guide bushings.
- Offenhauser #1069 polished aluminum "425" cylinder heads.
- Offenhauser #1078 polished aluminum single quad intake manifold with Holley 650-cfm double-pumper carburetor. Speedway Motors "Mr. Roadster" air scoop.
- Mallory dual-point distributor and Accel chrome coil. Taylor 8-mm spark plug wires. GM chrome alternator.
- 1949 Mercury chrome water pumps. Polished stainless steel 18″ flexfan.
- Speedway Motors Cermakrome coated exhaust headers.
- Gene Benson's "Flat-O-Matic" Ford C-4 automatic transmission conversion kit.

NOTE: The estimated output of this engine is 215 hp @ 4,500 rpm and 289 ft-lb torque @ 3,000 rpm.

SHORT BLOCK

Block:	FORD "FLATHEAD".	Bore:	3.375 in	Stroke:	4.000 in
Cylinders:	8	Cyl Vol:	586.4 cc	Total Vol:	286.3 ci

CYLINDER HEADS

Cylinder Heads:	Low Performance/Stock Ports And Valves		
Air Flow File:	***		
Intake Valves:	1	Exhaust Valves:	1
Intake Valve:	1.600 in	Exhaust Valve:	1.500 in

COMPRESSION

Compression Ratio:	8.60	Combustion Space:	77.2 cc

INDUCTION

Induction Flow:	650.0 cfm @ 1.5 inHg	Fuel:	Gasoline
Manifold Type:	Dual-Plane Manifold	N20:	0.0 lbs/min

Blower:	None			Intercooler:	*** %
Flow:	*** cfm	Pressure Ratio:	***	Boost Limit:	*** psi
Speed:	*** rpm	Belt Gear Ratio:	***	Surge Flow:	*** cfm
Eff:	*** %	Internal Gear Ratio:	***		

EXHAUST

Exhaust System:	H.P. Manifolds And Mufflers

CAMSHAFT

Camshaft Type:	ISKY "88 GRIND".	Cam File:	***
Lifter:	Solid	Lobe Center:	110.0
Cam Specs @:	0.050-Lift	Valve Overlap:	4.0
Int Lift@Valve:	0.324 in	Int Duration:	224.0
Exh Lift@Valve:	0.322 in	Exh Duration:	224.0
Nominal Timing		Timing@ Adv(+)/Ret(-):	0.0

IVO (BTDC):	5.0	IVC (ABDC):	39.0	IVO:	5.0	IVC:	39.0
EVO (BBDC):	45.0	EVC (ATDC):	-1.0	EVO:	45.0	EVC:	-1.0
ICA (ATDC):	107.0	ECA (BTDC):	113.0	ICA:	107.0	ECA:	113.0

CALCULATED POWER AND ENGINE PRESSURES

Engine RPM	Power (Fly)	Torque (Fly)	Int Man Pressure	Vol Eff %	IMEP Pressure	FMEP Pressure	BMEP Pressure
2000	104	272	14.68	69.9	189.8	18.2	145.4
2500	132	278	14.66	72.0	185.9	19.9	148.3
3000	165	289	14.64	76.1	190.5	21.7	154.2
3500	190	284	14.61	78.1	186.2	23.6	151.9
4000	208	272	14.58	78.8	180.0	25.7	145.6
4500	215	251	14.55	77.3	170.2	28.0	134.1
5000	211	222	14.52	74.5	156.1	30.4	118.6
5500	192	183	14.49	69.6	136.6	32.9	97.8
6000	163	143	14.49	64.0	116.4	35.6	76.2
6500	126	102	14.49	58.3	96.1	38.5	54.4
7000	83	62	14.49	52.9	76.8	41.4	33.3
7500	40	28	14.51	48.1	60.4	44.6	14.9
8000	0	0	14.52	43.3	43.3	47.8	-4.3
8500	0	0	14.53	38.9	28.9	51.3	-21.1
9000	0	0	14.55	35.1	15.8	54.8	-36.8
9500	0	0	14.56	31.7	5.1	58.5	-50.4
10000	0	0	14.58	28.4	-4.8	62.4	-63.4
10500	0	0	14.59	25.5	-13.7	66.4	-75.6
11000	0	0	14.60	22.7	-21.5	70.5	-86.8

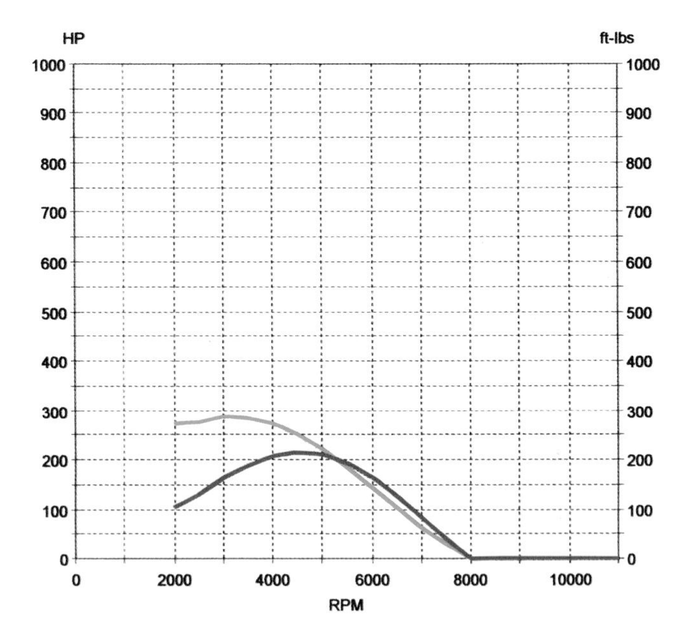

I built this Ford flathead V-8 286-ci engine over 10 years ago and sold it 7 years ago to a fine gentleman living in Colorado.

Ford Flathead V-8 260-ci Performance Street Engine

This engine consisted of the following:

- 1950 Canadian Ford engine block; full-flow oil system; block bored 0.030″ over to 3.2175″; engine block parallel decked; intake and exhaust ports fully ported and polished; Mercury 4″-stroke cast alloy steel crankshaft.
- 1950-53 Ford connecting rods, casting #8BA-6205A. Ross Racing Pistons forged aluminum pistons with Ross Racing Pistons moly rings.
- Melling #M-19 oil pump and 1949-53 Ford passenger car oil pan.
- Crane Cams #BF5528 400 grind camshaft; Johnson adjustable lifters; 1.60″ stainless steel intake and exhaust valves; Iskenderian #185-G single valve springs; Speedway Motors new valve guide bushings.
- Offenhauser #1069 polished aluminum "400" cylinder heads.
- Offenhauser #1075 polished aluminum regular dual-carb intake manifold with 2 x Holley 94 carburetors.
- MSD electronic distributor; MSD chrome coil; MSD ignition box. Taylor 8-mm spark plug wires. GM chrome alternator.
- 1949-53 Ford passenger car water pumps.
- Fenton cast iron exhaust headers.

NOTE: The estimated output of this engine is 208 hp @ 5,500 rpm and 229 ft-lb torque @ 4,000 rpm.

SHORT BLOCK

Block: FORD "FLATHEAD". Bore: 3.218 in Stroke: 4.000 in
Cylinders: 8 Cyl Vol: 533.1 cc Total Vol: 260.3 ci

CYLINDER HEADS

Cylinder Heads: Low Performance/Stock Ports And Valves
Air Flow File: ***
Intake Valves: 1 Exhaust Valves: 1
Intake Valve: 1.600 in Exhaust Valve: 1.600 in

COMPRESSION

Compression Ratio: 8.50 Combustion Space: 71.1 cc

INDUCTION

Induction Flow: 320.0 cfm @ 1.5 inHg Fuel: Gasoline
Manifold Type: Dual-Plane Manifold N20: 0.0 lbs/min

Blower: None Intercooler: *** %
Flow: *** cfm Pressure Ratio: *** Boost Limit: *** psi
Speed: *** rpm Belt Gear Ratio: *** Surge Flow: *** cfm
Eff: *** % Internal Gear Ratio: ***

EXHAUST

Exhaust System: H.P. Manifolds And Mufflers

CAMSHAFT

Camshaft Type: CRANE CAMS "400". Cam File: ***
Lifter: Solid Lobe Center: 111.0
Cam Specs @: 0.050-Lift Valve Overlap: 22.0
Int Lift@Valve: 0.396 in Int Duration: 244.0
Exh Lift@Valve: 0.396 in Exh Duration: 244.0
Nominal Timing Timing@ Adv(+)/Ret(-): 0.0

IVO (BTDC): 14.0 IVC (ABDC): 50.0 IVO: 14.0 IVC: 50.0
EVO (BBDC): 56.0 EVC (ATDC): 8.0 EVO: 56.0 EVC: 8.0
ICA (ATDC): 108.0 ECA (BTDC): 114.0 ICA: 108.0 ECA: 114.0

Engine RPM	Power (Fly)	Torque (Fly)	Int Man Pressure	Vol Eff %	IMEP Pressure	FMEP Pressure	BMEP Pressure
2000	73	191	14.62	61.8	150.7	18.2	112.3
2500	97	204	14.60	65.2	154.2	19.9	119.9
3000	125	219	14.54	70.3	162.6	21.7	128.7
3500	152	228	14.45	74.7	166.9	23.6	133.9
4000	175	229	14.33	77.5	168.4	25.7	134.6
4500	194	226	14.19	79.2	168.9	28.0	132.9
5000	205	215	14.04	79.4	164.5	30.4	126.5
5500	208	198	13.90	78.7	156.5	32.9	116.6
6000	201	176	13.76	76.3	145.1	35.6	103.3
6500	182	147	13.67	72.4	129.8	38.5	86.2
7000	156	117	13.62	68.6	114.4	41.4	68.8
7500	128	89	13.59	64.4	100.3	44.6	52.6
8000	93	61	13.59	60.9	85.7	47.8	35.7
8500	57	35	13.58	57.1	73.2	51.3	20.7
9000	15	9	13.59	53.7	60.3	54.8	5.2
9500	0	0	13.61	50.0	47.7	58.5	-10.2
10000	0	0	13.65	47.0	37.8	62.4	-23.2
10500	0	0	13.68	44.2	27.0	66.4	-37.2
11000	0	0	13.71	41.0	17.2	70.5	-50.3

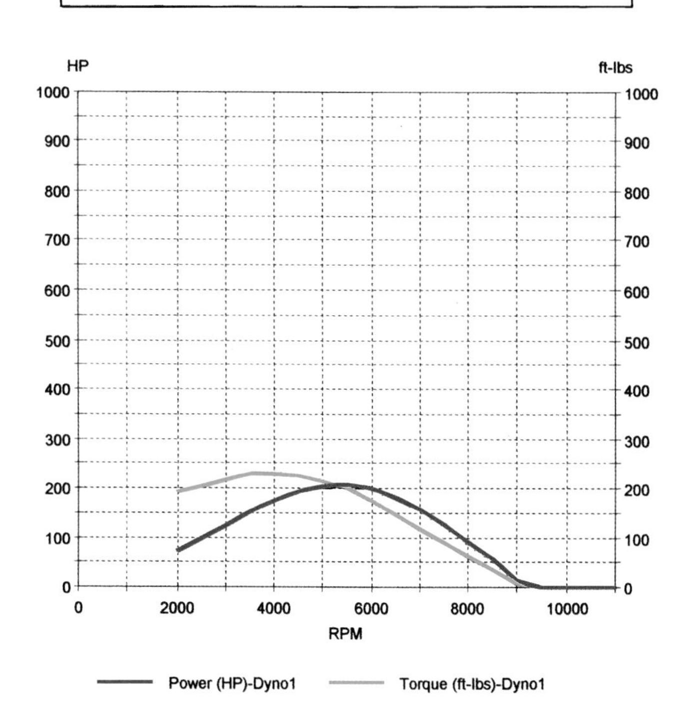

Ford Flathead V-8 260-ci Performance Street Engine, continued

This Ford flathead V-8 260-ci engine is on a wooden test stand built by the owner. When I first saw this monstrosity (the engine stand), I thought it had been built by someone out on a day pass from the funny farm! The engine was built by Luke's and installed in a daily-driven 1950 Ford two-door coupe.

Ford Flathead V-8 276-ci Performance Street Engine

NOTE: The estimated output of this engine is 221 hp @ 5,000 rpm and 286 ft-lb torque @ 3,000 rpm.

CALCULATED POWER AND ENGINE PRESSURES

Engine RPM	Power (Fly)	Torque (Fly)	Int Man Pressure	Vol Eff %	IMEP Pressure	FMEP Pressure	BMEP Pressure
2000	102	267	14.66	70.7	193.2	18.2	148.3
2500	130	274	14.63	72.9	189.7	19.9	151.7
3000	163	286	14.60	77.2	195.3	21.7	158.6
3500	189	284	14.55	79.4	191.9	23.6	157.2
4000	209	274	14.49	80.2	186.8	25.7	151.9
4500	220	257	14.43	79.3	179.1	28.0	142.6
5000	221	232	14.37	76.9	166.6	30.4	128.5
5500	209	199	14.32	73.2	150.1	32.9	110.5
6000	183	160	14.30	67.7	129.8	35.6	88.8
6500	152	123	14.29	62.5	110.5	38.5	68.0
7000	113	84	14.30	57.2	91.1	41.4	46.8
7500	71	50	14.31	52.2	74.0	44.6	27.7
8000	24	16	14.33	47.8	57.3	47.8	8.9
8500	0	0	14.35	43.4	42.6	51.3	-8.1
9000	0	0	14.38	39.5	29.1	54.8	-24.3
9500	0	0	14.40	35.8	16.4	58.5	-39.7
10000	0	0	14.43	32.5	6.0	62.4	-53.1
10500	0	0	14.46	29.4	-4.3	66.4	-66.7
11000	0	0	14.48	26.7	-12.1	70.5	-78.0

SHORT BLOCK

Block: FORD "FLATHEAD". Bore: 3.313 in Stroke: 4.000 in
Cylinders: 8 Cyl Vol: 565.1 cc Total Vol: 275.9 ci

CYLINDER HEADS

Cylinder Heads: Low Performance/Stock Ports And Valves
Air Flow File: ***
Intake Valves: 1 Exhaust Valves: 1
Intake Valve: 1.600 in Exhaust Valve: 1.600 in

COMPRESSION

Compression Ratio: 9.10 Combustion Space: 69.8 cc

INDUCTION

Induction Flow: 480.0 cfm @ 1.5 inHg Fuel: Gasoline
Manifold Type: Dual-Plane Manifold N20: 0.0 lbs/min

Blower: None Intercooler: *** %
Flow: *** cfm Pressure Ratio: *** Boost Limit: *** psi
Speed: *** rpm Belt Gear Ratio: *** Surge Flow: *** cfm
Eff: *** % Internal Gear Ratio: ***

EXHAUST

Exhaust System: H.P. Manifolds And Mufflers

CAMSHAFT

Camshaft Type: CROWER "STREET" Cam File: ***
Lifter: Solid Lobe Center: 110.0
Cam Specs @: 0.050-Lift Valve Overlap: 4.0
Int Lift@Valve: 0.322 in Int Duration: 224.0
Exh Lift@Valve: 0.320 in Exh Duration: 224.0
Nominal Timing Timing@ Adv(+)/Ret(-): 0.0

IVO (BTDC): 6.0 IVC (ABDC): 38.0 IVO: 6.0 IVC: 38.0
EVO (BBDC): 46.0 EVC (ATDC): -2.0 EVO: 46.0 EVC: -2.0
ICA (ATDC): 106.0 ECA (BTDC): 114.0 ICA: 106.0 ECA: 114.0

This is the Ford flathead V-8 engine described in Section I. The owner installed it in a daily-driven 1934 Ford five-window coupe. The engine was built by Luke's Custom Machine & Design.

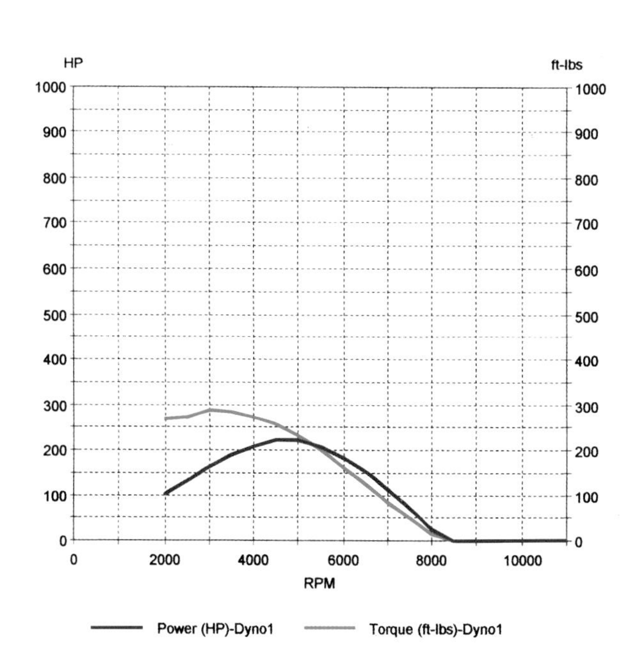

Ford Flathead V-8 265-ci Blown Street Engine

NOTE: The estimated output of this engine is 307 hp @ 6,000 rpm and 312 ft-lb torque @ 4,500 rpm.

CALCULATED POWER AND ENGINE PRESSURES

Engine RPM	Power (Fly)	Torque (Fly)	Int Man Pressure	Vol Eff %	IMEP Pressure	FMEP Pressure	BMEP Pressure
2000	100	263	14.96	75.4	197.1	18.2	151.6
2500	136	285	15.49	81.7	204.2	19.9	164.6
3000	170	298	16.02	86.7	209.8	21.7	171.8
3500	205	307	16.53	91.6	213.1	23.6	177.1
4000	237	310	17.04	95.1	215.6	25.7	179.1
4500	267	312	17.54	97.8	218.7	28.0	179.9
5000	290	304	18.03	99.0	216.3	30.4	175.4
5500	303	289	18.52	99.2	209.8	32.9	166.8
6000	307	269	19.01	98.1	200.0	35.6	155.0
6500	301	243	19.50	95.8	187.0	38.5	140.1
7000	284	213	20.01	92.7	171.8	41.4	123.0
7500	260	182	20.39	88.1	156.0	44.6	105.2
8000	228	150	20.38	82.7	139.4	47.8	86.4
8500	195	121	20.38	77.3	125.0	51.3	69.6
9000	168	98	20.39	73.3	114.9	54.8	56.7
9500	128	71	20.39	68.5	101.9	58.5	40.9
10000	97	51	20.41	64.8	93.5	62.4	29.4
10500	57	29	20.41	61.0	83.9	66.4	16.5
11000	12	6	20.42	57.0	73.9	70.5	3.2

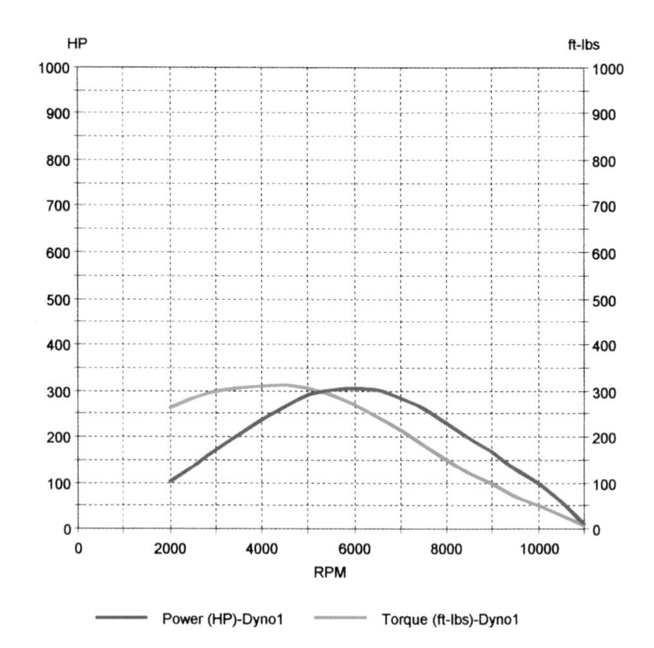

SHORT BLOCK

Block: FORD "FLATHEAD". Bore: 3.248 in Stroke: 4.000 in
Cylinders: 8 Cyl Vol: 543.1 cc Total Vol: 265.1 ci

CYLINDER HEADS

Cylinder Heads: Low Performance/Stock Ports And Valves
Air Flow File: ***
Intake Valves: 1 Exhaust Valves: 1
Intake Valve: 1.600 in Exhaust Valve: 1.600 in

COMPRESSION

Compression Ratio: 8.00 Combustion Space: 77.6 cc

INDUCTION

Induction Flow: 650.0 cfm @ 1.5 inHg Fuel: Gasoline
Manifold Type: Forced Induction N20: 0.0 lbs/min

Blower: Roots- BDS 471 (Street) Intercooler: *** %
Flow: 260.0 cfm Pressure Ratio: *** Boost Limit: 6.2 psi
Speed: *** rpm Belt Gear Ratio: 0.86 Surge Flow: *** cfm
Eff: 55.0 % Internal Gear Ratio: ***

EXHAUST

Exhaust System: Forced Induction Exhaust

CAMSHAFT

Camshaft Type: CROWER BLOWER. Cam File: ***
Lifter: Solid Lobe Center: 112.0
Cam Specs @: 0.050-Lift Valve Overlap: 14.0
Int Lift@Valve: 0.350 in Int Duration: 238.0
Exh Lift@Valve: 0.348 in Exh Duration: 238.0
Nominal Timing Timing@ Adv(+)/Ret(-): 0.0

IVO (BTDC): 11.0 IVC (ABDC): 47.0 IVO: 11.0 IVC: 47.0
EVO (BBDC): 55.0 EVC (ATDC): 3.0 EVO: 55.0 EVC: 3.0
ICA (ATDC): 108.0 ECA (BTDC): 116.0 ICA: 108.0 ECA: 116.0

The Ford flathead V-8 engine described in Section II installed in a daily-driven 1936 Ford three-window coupe. The engine was built by Luke's.

Ardun V-8 284-ci Performance Street Engine

NOTE: The estimated output of this engine is 300 hp @ 5,500 rpm and 323 ft-lb torque @ 4,000 rpm.

CALCULATED POWER AND ENGINE PRESSURES

Engine RPM	Power (Fly)	Torque (Fly)	Int Man Pressure	Vol Eff %	IMEP Pressure	FMEP Pressure	BMEP Pressure
2000	111	292	14.66	72.8	203.9	18.4	157.2
2500	142	297	14.63	74.8	199.3	20.1	159.9
3000	175	306	14.59	77.2	201.9	22.0	164.3
3500	212	318	14.54	81.6	207.1	24.1	171.0
4000	246	323	14.46	84.6	210.4	26.3	173.7
4500	275	321	14.38	85.9	211.4	28.7	172.4
5000	294	309	14.29	86.1	207.3	31.2	166.2
5500	300	287	14.20	84.5	197.1	33.8	154.0
6000	293	256	14.13	81.3	182.7	36.7	137.7
6500	269	217	14.08	76.5	163.6	39.7	116.9
7000	242	181	14.06	72.3	146.2	42.8	97.6
7500	208	145	14.04	67.4	128.9	46.1	78.1
8000	162	107	14.05	62.5	110.3	49.5	57.3
8500	117	72	14.07	58.0	94.3	53.1	38.9
9000	65	38	14.09	53.7	78.6	56.9	20.5
9500	10	6	14.12	49.6	64.0	60.8	3.0
10000	0	0	14.15	45.9	51.4	64.9	-12.7
10500	0	0	14.18	42.6	39.0	69.1	-28.4
11000	0	0	14.21	39.0	26.8	73.5	-44.0

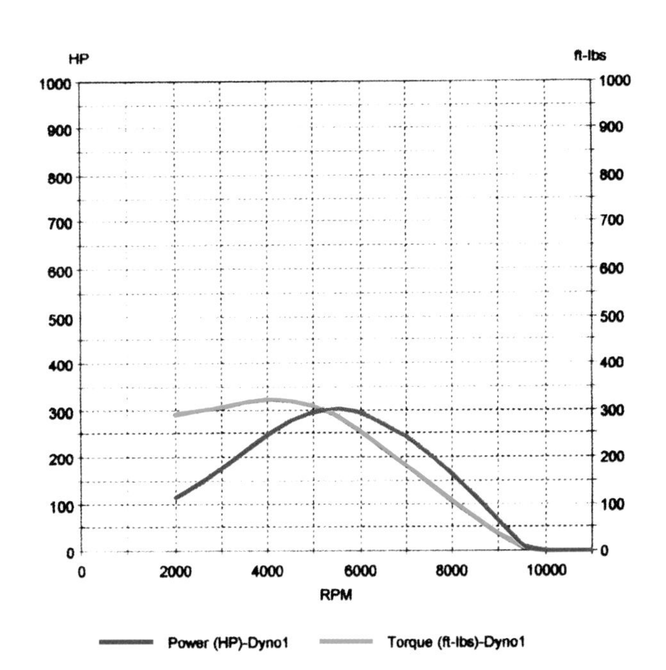

This is the Ardun V-8 engine built by Luke's and described in Section III. The owner installed it in a daily-driven 1932 Ford Roadster original 1950s era hot rod.

SHORT BLOCK

Block:	ARDUN.	Bore:	3.313 in	Stroke:	4.125 in
Cylinders:	8	Cyl Vol:	582.7 cc	Total Vol:	284.5 ci

CYLINDER HEADS

Cylinder Heads:	Canted/Oval Pocket Ported, Stock Valves		
Air Flow File:	***		
Intake Valves:	1	Exhaust Valves:	1
Intake Valve:	1.750 in	Exhaust Valve:	1.500 in

COMPRESSION

Compression Ratio:	8.50	Combustion Space:	77.7 cc

INDUCTION

Induction Flow:	480.0 cfm @ 1.5 inHg	Fuel:	Gasoline
Manifold Type:	Dual-Plane Manifold	N20:	0.0 lbs/min

Blower:	None			Intercooler:	*** %
Flow:	*** cfm	Pressure Ratio:	***	Boost Limit:	*** psi
Speed:	*** rpm	Belt Gear Ratio:	***	Surge Flow:	*** cfm
Eff:	*** %	Internal Gear Ratio:	***		

EXHAUST

Exhaust System:	Small-Tube Headers With Mufflers

CAMSHAFT

Camshaft Type:	CROWER "STREET"	Cam File:	***
Lifter:	Solid	Lobe Center:	110.0
Cam Specs @:	0.050-Lift	Valve Overlap:	7.0
Int Lift@Valve:	0.398 in	Int Duration:	227.0
Exh Lift@Valve:	0.398 in	Exh Duration:	227.0
Nominal Timing		Timing@ Adv(+)/Ret(-):	0.0

IVO (BTDC):	7.5	IVC (ABDC):	39.5	IVO:	7.5	IVC:	39.5
EVO (BBDC):	47.5	EVC (ATDC):	-0.5	EVO:	47.5	EVC:	-0.5
ICA (ATDC):	106.0	ECA (BTDC):	114.0	ICA:	106.0	ECA:	114.0

CLOSING COMMENTS

At the beginning of this book, I mentioned that the prices quoted did not include taxes or shipping and handling charges. Some additional facts about the prices should be mentioned. The prices are the "rock bottom," based on the presumption that the owner of the engine would purchase all the parts and take his own engine to a machine shop. If an engine building shop purchased all the parts for the owner and arranged for the machining work, there would be a markup on the price of the parts and the machining work. This markup is usually in the 20% range, because the engine building shops are not banks and they must account for the shop time it takes to order, receive, ship, and inspect parts.

Be prepared to give the engine building shop a down payment for the engine work, and you will probably have to "pay as you go" if your engine is a big-ticket item like the ones described in this book. You can bet that most engine building shops have been "burned" in the past by customers who had eyes bigger than their wallets or were just plain jerks!

If you are going to assemble your own engine, I highly recommend you do not attempt to do this after finishing the better part of a keg of ale! Take your time when assembling a motor and do it in stages. Remember, you are not part of the pit crew of a NASCAR race team! Check and re-check clearances. The extra time you take to assemble the engine will prevent the possibility of a serious and costly mistake.

When you decide to assemble your flathead motor, I suggest you lock yourself in your garage. We all have friends or acquaintances who consider themselves the ultimate experts when it comes to engine building. They can quote part numbers, camshaft specifications, and generally bore you to death! These are the same people who have never built an engine or vehicle themselves. I have always wondered what would be the end result if they did attempt to build an engine. I guess it would be like giving a monkey a loaded gun! It is your engine, so build it your way without interference.

The engines I have described in this book should prove to be very reliable and provide years and miles of pleasure for the owners. Just remember to change the oil and oil filter every few thousand miles.

I have thoroughly enjoyed writing this book because it has brought back a lot of fond memories. I particularly liked assisting with the build up of the three engines described in this book. Now it is time for you to build your own flathead, fire it up, and get on with some real nostalgia hot rodding. Remember to drive safely and sanely. Good luck!

RESOURCES

Following is a list of the parties and parts sources I believe are important to know about when building a Ford flathead V-8 engine. The companies with a brief explanation are the ones I deal with on a regular basis. I have not received any commercial or financial considerations from these companies for mentioning them. This is actually quite unfortunate because I have always made a point of telling people that my car trunk is unlocked and any jugs of booze, bulging unmarked envelopes, etc., they would like to donate would be greatly appreciated!

A number of excellent speed equipment manufacturers and engine building shops are located inNorth America. Some of these facilities have been mentioned in other publications and hot rod magazine articles pertaining to the Ford flathead V-8 engine. I have not mentioned them in this book because I have not used their services when I have built any of my own engines, and I am hesitant about recommending a company with whom I have had no personal experience. It is definitely not intended as a snub of anyone or any business.

Hundreds of manufacturers and parts outlets are positioned throughout North America, and I would probably end up with a book the size of the *Encyclopedia Britannica* if I listed them all. I have mentioned a few of those outlets. Most readers will have their own local source for parts. *Hemmings Motor News* is an excellent source for flathead parts and is available at better news stands or online at: www.hemmings.com.

I should say a few words about the eBay website. I have bought parts through eBay listings without problem, but I am cautious and only buy from high-rated sellers. The one thing I have noticed recently is the outrageous prices that some people selling goods are asking. I can fully appreciate that certain Ford flathead V-8 items are getting harder to find, and as a result, the price increases. This is the old law of supply and demand. My advice is, if the asking prices for goods are out of touch with reality, then do not buy them. Walk away and wait, because something will always turn up. These ridiculous eBay prices are ruining the market because they are now being reflected at swap meets.

Buying used engine parts is risky business. Remember the old adage: "buyer beware." Many of the parts required to build a Ford flathead V-8 engine will be used. If you do not know what to look for in the way of wear in specific used items, take a friend along who does know, or only buy from a reputable dealer. Do not pretend to know something when you do not; know your own limitations!

ARDUN ENTERPRISES
Don Ferguson
P.O. Box 205
Wilmington, California 90744
Tel.: (323) 775-6803
Fax: (310) 834-9904
Website: www.ardun.com

BENSON'S FLAT-O-PRODUCTS
Gene Benson
2195 Commercial N.E.
Salem, Oregon 97303
Tel.: (503) 364-2934
Fax: (503) 364-5108

BLOWER DRIVE SERVICE
12140 E. Washington Boulevard
Whittier, California 90606
Tel.: (562) 693-4302
Fax: (562) 696-7091
Website: www.blowerdriveservice.com

CRANE CAMS
530 Fentress Boulevard
Daytona Beach, Florida 32114
Tel.: (386) 252-1151
Tech Line: (386) 258-6174
Fax: (386) 258-6167
Website: www.cranecams.com

CROWER CAMS & EQUIPMENT COMPANY
3333 Main Street
Chula Vista, California 91911-5899
Tel.: (619) 422-1191
Fax: (619) 422-9067
Website: www.crower.com

I have been buying only Crower camshafts and valvetrain parts from Crower Cams for my own engines over the past number of years. I believe that Crower produces the best quality camshaft components at an affordable price.

Jerry MacLaughlin of their Technical Department has been most accommodating with any questions I have had over the years relating to camshafts and specific applications. The recommended products he has supplied have always worked superbly. There is no question of the quality of Crower products when a lot of the stock car racing teams and a number of famous drag racing teams are using Crower camshafts and components.

Jerry recommended the three different types of camshafts for the engines described in this book. These camshafts really work! The next time I am in Southern California, I shall make every effort to visit the Crower Cams & Equipment facility and meet Jerry. You have been forewarned, Jerry!

CUNNINGHAM RODS
550 West 172nd Street
Gardena, California 90248
Tel.: (310) 538-0605
Fax: (310) 538-0695
Website: www.cunninghamrods.com
E-mail: staff@cunninghamrods.com

EDELBROCK CORP.
2700 California Street
Torrance, California 90503
Tel.: (310) 781-2222
Fax: (310) 320-1187
Website: www.edelbrock.com

EGGE PARTS HOUSE
11707 Slauson Avenue
Sante Fe Springs, California 90670
Tel.: (800)-886-3443 or (562) 945-3419
Fax: (562) 693-1635
Website: www.egge.com
E-mail: info@egge.com

FLATATTACK RACING PRODUCTS
c/o Dave Dooley
1002 Bighorn Drive
Jefferson City, Missouri 65109
Tel.: (573) 893-4044
Website: www.flatattackracing.com
E-mail: flathead46@hotmail.com
In Australia:
Mike Davidson
Tel.: 61-8-8362-1255
Fax: 61-8-8362-1515
E-mail: mrd@bold.net.au

HIGH PERFORMANCE ENGINES
4329 Buchanan Street
Burnaby, B.C. V5C 3X7
Canada
Tel.: (604) 299-6131
Fax: (604) 299-6017

High performance Engines was founded by Bud Child close to 40 years ago. Bud has retired and now only comes to the shop five and a half days a week! His son Dave is running the business and I am certain pays his father less than the minimum wage allowed by law.

High Performance Engines has performed the machine work on all my engines for the past 30 years. Their work is superb and reasonably priced. This shop builds engines for customers from all over the Pacific Northwest and many of these engines have produced drag racing and drag boat winners.

My thanks to Dave Child for providing me with current prices applicable to the machine work normally performed on automotive engines and for allowing me access to his shop in order to take photographs of the various machining procedures applicable to the Ford flathead V-8 engine. I would also like to thank him for not charging me for the time I spent in his shop taking those photographs!

ISKENDERIAN RACING CAMS
16020 South Broadway
Gardena, California 90248
Tel.: (323) 770-0930
Fax: (310) 515-5730
Website: www.iskycams.com

Ed "The Camfather" Iskenderian has been involved in camshaft manufacturing since shortly after World War II. His name is synonymous with camshafts. The Iskenderian Racing Cams "400 JR" camshaft is probably one of the most famous flathead camshafts ever produced. The single and dual flathead valve springs available today from Iskenderian Racing Cams are fine quality items. I have purchased camshafts and components from Iskenderian Racing Cams and I found their service to be very professional, friendly, and the shipping of their products was prompt.

J & M AUTOBODY & PAINT
1764 Powell Street
Vancouver, B.C. V5L 1H7
Canada
Tel.: (604) 254-5505
Fax: (604) 254-4114

J & M Autobody & Paint (formerly J & M Fiberglass Enterprises) started out over 30 years ago with the repair and restoration of Corvettes. Jerry Olsen and Larry Woida are the founders and owners of that fine establishment. They have been spraying every type of paint imaginable on cars, automobile frames, engines, boats, and helicopters for decades. The Pearl Teal basecoat/clearcoat paint they applied to my 1969 Corvette resulted in an award for the best paint in a custom car show with over 500 vehicles. It does not matter where you live in North America; if you want the best paint job, bring your engine and parts (and even your whole car) to these people.

JITNEY AUTO PARTS (For Canadian Customers)
Mr. Keith Lee
P.O.Box 23048, Sub 31
Saskatoon, Saskatchewan S7J 5H3
Tel.: (306) 668-3673
Fax.: (306) 668-3658

Keith Lee, the owner, stocks just about all the name brand speed equipment required for a "flathead" engine. He will ship anywhere in Canada. This is a good way to save a lot on the import brokerage and associated costs. His prices are very competitive.

JOBLOT AUTOMOTIVE
P.O. Box 75
98-11 211th Street
Queens Village, New York 11429
Tel.: (718) 468-8585
Fax: (718) 468-8686
Website: www.joblotauto.com
E-mail: joblot@joblotauto.com

DOUG KING ENTERPRISES
Tel.: (510) 537-3909

LUKE'S CUSTOM MACHINE & DESIGN
1457 Charlotte Road
North Vancouver, B.C. V7J 1H1
Canada
Tel.: (604) 980-8617
Fax: (604) 980-8656

Owner Luke Balogh has operated his business for the past 25 years, although he has been heavily involved in performance engine and custom automobile building for over 30 years. Luke has been an accomplished drag racer, and he raced at the Bonneville Salt Flats in the 1980s, setting a record there. He has been building a blown early Chrysler hemi-equipped 1934 Ford five-window coupe for the past 22 years. This vehicle, when completed, will most likely be one of the finest 1934 Fords ever built.

Luke is a professional machinist by trade. He specializes in all types of lathe and milling machine assignments and is an expert welder. Luke is renowned for his aluminum designs, fabrication, and welding. He has built a variety of engines over the years, but his preference is for the rare Ardun engine, the early Chrysler hemis, and the venerable Ford flathead V-8. The engines described in this book were all built at Luke's.

Luke produces excellent blower kits that consist of professionally assembled supercharger cases, blower snouts, and pulleys. The splines on his blower snout shafts incorporate the largest depth presently offered in the industry. The "sculptured" blower snout he produces is truly a work of art. I have one of these snouts on my own blown engine, and it is the immediate focus of everyone's attention.

Luke sold a blown Ardun engine a few years ago to Ken Roble, the president of Ross Racing Pistons. That engine is presently on display at Ross's office in El Segundo, California and has now become the altar for all loyal flathead and Ardun pilgrims!

MANLEY PERFORMANCE PARTS
1960 Swarthmore Avenue
Lakewood, New Jersey 08701
Tel.: (732) 905-3366
Fax: (732) 905-3010
Website: www.manleyperformance.com
E-mail: sales@manleyperformance.com

MOONEYES USA
10820 South Norwalk Boulevard
Sante Fe Springs, California 90670
Tel.: (562) 944-6311
Fax: (562) 946-2961
Website: www.mooneyes.com
E-mail: info@mooneys.com

MOTION SOFTWARE, INC.
535 West Lambert Road, Building E
Brea, California 92821-3911
Tel.: (714) 255-2931
Fax: (714) 255-7956
Website: www.motionsoftware.com
E-mail: support@motionsoftware.com

Motion Software produces the computer program used for the dyno tests shown in the Dyno Printouts section. This an excellant way to compare camshafts, compression ratios, carburetion, etc., in order to determine the best combination for a particular engine. The Dyno 2000 Advanced Engine Simulation booklet is available online as are upgrades.

OFFENHAUSER SALES
P.O. Box 32218
Los Angeles, California 90032
Tel.: (323) 225-1307

PACIFIC FASTENERS
3934 East 1st Avenue
Burnaby, B.C. V5C 5S3
Canada
Tel.: (604) 294-9411
Fax: (604) 294-4730
Website: www.pacificfasteners.com
E-mail: pacfast@pacificfasteners.com

Pacific Fasteners (U.S.)
2411 South 200 Street
Seattle, Washington 98198
Tel.: (206) 824-0416
Fax: (206) 878-1041

Pacific Fasteners is one of the best sources for quality stainless steel bolts, washers, nuts, screws, rods, cotter pins, and so forth. These people seem to stock everything required for an engine. They even stock stainless steel fillister-head machine screws used on the Holley 94 and Stromberg 97 carburetors. You can buy bolts individually or in bulk quantities, but there is usually a $5.00 minimum for orders. They will ship FedEx or U.P.S. to just about anywhere.

REDI-STRIP METAL CLEANING CANADA
7961 Vantage Way
Delta, B.C. V4G 1A6
Canada
Tel.: (604) 946-7761
Fax: (604) 946-5936

Redi-Strip Metal Cleaning Canada Ltd. has been in business for 20 years. This company specializes in all types of metal cleaning, from engine blocks to entire automobile body shells. They do excellent work and their prices are reasonable. About five years ago, this company started a division specifically for the high temperature coating (H.T.C.) of exhaust components. This is a quality process that works. I had an entire exhaust system on one of my cars high temperature coated by these people. It looks great!

Hot tanking alone does not remove all the internal mess from an engine block. "Redi-stripping" is a process that does, resulting in a squeaky clean block. After 50 years, I can guarantee there is a lot of rust and sludge residue in the water passages of a Ford flathead V-8 engine block. A good machine shop will most likely insist an engine block be "redi-stripped" before they seriously attack it. The end result is worth the cost of the shipping.

Other companies in North America may provide a similar service, but Redi-Strip Metal Cleaning Canada is the only company in North America that strips entire automobile bodies.

THE ROD SHOP
Ken Austin
P.O. Box 111
Newburg, Oregon 97132
Tel.: (503) 537-2700.

ROSS RACING PISTONS
625 South Douglas
El Segundo, California 90245
Tel.: (800) 392-7677 or (310) 536-0100 (tech line)
Fax: (310) 536-0333
Website: www.rosspistons.com

In June 2001 I visited Ross Racing Pistons and met Ken Roble, the president. I have been buying all my pistons from Ross for the past number of years, and I thought it was time to meet Ken. He has been a hot rodder and an avid flathead owner and builder for most of his life. He is an extremely talented tool and die maker responsible for a lot of the tooling at his company. Ken is the proud owner of a blown Ardun engine that Luke Balogh built for him, and he has that classic beauty parked next to his desk. I doubt if that engine will ever be installed in a car, because Ken insists "it is too pretty."

I was given the grand tour of the Ross facilities, and I was more than suitably impressed. Ross produces top-quality pistons using state-of-the-art CNC machining technology. The result is one of the best pistons money can buy, at a very affordable price. Ross produces pistons for various engines in sizes from lawn mowers to aircraft. They can custom build just about any type of piston. Thank you, Ken, for the great tour!

Ken spent a lot of time developing a Ford flathead piston based on Art Sparks' original design, and he considers the end result to be a labor of personal love. Ross Racing Pistons stocks these Ford and Mercury forged aluminum pistons, and they are available in bores of 3 5/16″, 3 5/16″ + 0.030″, or 3 3/8″, and strokes of 3 3/4″, 4″, or 4 1/8″. Your order can usually be shipped out within two days, providing you pay for the parts! These pistons are complete with aircraft-quality piston pins, Spiro Lox retainers, and the original Grant piston rings. This is a fantastic deal for the price. I do not understand why anyone would purchase a set of the old-style cast pistons when this setup can be obtained for only a few more dollars. These pistons are quality!

RPM CATALOG
Dale Wilch
P.O. Box 12301
Kansas City, Kansas 66112
Tel.: (913) 788-3219
Fax: (913) 788-9682
Website: www.rpmcat.com
E-mail: info@rpmcat.com

Owner Dale Wilch has been selling used speed equipment for years. Once in awhile, he has some interesting vintage Ford flathead V-8 multiple carburetor intake manifolds and other parts for sale on his website. I have purchased items from him in the past and found his service to be courteous, efficient, and prompt. His prices are competitive.

Recently, Dale has been selling some very high-quality stainless steel intake and exhaust valves for small-block Chevrolet engines. The exhaust valves are 1.61″ diameter, one-piece stock length, hardened tips, 1 1/32″ stem diameter, and swirl polished. These valves are manufactured in Argentina and they sell for $50.00 (U.S.) for eight valves. I have used these valves in one of my own engines designed for street use, and they perform as well as any name-brand valve at a lot less cost. These valves will work perfectly in the Ford flathead V-8 engine.

SI INDUSTRIES
2175-A Agate Court
Simi Valley, California 93085
Tel.: (805) 582-0085
Fax: (805) 582-0845
Website: www.sivalves.com

SMITH BROTHERS PUSHRODS
62968 Layton Avenue, Suite 1
Bend, Oregon 97701
Tel.: (800) 367-1533 or (541) 388-8188
Fax: (541) 389-8840
Website: www.pushrods.net
E-mail: smithbros@bendcable.com

SPEEDWAY MOTORS
P.O. Box 81906
Lincoln, Nebraska 68501
Tel.: (402) 323-3200
Fax: (402) 323-3211
Website: www.speedwaymotors.com
E-mail: sales@speedwaymotors.com

I have been buying parts for hot rods and Ford flathead engines for my own use since 1983 from Speedway Motors. They have always been prompt and efficient when filling orders. The flathead reproduction parts they provide are of high quality, and their prices are competitive. This is one of the best sources for flathead engine parts. Speedway Motors must be doing something right because 2002 is their fiftieth year in business!

Bill "Speedy" Smith, the founder and owner of Speedway Motors, probably has the world's foremost collection of Ford flathead V-8 engines—everything from stock to wildly modified. One day I hope to go to view this amazing assortment of Henry Ford's finest!

SUMMIT RACING EQUIPMENT
P.O. Box 909
Akron, Ohio 44309-0909
Tel.: (800) 230-3030
Fax: (330) 630-5333
Website: www.summitracing.com

TATOM CUSTOM ENGINES
P.O. Box 2504
Mount Vernon, Washington 98273
Tel.: (360) 424-8314
Fax: (360) 424-6717
Website: www.tatom.com
E-mail: flatheads@tatom.com

VINTAGE SPEED 2001
Charles Price
1916 – 63rd Court
Vero Beach, Florida 32966
Tel.: (772) 788-0809
Fax: (772) 569-7028
Website: www.vintagespeed.com

Charles Price is the owner of Vintage Speed. I have been buying Holley 94 carburetor parts from Charlie for over two years now. I have found his service to be prompt and efficient and his prices reasonable. There are a lot of used Ford flathead V-8 intake manifolds, cylinder heads, and other interesting parts on Charlie's website.

Charlie is well known for his knowledge of early carburetors, particularly the Stromberg 97 and the Holley 94. He built the intake setup for the Beach Boys' original hot rod. He sells excellent quality extended and oversize throttle shafts plus he seems to have every small part imaginable for the early carburetors. If you require carburetor parts, call Charlie!

J.C. WHITNEY & COMPANY
P.O. Box 3000
LaSalle, Illinois 61301-0300
Tel.: (877) 927-7427
Fax: (800) 537-2700
Website: www.jcwhitney.com

WILKINSON'S AUTOMOBILIA
2531 Ontario Street
Vancouver, B.C. V5T 2X7
Canada
Tel.: (604) 873-6242
Fax: (604) 873-6259
Website: www.eautomobilia.com
E-mail: info@wilkinsonsauto.com

This is one of the finest sources of vintage and current automotive books, shop manuals, chassis manuals, and hot rod magazines. Some of the publications they have go back to the early part of the twentieth century. They seem to have just about everything. These people are extremely helpful and friendly.

INDEX